THROUGH THE
LOOKING GLASS

Society for the Promotion of Byzantine Studies

Publications
7

THROUGH THE LOOKING GLASS

BYZANTIUM THROUGH BRITISH EYES

Papers from the Twenty-ninth Spring Symposium of
Byzantine Studies, London, March 1995

edited by

Robin Cormack and Elizabeth Jeffreys

ASHGATE
VARIORUM

Aldershot • Burlington USA • Singapore • Sydney

Copyright © 2000 by the Society for the Promotion of Byzantine Studies
Hon. Secretary, James Crow, Dept of Archaeology, The University,
Newcastle-upon-Tyne NE1 7RU

Published by Variorum for the Society for the Promotion of Byzantine Studies

Ashgate Publishing Limited
Gower House, Croft Road
Aldershot, Hampshire GU11 3HR
Great Britain

Ashgate Publishing Company
131 Main Street
Burlington Vermont 05401
USA

ISBN 0–86078–667–6

Ashgate website: http://www.ashgate.com

British Library Cataloguing-in-Publication Data

Through the Looking Glass: Byzantium through British Eyes.
– (Society for the Promotion of Byzantine Studies
publication 7)
1. Byzantine Empire – History – Congresses
I. Cormack, Robin   II. Jeffreys, E. M. (Elizabeth M)
III. Society for the Promotion of Byzantine Studies
949.5'02

U.S. Library of Congress Cataloging-in-Publication Data

The Library of Congress Card Number was preassigned as:
00-100090

This volume is printed on acid free paper.

Typeset by   Manton Typesetters, Louth, Lincolnshire, UK

Printed in Great Britain by MPG Books Ltd, Bodmin, Cornwall

SOCIETY FOR THE PROMOTION OF BYZANTINE STUDIES – PUBLICATION 7

Contents

Section III   Interpreters

Section IV   Other perspectives

Section V   Encounters with the imagined Byzantium

Acknowledgements

The twenty-ninth Spring Symposium was held at King's College, London, in March 1995 under the patronage of the Trustees of the British Museum and the aegis of the Society for the Promotion of Byzantine Studies. The symposium was helped by generous support from the Hellenic Foundation, the Leventis Foundation, the British Academy and the Bank of Cyprus, and with the hospitality of the Centre for Hellenic Studies, King's College. The symposiarch was David Buckton (British Museum) and the organizing committee consisted of Robin Cormack (Courtauld Institute of Art), Rowena Loverance (British Museum) and Charlotte Roueché (King's College London). The communications were organized by Kara Hattersley-Smith. The Society for the Promotion of Byzantine Studies is – as usual – deeply grateful to all these persons and institutions which enabled the symposium to take place. An especial debt of gratitude is owed to the Trustees of the British Museum and its Director, Dr. R. G. W. Anderson, partly for stimulus provided by the exhibition 'Byzantium. Treasures of Byzantine Art from British Collections' which opened concurrently with the symposium, but also for generous support given to the organisation of the symposium and to the publication of the papers. The exhibition catalogue, edited by David Buckton and published by the British Museum (1994), is a frequent reference point in the papers published here, as it was in the course of the symposium itself. The Editors would like to thank Daniel Farrell for compiling the index.

List of abbreviations

ABSA	Annual of the British School at Athens
BICS	Bulletin of the Institute of Classical Studies
BMGS	Byzantine and Modern Greek Studies
CBM	Corpus der byzantinischen Miniaturenhandschriften
DChAE	Δελτίον τῆς Χριστιανικῆς Ἀρχαιολογικῆς Ἑταιρείας
DNB	Dictionary of National Biography
DOP	Dumbarton Oaks Papers
GRBS	Greek, Roman and Byzantine Studies
HThR	Harvard Theological Review
JEH	Journal of Ecclesiastical History
JHS	Journal of the Historical Society
JRS	Journal of Roman Studies
JThS	Journal of Theological Studies
ODB	Oxford Dictionary of Byzantium
OED	Oxford English Dictionary
PBA	Proceedings of the British Academy
PG	Patrologia Graeca
REG	Revue des Etudes Grecques
ZRVI	Zbornik Radova Vizantoloskog Instituta

List of figures

Preface

The Spring Symposium in London in 1995 explored the ways in which British scholars, travellers, novelists, architects, churchmen, gentlemen, critics came into contact with Byzantium and how they perceived what they saw. The questions were treated chronologically so that Byzantium could be treated both as a source of influence on British culture as well as an 'idea' which British culture constructed in different ways in different periods of history. Papers dealt with the collecting of Byzantium, and in particular with the attitudes towards Greek manuscripts exhibited by classical scholars, with the appreciation of Byzantine manuscripts in the nineteenth century and with the changing ways in which manuscripts have been taken to illuminate Byzantium. Robert Curzon, whose manuscripts form a significant section of those now in the British Library, emerged as a perceptive nineteenth-century critic of Byzantine culture.

The influence of concepts of Byzantium on British poetry and the novel were also covered; and Ruskin was included in the treatment of the literary view of Byzantium. A series of case studies looked at individual historians and Byzantinists, and particular coverage was given to Bury, Baynes, Toynbee, Dawkins, Dalton. The British view of Byzantium was contrasted with two case studies from elsewhere in Europe (France and Russia). The aim of the papers of the symposium was to document the various ways in which Byzantium entered the British imagination and formed the national consciousness of the culture and its history. It is hoped that the selection included in this volume will achieve the same result.

Introduction: Through the Looking Glass –
Byzantium through British Eyes

Robin Cormack

The theme of the Symposium was an exploration of the British view of Byzantium. Amongst all else it gave the opportunity to provide a historical framework to the British Museum's major exhibition of Byzantine art, 'Byzantium. Treasures of Byzantine Art and Culture from British Collections'.[1] This exhibition put on display over two hundred and fifty treasures of Byzantine art from more than thirty collections in the United Kingdom, and it showed a range of media from manuscripts to fragments of monumental mosaics, including icons from the National Collection of Icons held in the British Museum. This exhibition supplied visual materials which were treated in several of the papers and gave an extra, invaluable dimension to the whole symposium. The Director, Dr. R. G. W. Anderson gave the opening address at the symposium, and quoted the anecdote recorded in the exhibition catalogue introduction: that in 1860 Panizzi, the museum's principal librarian in answer to the question whether there were 'Byzantine, Oriental, Mexican and Peruvian antiquities stowed away in the basement?' gave the reply, 'Yes, a few of them; and, I may well add, that I do not think it any great loss they are not better placed than they are'.

The theme of the symposium was an exploration of the British view of Byzantium, and its strategy was not so much to focus on how the words 'Byzantium' and 'Byzantine' have been variously given different and revealing meanings in British writing and thinking, but what 'Byzantium' meant at different times to different individuals and groups. The organization of this debate was best carried out, the organizing commit-

---

[1] D. Buckton, ed., *Byzantium: Treasures of Byzantine Art and Culture from British Collections* (London [British Museum], 1994).

tee decided, by treating the British viewing of the Byzantine world and all its constituent elements as a chronological continuum which could be sampled and analysed at various times (though the chronological component has not been emphasised in the papers published here). This decision meant that the approach of the symposium was more than an examination of the historiography of Byzantium, but included historical enterprises and relationships over the course of British history from the Middle Ages onwards. The copying of a Byzantine motif in medieval art was understood to be as revealing a way of defining Byzantium as any Enlightenment historian's characterisation of the nature of Byzantine society. One outcome of the symposium was to appreciate the shifting and ambivalent attitudes of the British towards Byzantium, and to reveal the relativism that must be taken into account in the study of that culture. In this sense the symposium might be said to be a 'post-modernist' exploration of the meaning of Byzantium; or at least to genuflect towards the spirit of Lewis Carroll from whom our title was taken.

This final publication, regrettably delayed, but brought to completion by the editorship of Elizabeth Jeffreys, presents most of the papers given. The paper by David Womersley on 'Gibbon and Byzantium: classical example and commercial society in the reign of Justinian I' was not intended for publication here, and represented just one part of his major work on editing and commenting on Edward Gibbon (1737–94).[2] Although *The Decline and Fall of the Roman Empire*, which occupied Gibbon from its anecdotal origin in Rome as he 'sat musing amidst the ruins of the Capitol' on 15 October 1764, has been the greatest influence on the British construction of Byzantium ever since, these papers acknowledge this fact without joining the broader Gibbon industry.[3] For some this may suggest the criticism that this volume will be presenting Hamlet without the Prince; but the defence is that the volume sets out wider perspectives of Britain and Byzantium and in this aim too much emphasis on Gibbon and his hostile interpretation of Byzantium and Medieval Christianity would have been a distortion of the more positive side of British thinking. Nevertheless one should say the obvious, and signal Gibbon's dominant and pessimistic influence over Byzantine history writing. Some will want to speculate that without Gibbon the story of Byzan-

---

[2] E. Gibbon, *The Decline and Fall of the Roman Empire*, ed. D. Womersley (London, 1995); E. Gibbon, *The Decline and Fall of the Roman Empire*, facsimile edition with an introduction by D. Womersley (London, 1997); D. Womersley, ed., *Religious scepticism: contemporary responses to Gibbon* (Bristol, 1997); D. Womersley, ed., *Edward Gibbon: bicentenary essays* (Oxford, 1997).

[3] A relevant publication here is R. McKitterick and R. Quinault, eds, *Edward Gibbon and Empire* (Cambridge, 1997).

tium might have assumed a different, perhaps greater, role in British education. But it would be too simple to suppose that one historian was single-handedly responsible for the British perception of the whole Byzantine world, and this volume sets out a more complex set of evidence, some from the period before Gibbon and some showing the diversity of thinking about Byzantium, despite the existence of *Decline and Fall*. There are, as this symposium demonstrated, many other factors other than the Enlightenment which have influenced the ways in which Britain saw the nature of this Mediterranean culture. It hopes to redress the balance, to map out some of the overlooked stages in the development of Byzantine historiography. Accordingly the paper by Averil Cameron assesses the nature of historical approaches of historians who can hardly be said to work simply in the 'shadow' of Gibbon.

The coverage of our subject was selective in another significant way too. The symposium was planned as an exploration of past circumstances, endeavours and attitudes by living researchers. Hence there was no paper on the work of the Hon. Sir Steven Runciman who was present as a symposiast and discussant, contributing himself both anecdotal and intellectual observations and giving the closing remarks.[4] Perhaps future publications of symposia of this kind ought to include a record of discussions, as an integral part of that exercise of interpreting both past activities and present reactions. Some contributions were intended as publication for elsewhere, such as Cyril Mango, 'The British Discovery of Constantinople: the Golden Gate reliefs', Annabel Wharton, 'Westminster Cathedral and the architectures of empire', Bryony Llewellyn, 'Fact and Fiction: western representations of Hagia Sophia', Donald Nicol, 'The Emperor Manuel II in London, 1400–1401', and A. Bryer, 'Nicander and Henry VIII'. One symposiast, Robert Nelson, has published a relevant study of the place of Byzantine art in global art history.[5]

The outcome of the symposium was to identify a diversity of strategies among those engaged in the study or the appropriation of Byzantium. Whether these amount to a sum national construction of Byzantium may perhaps be doubted, but the comparison with France, made by Jean-Michel Spieser, who focussed on Du Cange, documents how a political programme concerned with the idea of empire and the glorification of France did promote there a specific and different kind of historical interest in Byzantium and its relation to Rome.[6] The comparison with

---

[4] See also Steven Runciman, *A Traveller's Alphabet. Partial Memoirs* (London, 1991).

[5] Robert S. Nelson, 'The map of art history', *Art Bulletin* 79 (1997), 29–40.

[6] The effects of the French interest in Byzantium can be quantified by the manner and

Russia, however, contributed by Olga Etinhof, demonstrated a similarity with Britain in treating Byzantium as a collector's realm. Since the Middle Ages this too had been one pattern of British activity, but in a variety of methods, either by using Byzantine art as a source of inspiration (discussed by Barbara Zeitler) or by the more practical collection of manuscripts. The major activity of the British in collecting medieval manuscripts was given emphasis in the symposium, either as a positive quest as in the case of Robert Curzon (discussed by Robin Cormack and Zaga Gavrilović) or as part of the pursuit of the Classical (documented by Pat Easterling) or bound up with ecclesiastic and diplomatic relations with the Levant (in the papers of Jonathan Harris and Colin Davey). John Lowden risked a figure for the number of Greek manuscripts in Britain: he counted 3,230, of which only about 120 contain pictorial illustrations. As for the collected Byzantine antiquities in the basement of the British Museum, these were rescued by the interest and research of O. M. Dalton, whose curatorial (and other activities) are chronicled here by C. J. S. Entwistle (who properly also quotes the Panizzi soundbite). A context was provided by the systematic paper given in the symposium (not included here) on 'Museums and Collections of Byzantine and Post-Byzantine art in Greece since George Lampakis' by Panayotis Vocotopoulos.

Collecting was, in view of the stimulus of the British Museum exhibition, a major theme of the symposium, but travel and perception of Byzantium and the viewing of Byzantium in the field was significantly investigated, as in the case of Robert Curzon's travels and their subsequent publication and popularity with the British reading public. The nature of John Ruskin's perceptions are covered by Michael Wheeler. British fieldwork, excavation and conservation in the Byzantine lands are covered by Haris Kalligas, Mary Whitby and David Winfield, and were the subject of a paper at the symposium by Rowena Loverance.

The literary appearance of Byzantium in poetry and novel writing was treated by David Ricks and Liz James, revealing that the culture had its influences on both high and popular writings. Here the influence of Gibbon is particularly strong – and enduring. Significantly the papers of Averil Cameron and Peter Mackridge who cover two high profile holders of inaugural chairs of Byzantine and Modern Greek studies, Arnold Toynbee, the first holder of the Koraes chair at King's College London, and R. M. Dawkins, the first holder of the Bywater and Sotheby chair of Byzantine and Modern Greek Language and Literature at Oxford, portray maverick scholars with pronounced meth-

period of the acquisition of Byzantine art; see Robin Cormack, 'The French construction of Byzantium: reflections on the Louvre exhibition of Byzantine art', *Dialogos* 1 (1994), 28–41.

ods of approach. They make the point that the work of both professors has remarkable echoes in current studies: Toynbee has relevance for the current explorations of global history, and Dawkins for the history of 'mentalités'.[7]

The papers which follow in this volume therefore have some coherence in identifying a few of the constants in the British perception of Byzantium. But they also show the extraordinary diversity of interests and pursuits which Byzantium has stimulated. At the end of the symposium a group of symposiasts who represented practitioners of the field, one from each decade between 1920 and 1990, were questioned by Margaret Mullett as a group about the necessary tools of the subject. The consistent reply from the upper age group was emphatically to declare knowledge of Greek as the priority for research into Byzantine studies, but it was not the universal belief of the whole group. None of the papers explored how far the particular type of training in Latin and Greek in British education might have influenced Byzantine studies. The reasons for the rise and fall of Classics in British education has been recently investigated,[8] but how the knowledge of Byzantine Greek (or lack of it) will influence the popularity of Byzantium in future or the character of its study is an open question. But a feature of the turn of the millennium is that the British Museum exhibition has been followed by equally popular exhibitions in New York and Germany, and that the frequency of further Byzantine displays seems sure to accelerate. These papers emphasize that the future of the subject depends on the character of its past.

---

[7] See also R. Clogg, *Politics and the Academy. Arnold Toynbee and the Koraes Chair* (London, 1986) and A. A. M. Bryer, 'Byzantine and Modern Greek Studies: a partial view', *BMGS* 12 (1988), 1–26. For the Scottish endowment of a lectureship in post-classical and modern Greek at St Andrews, see R.J. Macrides, *The Scottish Connection in Byzantine and Modern Greek Studies* (St John's House Papers no 4, St Andrews, 1992).

[8] C. Stray, *Classics Transformed. Schools, Universities and Society in England 1830–1960* (Oxford, 1998).

Section I

Encounters with places

1. Byzantine 'purple' and Ruskin's St Mark's, Venice

Michael Wheeler

In Ruskin's unfinished late work entitled *St Mark's Rest* (1877–84) he describes the mosaics of the great eastern dome of St Mark's:

> The decorative power of the colour in these figures, chiefly blue, purple, and white, on gold, is entirely admirable, – more especially the dark purple of the Virgin's robe, with lines of gold for its folds; and the figures of David and Solomon, both in Persian tiaras, almost Arab, with falling lappets to the shoulder, for shade; David holding a book with Hebrew letters on it and a cross (a pretty sign for the Psalms); and Solomon with rich orbs of lace like involved ornament on his dark robe, cusped in the short hem of it, over gold underneath. And note in all these mosaics that Byzantine 'purple,' – the colour at once meaning Kinghood and its Sorrow, – is the same as ours – not scarlet, but amethyst, and that deep.[1]

Why did the colour purple mean so much to Ruskin? What is the significance for him of 'Byzantine "purple"', especially in St Mark's? And what is the relationship between 'Byzantine "purple"' and Solomon, whose 'Kinghood and its Sorrow' make him a type of Christ? These are the questions that I wish to address in this chapter.

In both the published works and the private diaries and notebooks of Ruskin, references to the colour purple abound. In the 1845 notebooks, for example, used on his formative first trip to Italy without his parents, we find the word 'purple' recurring frequently, and even capitalized in the margins of his descriptions of the art and sculpture of Genoa and

---

[1] *The Works of John Ruskin*, Library Edition, eds E. T. Cook and A. Wedderburn, 39 vols (London and New York, 1903–12), XXIV, 301–2. All further references to this edition are given thus in the text: *Works*, XXIV, 301–2. For further discussion of Ruskin's religious references, see M. Wheeler, *Ruskin's God* (Cambridge, 1999).

Lucca.[2] In his *magnum opus*, *Modern Painters*, he marvels at the purples in the natural landscape, and, particularly in volume IV (1856), in the rocks. Granite seen at a distance in the sunset has 'that peculiar reddish purple which is so strikingly the characteristic of the rocks of the higher Alps' (*Works*, VI, 140).[3] This 'reddish purple' differs from the 'Byzantine' bluish purple described in *St Mark's Rest*. In *The Queen of the Air*, his study on Greek myth published in 1869, Ruskin's discussion of the etymology of 'purple' points up the problem of defining the colour:

> As far as I can trace the colour perception of the Greeks, I find it all founded primarily on the degree of connection between colour and light; the most important fact to them in the colour of red being its connection with fire and sunshine; so that 'purple' is, in its original sense, 'fire-colour,' and the scarlet, or orange, of dawn, more than any other, fire-colour. I was long puzzled by Homer's calling the sea purple; ... he really means the gleaming blaze of the waves under wide light. ... a colour may be called purple because it is light subdued (and so death is called 'purple' or 'shadowy' death); or else it may be called purple as being shade kindled with fire, and thus said of the lighted sea; or even of the sun itself ...; or of golden hair ...; ... and then, to make the whole group of thoughts inextricably complex, yet rich and subtle in proportion to their intricacy, the various rose and crimson colours of the murex-dye, – the crimson and purple of the poppy, and fruit of the palm – and the association of all these with the hue of blood ... mingle themselves in, and renew the whole nature of the old word; so that, in later literature, it means a different colour, or emotion of colour, in almost every place where it occurs: and casts around for ever the reflection of all that has been dipped in its dyes. (*Works*, XIX, 379–80)

So Ruskin knew that 'Tyrian purple', the dye obtained from species of the gastropod molluscs *purpura* and *murex*, and the imperial or royal colour, was originally a crimson.[4] Furthermore, in this passage at least, he glories in the richness of association which the very indeterminacy of 'purple' makes possible.

The most important association for Ruskin is, however, biblical, as one might expect, and is explained in his definition of 'purpure', the 'third of the three secondary colours', in *Deucalion*, chapter VII, published in the year (1876) in which he began the long stay in Venice which gave rise to *St Mark's Rest*:

---

[2] The Ruskin Foundation, Lancaster University (The Ruskin Library), MS 5/5A. (The notebook is bound in purple leather.)

[3] For further examples see *Works*, VI, 158, 163, 171, 173, 305.

[4] In Byzantine aesthetics, according to G. Mathew, the imperial purple was probably a dark red, at least by the twelfth century: *Byzantine Aesthetics* (London, 1963), 147. Ray Haslam points out to me that the first edition of Ruskin's *Oxford Lectures on Art* (1870), which included his Inaugural, was published in purple cloth with gold embossed rules – 'purple' in the modern bluish-purple sense.

VI. Purpure. The true purple of the Tabernacle, 'blue, purple, and scarlet' [Exodus 25:4] – the kingly colour, retained afterwards in all manuscripts of the Greek Gospels; therefore known to us absolutely by its constant use in illumination. It is rose colour darkened or saddened with blue; the colour of love in noble or divine sorrow; borne by the kings, whose witness is in heaven [Job 16:19], and their labour on the earth. Its stone is the Jacinth, Hyacinth, or Amethyst, – 'like to that sanguine flower inscribed with woe' [Milton, *Lycidas*, 106]. (*Works*, XXVI, 186)[5]

Here, then, is a clue to Ruskin's thinking in my opening quotation, where he reflects upon the relationship between kingship and sorrow.

This association helps to explain why it is St Mark's above all that Ruskin values for the 'charm of colour' he finds it has 'in common with the greater part of the architecture, as well as of the manufactures, of the East' (*Works*, X, 58). This charm of colour is unique to what he calls the 'school of incrusted architecture' – '*the only one in which perfect and permanent chromatic decoration is possible*' (ibid.). Yet such beautiful colour is not to be associated with gaiety or festivity:

> ... the bright hues of the early architecture of Venice were no signs of gaiety of heart, ... the investiture with the mantle of many colours by which she is known above all other cities of Italy and of Europe, was not granted to her in the fever of her festivity, but in the solemnity of her early and earnest religion. ... her glorious robe of gold and purple was given her when first she rose a vestal from the sea, not when she became drunk with the wine of her fornication [Revelation 17:2]. (*Works*, X, 177)

This strongly evangelical emphasis upon judgement in *The Stones of Venice* helps to explain why Ruskin pays close attention to what he calls the 'Judgment Angle' of the Ducal Palace – the sculpture of Solomon in judgement which, significantly, faces the Baptistery of St Mark's. Elsewhere I have argued[6] that criticism on Ruskin and architecture, and on Ruskin and religion, has failed to recognize the significance for him of key

---

[5] For an explanation of the colour purple in the Priests' Code, see J. Hastings, *Dictionary of the Bible*, second edn, rev. by F. C. Grant and H. H. Rowley (Edinburgh, 1963), 170. Among other passages in which Ruskin refers to the colours of the tabernacle, see especially *Works*, X, 175; VI, 113. 'Moreover thou shalt make the tabernacle with ten curtains of fine twined linen, and blue, and purple, and scarlet: with cherubims of cunning work shalt thou make them' (Exodus 26:1); 'And of the blue, and purple, and scarlet, they made cloths of service, to do service in the holy place, and made the holy garments for Aaron; as the Lord commanded Moses. / And he made the ephod of gold, blue, and purple, and scarlet, and fine twined linen. / And they did beat the gold into thin plates, and cut it into wires, to work it in the blue, and in the purple, and in the scarlet, and in the fine linen, with cunning work' (Exodus 39:1–3).

[6] See 'Ruskin among the ruins: tradition and the temple', in *The Lamp of Memory: Ruskin, tradition and architecture*, ed. M. Wheeler and N. Whiteley (Manchester, 1992), 77–97.

biblical terms such as 'ruin' (meaning fall) and 'restoration' (of Israel), and of the powerful symbolism associated with the temple in Jerusalem, where the earthly and the eternal meet, and where both the fall and God's judgement are continually enacted.[7] In my view the biblical type of the temple and its associated symbolism underpin Ruskin's whole critique of architecture, which must be read in the context of evangelical apocalyptic. The famous description of St Mark's, Venice, for example, in the second volume of *The Stones of Venice*, is remarkable not least for its subtle intertextual relations – a conflation of Old and New Testament prophecy, of visions of earth and heaven, of physical and spiritual temples (*Works*, X, 82–3). The *raising* of Solomon's temple in 1 Kings 6 is folded into the description in Revelation 21 of the heavenly Jerusalem which came *down* from God out of heaven, when 'the first heaven and the first earth were passed away; and there was no more sea'.[8] Like Torcello, although richer symbolically, St Mark's is a sign of mediation between earth and heaven, and of a present hope of future restoration – ideas that are prepared for in echoes of the 'broken walls' of Jerusalem, the 'goodly stones' of the temple here applied to the Doge's Palace, and St Paul's call to the Romans to be 'transformed'.[9] The appallingly crude restoration work carried out on St Mark's, which later became the subject of one of Ruskin's more successful protest campaigns,[10] takes on added significance when one considers the moral and religious freight which the building's symbolic sculpture had for him. His richest sign of salvation from ruin was being ruined.

It was during his stay in Venice in 1876–77 with the intention of rewriting *The Stones of Venice* that Ruskin was introduced to Count Zorzi and became most deeply involved in the campaign to save St Mark's from further damage. In a letter to Zorzi, published in the Count's book on the

---

[7] See, e.g., K. O. Garrigan, *Ruskin on Architecture: his thought and influence* (Madison and London, 1973), and R. E. Fitch, *The Poison Sky: myth and apocalypse in Ruskin* (Athens, Ohio and London, 1982).

[8] See particularly 1 Kings 6:3, 20–22, 24, 29 and Revelation 21:12, 21. Later in the chapter Ruskin writes of the 'glory of the temple' that is St Mark's, and quotes 1 Kings 10:9 (cf. also Genesis 18:19, Proverbs 21:3, Jeremiah 22:15) as the sound in the echo of its vaults, 'that one day shall fill the vault of heaven, – "He shall return to do judgment and justice"' (*Works*, X, 141). He also explicitly links St Mark's with Solomon's temple in his *Guide to the Academy at Venice*, 1877 (*Works*, XXIV, 164), and with the cleansing of the temple in *The Stones of Venice* (*Works*, X, 84). In *St Mark's Rest*, 1877, he links the Tyrian 'Thronos' with Solomon's (*Works*, XXIV, 243), and in an unpublished passage writes of 'Venice in her Tyrian time, parallel in the history of Israel to the reign of Solomon in alliance with Hiram' (*Works*, XXIV, 445).

[9] See, e.g., 2 Kings 25:10, Luke 21:5, Romans 12:2. In *Stones* I, chapter 5, 'The Wall Veil', Ruskin describes 'a fragment of [nature's] building among the Alps' as a 'group of broken walls, one of them overhanging' (*Works*, IX, 85).

[10] See R. Hewison, *Ruskin and Venice* (London, 1974), 28–9.

restoration work (1877), Ruskin laments recent developments, recalling how in 1876 he took back to London 'for principal illustration, and, to my bitter sorrow, was able to hold in my hand, and show to my scholars, pieces of the white and purple veined alabasters, more than a foot square, bought here in Venice out of the wrecks of restoration' (*Works*, XXIV, 408).[11] He also remembers nostalgically 'the bright recess of your Piazzetta, by the pillars of Acre' where he once spent so many 'happy and ardent days' (*Works*, XXIV, 405–6). The mosaics 'especially were of such exquisite intricacy of deep golden glow between the courses of small pillars, that those two upper arches [of the south side, which had then been 'restored'] had an effect as of peacock's feathers in the sun, when their green and purple glitters through and through with light. But now they have the look of a peacock's feather that has been dipped in white paint' (*Works*, XXIV, 407–8). Unrau has compared the present structure of St Mark's with a photograph of the early 1860s which identifies 'particular slabs of the purple-veined marbles which were removed'.[12] As if to compensate for this loss of colour, Ruskin was later to make a number of drawings on purple paper, including one of the pillars of Acre.[13]

Ruskin had commented on the peacock as a favourite symbol of resurrection in Byzantine art in *The Stones of Venice* (*Works*, X, 171), and was to

---

[11] He adds that, in his youth, he painted 'literally vein for vein' the 'same veined purple alabaster as St Mark's that were to be found at the Gothic palace at San Severo' (*Works*, XXIV, 409; cf. X, 308). Ruskin wrote urgently to his cousin Joan Severn at Brantwood, on 24 February 1877, asking her to send him this drawing 'of the purple veined marble' so that he could fulfil his promise to the Count that he would exhibit it in Venice by the time the book appeared: Lancaster MS L41.

[12] John Unrau, *Ruskin and St Mark's* (London, 1984), 127.

[13] *The Pillars of Acre and Southwest Portico of St Mark's* (reversed image), 1879; pencil and watercolour heightened with white on purple paper (152 × 89), British Museum. The drawing figured in an 'Exhibition of Drawings and Sketches' in the British Museum in 1901. The Guide read (p. 61): 'A very characteristic example of Mr. Ruskin's remarkable power of eye and hand in expressing the detail and character of sculptured ornaments. He loved the colour purple, and has translated the material of these columns into that colour for his pleasure' (*Works*, XXXVIII, 298). Hewison notes that 'Ruskin's works on purple-tinted paper form a distinct group; some of them are dated 1879, and it is reasonable to attribute the whole group to that year. It is likely that Ruskin made the series as an indirect consequence of the request from Norton to copy the large drawing of the north-west portico of St Mark's. It may be an indication of Ruskin's mental confusion that he was not concerned which way round the subject appeared' (*Ruskin and Venice*, 90; Hewison reproduces John Hobbs's daguerreotype of the subject, probably Lancaster Daguerreotype 5, on the same page). The British Museum has another drawing on purple paper: *Jean d'Acre Pillar, Venice*, watercolour, with white (280 × 222). A drawing of *Palazzo Bernardo a S. Polo* (Lancaster 1578) is on purple-coated paper, and is based on Lancaster Daguerreotype 24. (Daguerreotypes themselves have been said to have a purple tint, and this is certainly pronounced where the copper plate is exposed through deterioration, as in this case.)

write to Rooke in 1879: 'The real *fact* is that all Byzantine mosaic (and all Eastern colour) has splendour for its first object – and its type is the peacock's tail. If your drawings glow and melt like that you are right' (*Works*, XXX, lviii). In July 1872 John Bunney, another of Ruskin's copyists, had given Ruskin a box, 2⅞ inches in diameter, containing fragments of mosaic and labelled, 'One of the Eyes of the Peacock's tail from old pavement in North Aisle of St Mark's Venice destroyed when the pavement was removed in April 1872' – literally the stones of Venice.[14] And peacocks – here part of the design for the cover of *The Stones of Venice* in which Ruskin had a hand (see Figure 1.1) – were associated in his mind with Solomon who, 'in his wisdom ... sent his ships to Tarshish for ... gold, and silver, ivory, and apes, and peacocks' (*Works*, XXVIII, 465–6).

By January 1877 Ruskin's plans for the revised version of *The Stones of Venice*, which he now regarded as insolently evangelical in tone, had been abandoned in favour of the new project, *St Mark's Rest*, which he began at the same time as his finest architectural drawing – a large drawing of what he called the 'gold and purple' northwest portico (*Works*, XXIV, xxxvi). 'Throughout the whole façade of St Mark's', Ruskin was to write in 1879, 'the capitals have only here and there by casualty lost so much as a volute or an acanthus leaf, and whatever remains is perfect as on the day it was set in its place, mellowed and subdued only in colour by time, but white still, clearly white; and grey still, softly grey; its porphyry purple as an Orleans plum, and the serpentine as green as a greengage' (*Works*, XXIV, 419).

The first seven chapters of *St Mark's Rest*, and chapter 10, appeared in 1877; chapters 8 and 11 in 1879 (following the first terrible period of dementia in 1878); the rest in 1884. It is in chapter 5, 'The Shadow on the Dial', that Ruskin defines the third period in the history of Venice (1301 to 1530) as being 'that of religious meditation, as distinct, though not withdrawn from, religious action' (*Works*, XXIV, 255). He adds, 'The entire body of her noble art-work belongs to this time.' He then describes the craft guilds:

> Protected and encouraged by a senate thus composed, distinct companies of craftsmen, wholly of the people, gathered into vowed fraternities of social order; and, retaining the illiterate sincerities of their religion, laboured in unambitious peace, under the orders of the philosophic aristocracy; – built for them their great palaces, and overlaid their walls, within and without, with gold and purple of Tyre, precious now in Venetian hands as the colours of heaven more than of the sea. (*Works*, XXIV, 257)

---

[14] Hewison, *Ruskin and Venice*, 96.

But *St Mark's Rest* itself is far from being a restful, ordered text: its confusions and disappointments reflect Ruskin's state of mind during this stay in Venice, much of which is devoted to an obsessive study of Carpaccio's St Ursula series, now inextricably associated in Ruskin's dreams with the spirit of Rose la Touche, who had died in 1875.[15] On Sunday 20 May 1877, however, towards the end of his work on St Mark's, the discovery of a particular mosaic brightens him – 'a mosaic of upright figures in dresses of blue, green, purple, and white, variously embroidered with gold' (*Works*, XXIV, 294; see Figure 1.2). Ruskin made his own watercolour *Study of Mosaic of the Doge and his People* on the spot, and four days later was homeward bound, his head full of it. Two years later he recorded in chapter 8 of *St Mark's Rest*, 'The Requiem', that this remained the 'most precious "historical picture"' to his mind 'of any in worldly gallery, or unworldly cloister, east or west' (*Works*, XXIV, 296). And we have a second drawing of the Doge and his people made on 20 May 1877, for Ruskin had asked Charles Fairfax Murray to join him that day and bring his drawing materials: 'I am going up into the gallery, behind the organ at St Mark's, to study a mosaic plainly visible, and of extreme beauty and importance. A sketch of it … will be the most important work you or I have yet done in Venice' (*Works*, XXIV, xl). The mosaic was important to Ruskin, I believe, because it depicts not only the harmony between church, people and Doge that is so sadly lacking in the modern world, but the Doge is shown to be 'serene of mind'. The restless author of *St Mark's Rest* comments, 'Most Serene Highnesses of all the after Time and World, – how many of you knew, or know, what this Venice, first to give the title, meant by her Duke's Serenity! and why she trusted it?' (*Works*, XXIV, 296).

A few pages later in the same chapter is Ruskin's description of the eastern dome with which I began. 'My notes have got confused', he confesses to the reader, 'and many lost; and now I have no time to mend the thread of them: I am not sure even if I have the list of the Prophets complete' (*Works*, XXIV, 300). He does, in fact, but, as Cook and Wedderburn note, he misreads some of the inscriptions on a dome that is 'blackened with age and from candles'. In order to keep a true record of the mosaics and to endow the Guild's collection in Sheffield with suitable original illustrations of what he describes in his books, Ruskin commissions drawings from his copyists, among them T. M. Rooke, whose *Christ surrounded by prophets on the eastern cupola of St Mark's* (1879) is shown in Figure 1.3. On 20 July 1879 Ruskin wrote from Brantwood

---

[15] See V. Akin Burd, *Christmas Story: John Ruskin's Venetian Letters of 1876–1877, with an introductory essay on Ruskin and Spiritualists, his Quest for the Unseen* (Newark, NJ and London, 1990).

instructing Rooke, 'Do not be hampered by any idea of putting the drawings together so as to show united grouping and effect. That must be done by perspective drawings and quite other methods of work … *Your* work is to give the facts point blank of each figure, as fully as you can, caring nothing for junction' (*Works*, XXX, lvii). Having seen some of Rooke's work, he wrote again on 23 November:

> I am entirely pleased with them as documentary work: but they still – and even more than hitherto, disappoint me in colour, possessing none of the *charm*, to my own eyes, of the originals; but only their dignity and sobriety. I think this may be partly owing to the state of your health – and partly to your reading always on the sober – as I do on the gaudy, side of colour …[16]

Unrau believes that Rooke's drawing of the eastern dome 'suggests grounds for this dissatisfaction': 'The "decorative power" of the blues and purples is not absent from Rooke's attempt, but their infinite tonal ranges (from blackish blue through vivid blue to bluish white; from darkest violet to lilac grey) defeat him utterly.'[17] But then, as Unrau also points out, Ruskin was asking for the impossible.

He was also asking John Bunney – best known for his large and laborious painting of the west front of St Mark's – 'to make a sketch … of the David and Solomon, of the apse cupola', not in competition with or opposition to Rooke, he hastens to add, but in order to get the 'facts' of the colours in a way that is more habitual to him.[18] Bunney's drawing of David and Solomon certainly pays close attention to those facts, as Ruskin wished; and even Rooke, presumably under instruction from Ruskin, places at the centre of his drawing, not the Virgin, which would be conventionally correct, but Solomon, whose inscription Ruskin translates as 'Who is this that ascends as the morning?' (Canticles 6:9).

Let us return to the passage I quoted at the beginning, in which Ruskin describes the figures on the eastern dome in 'The Requiem':

> The decorative power of the colour in these figures, chiefly blue, purple, and white, on gold, is entirely admirable, – more especially the dark purple of the Virgin's robe, with lines of gold for its folds; and the figures of David and Solomon, both in Persian tiaras, almost Arab, with falling lappets to the shoulder, for shade; David holding a book with Hebrew letters on it

---

[16] Unrau, *Ruskin and St Mark's*, 208.

[17] Unrau, *Ruskin and St Mark's*, 208.

[18] Unrau, *Ruskin and St Mark's*, 208. On 22 January 1880 Bunney was paid nine pounds 'for the drawing of two Prophets on dome of choir', according to Guild of St George accounts associated with 'Memorial Studies of St. Mark's (Venice) Fund' (*Works*, XXX, 63). The drawing is at Lancaster under the title *Venice – Mosaics in St. Mark's* (Lancaster 127), and is a detailed study in the colours of the robes and inscriptions of David and Solomon, as well as of the background gold of the eastern dome.

and a cross (a pretty sign for the Psalms); and Solomon with rich orbs of lace like involved ornament on his dark robe, cusped in the short hem of it, over gold underneath. And note in all these mosaics that Byzantine 'purple,' – the colour at once meaning Kinghood and its Sorrow, – is the same as ours – not scarlet, but amethyst, and that deep. (*Works*, XXIV, 301–2)

I suggested earlier that the biblical type of Solomon's temple and its associated symbolism underpin Ruskin's whole critique of architecture. And there is more, for in *Unto this Last* Ruskin marks his transition to more overt social polemics by invoking Solomon as a 'Jew merchant' whose Proverbs offers a radical alternative to Victorian *laissez-faire* capitalist economics (*Works*, XVII, 57).[19] Indeed, I believe that much of Ruskin's literary project, particularly in the middle and later periods, was an attempt to write the nineteenth-century equivalent of the Old Testament wisdom literature that is associated with Solomon.[20] More specifically, I have suggested here that Solomon and his temple are closely linked with St Mark's, Venice in Ruskin's mind.[21] An image of Solomon seems to have played a role in his religious development, as Ruskin was copying Veronese's *Presentation of the Queen of Sheba to Solomon* when he underwent what he later described as his 'unconversion' from evangelical dogma in Turin in 1858. He wrote to his father on 9 August that year:

The way I took a fancy to his Solomon was especially on account of a beautiful white falcon on a falconer's fist, which comes against his dark purple robe – I thought it was only a pretty trick of colour; but as I worked on I saw that the white falcon was exactly and studiously under the head of one of the lions which sustain the throne, so that the sitting figure is sustained by the lion and eagle, who were the types of the Divine and Human power in Christ; and to show that he really meant to indicate thus Solomon's typical character, he has made one of the elders on the steps of the throne point to Solomon with a jewelled cross – a tremendous licence, by the way, as I imagine the Jews at that period would have avoided any

---

[19] In the penultimate paragraph of the previous chapter, Ruskin writes of gold coins as 'a kind of Byzantine harness or trapping', and adds, 'In fact, it may be discovered that the true veins of wealth are purple – and not in Rock, but in Flesh – perhaps even that the final outcome and consummation of all wealth is in the producing as many as possible full-breathed, bright-eyed, and happy-hearted human creatures' (*Works*, XVII, 55–6).

[20] Wheeler, *Ruskin's God*.

[21] A further illustration of this is in chapter 7 of *St Mark's Rest*, 'Divine Right', where Ruskin writes of the Doge Selve: 'this prince is one who has at once David's piety, and soldiership, and Solomon's love of fine things; a perfect man, as I read him, capable at once and gentle, – religious, and joyful, – in the extreme … Flaw he had, such as wisest men are not unliable to, with the strongest – Solomon, Samson, Hercules, Merlin the Magician.

Liking pretty things, how could he help liking pretty ladies?' (*Works*, XXIV, 274)

crosslet ornament as much as after the time of Christ; but it answers his purpose. (*Works*, XVI, xxxix)

Here, then, is another clue to that later, published description of the mosaic of Solomon in *St Mark's Rest*; of Solomon robed in purple, the colour of his kinghood and his sorrow; of Solomon the type of Christ who was clothed in purple, and 'when they had mocked him, they took off the purple from him, and put his own clothes on him, and led him out to crucify him' (Mark 15:20). Ruskin's attempt to persuade his copyists to get the colour right in their drawings of the mosaics of St Mark's is more than the fretting of a now mentally unstable perfectionist. A crucial period in which he lived with the monks at Assisi and also worked in Florence in 1874 had deepened his understanding of Roman Catholicism and the Franciscans. Rumours began to circulate in England that he had converted, and in the April *Fors Clavigera* of 1877, written in Venice, he denied them, explaining that he was in fact 'a "Catholic" of those Catholics, to whom the Catholic Epistle of St. James is addressed' (*Works*, XXIX, 92). His work on *St Mark's Rest* at this time is as much a religious as an aesthetic project. Byzantine 'purple' is not only a colour of great 'charm' for him; it is the colour of kingship and of sorrow, and thus, read typologically, the colour of redemption.

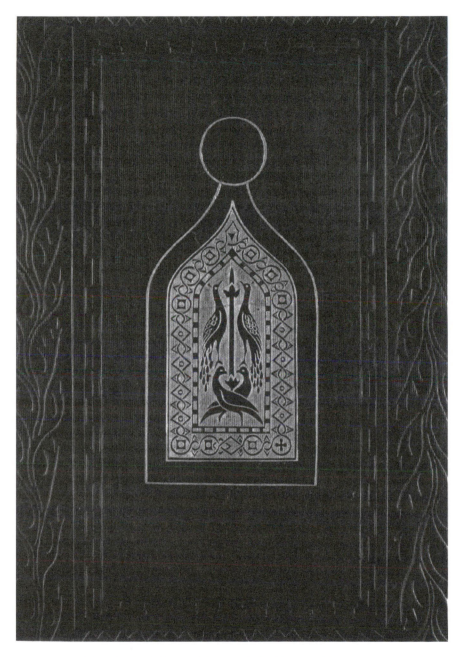

Fig 1.1. John Ruskin, Study of Mosaic of the Doge and his People *(1877),*
(photograph: Ashmolean Museum, Oxford)

Fig 1.2. T. M. Rooke, Christ surrounded by prophets on the eastern cupola of St Mark's (1879) (by permission of the Ruskin Gallery, Collection of the Guild of Saint George, Sheffield)

Fig. 1.3. John Ruskin, cover design for The Stones of Venice *(1851–53) (author's copy)*

2. Twin reflections of a Byzantine city: Monemvasia as seen by Robert Weir Schultz and Sidney H. Barnsley in 1890

Haris Kalligas

Robert Weir Schultz was born in 1860 in Scotland, where he was trained as an architect.[1] In 1885 he won the Golden Medal of the Royal Academy and the Travelling Scholarship of £200 that went with it. With Sidney Howard Barnsley, also an architect, who was five years younger, he set out in 1887, and together they visited Italy, Greece and Turkey. In Greece they worked for the British School on subjects that had to do with Ancient Greece: monuments, inscriptions, weapons and sculpture. The Report of the Director of the British School for the year 1888–89 shows Schultz busy recording remains from the classical period:

> In Greece the important work of making a fairly complete set of accurate drawings, to full scale, of Greek mouldings of the best period has been undertaken, and in great part carried out, by Mr. Schultz, who has been sent out by the School for this purpose.[2]

Around this time a strong interest in Byzantine monuments started to be expressed by a number of French scholars, Gabriel Millet in particular. In the later part of 1888 Millet undertook the responsibility for the restoration of an important monument of the middle Byzantine period:

[1] I would like to express my warmest gratitude to all the people who helped me in various stages with the material related to this paper, and in particular Michael Angold, Robin Cormack, Liza French, Hector Catling, the late Martin Price, Richard A. Tomlinson, Margaret Cogzell and Penny Wilson-Zarganis. I would also like to thank the British School at Athens for permission to study and publish material from the Notebooks. Biographical information on R. W. Schultz is based mainly on the book by Gavin Stamp, *Robert Weir Schultz, Architect, and his work for the Marquess of Bute. An Essay* (Mount Stuart, 1981).

[2] *JHS* 10 (1889), 274.

Daphni. The Prime Minister Trikoupis was persuaded to intervene to save the monument, which was in real danger, and the works began.[3]

Soon we find the British expressing similar interests. In the Minutes of the Annual General Assembly for the year 1889 of the British School at Athens there is a relevant paragraph:

Thus far the work to which reference has been made belongs to the field of classical archaeology. But an interesting and important feature in the year's record is the increased attention which is being given to architecture and art of the Byzantine age. The Greek Government has made grants towards the repair of the monastery of Daphni in Attica and of St Luke of Stiris in Boetia. These are among the finest examples of Byzantine work in Greece; the two churches at Stiris are said to be especially fine, though grievously dilapidated. With this province of work too, the British School has actively associated itself. The school has undertaken to prepare a series of plans and elevations of the chief Byzantine churches in Greece, with copies of their frescoes and mosaics. During the past year, Mr. Schultz, in conjunction with Mr. Barnsley – also a student of the School and of the Royal Academy – has been working at this subject. Another year, it is hoped, may suffice to complete their labours. This new manifestation of interest in the Byzantine period may be noted with great satisfaction, since it has sometimes been complained that, in Greece, classical monuments have been explored at the point of obliterating the remains of later ages.[4]

The material collected by the two architects during the years of their travels is deposited in the Archives of the British School at Athens; it is composed of architectural plans of various monuments, like Hosios Loukas and Kambia, Daphni, Saint Sophia of Monemvasia, together with photographs and their notebooks.

There are fifteen photographs of Monemvasia which show the rock and the city in the late nineteenth century and give valuable information (Figure 2.1). Their plans of Saint Sophia of Monemvasia are particularly important because part of the church has since collapsed.

The Notebooks (NB) have few notes and many sketches; in fact they are sketchbooks. Nineteen belonged to Robert Weir Schultz, and nine to Sidney Howard Barnsley. The material is in random order. Notes are few, almost rare, dates not always carefuly noted, particularly by Schultz. They sketched classical sculpture and mouldings and copied inscriptions; they recorded all sorts of things that may not have been relevant to

[3] Gabriel Millet, *Le monastère de Daphni. Histoire, architecture, mosaiques* (Paris, 1899), x.

[4] *JHS* 10 (1889), xlix. The understanding of all the facts regarding the survey, study and restoration of a number of Byzantine monuments during this period is not possible without further research being conducted in the Archives of both the French and the British Schools.

Fig 2.1. The Byzantine bridge in Monemvasia, 1890

classical art, such as boats, boots, figures, fireplaces and houses. Some
pleasures, like 'a little ouzo' in the guestroom of Hosios Loukas, next to
a nice fireplace, are mentioned. Names and addresses appear. In between the sketches, there are large sections of copied extracts from books
relating to various monuments or other subjects contained in the notebooks.

The sequence of their travels, which is not clear at first glance, can,
however, be reconstructed. Schultz's first sketches date from 1887, with
the last from Megalopolis in 1891. Barnsley's go from 1888 to 1890.

In Schultz's notebooks, after Italy, sketches of the classical mouldings
alternate with the survey of Daphni, where he had helped the French.[5]
During the first months of 1888 the two architects worked in Athens; in
the spring they are found in Mistra and a little later they visit Constantinople and Thessaloniki; then Italy. Early next year we find them working
at the Akropolis of Athens, then visiting Thessaloniki. In between Ephesos
is mentioned. The fact that copied extracts of books are dated July 1889
indicates that they might have been studying in the Library of the British
School during the warm months of the summer. In late autumn of the
same year they are found working in Hosios Loukas and Daphni and
also in parts of Attica, like Paiania and Kaisariani. At the end of the year
they are at Livadia. Except for a short trip to Athens they seem to have
spent March, April and some part of May 1890 in Mistra, whence they
visit Androusa, Samari, Andromonastiro, Leondari, Kalamata, Karytena,
Olympia, Isova, Stemnitza, Tripolis, Tegea, Mantineia and Argos – all
before the end of May.

After which they visit Monemvasia. It is the sketch of a window that
opens the series of views of the old city (Figures 2.2 and 2.3). Barnsley
takes care to note: Monemvasia, June 6, 1890. This is the first of a series of
sketches, most of which are twin appearances of the same subjects, drawn
by each of them. After the window Schulz sketches a house, which is a
well-known landmark of the lower city; in Barnsley the same house
follows after other subjects (Figures 2.4 and 2.5). A wooden ceiling is
sketched by each in ink, with measurements and details (Figure 2.6). It is
Barnsley who notes: 'Monemvassia'. Another twin sketch is that of the
well-known Stellakis house. In Barnsley it is labelled 'Monemvasia from
sea wall, Battlements of wall, June 8', and comes immediately after the
ceiling (Figures 2.7 and 2.8).[6] Another house, of which each made sketches,

---

    [5] Millet, *Daphni*, x.

    [6] This beautiful house had partly collapsed after the Schultz and Barnsley visit and was
restored recently, unfortunately without the knowledge of the carvings given by the Schultz
and Barnsley sketches. An oil painting made in the 1920s by George Maleas was used for the
restoration, together with a student survey from the 1950s. Neither shows any carvings.

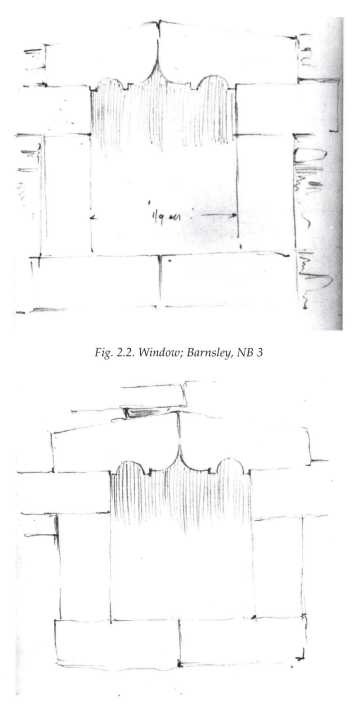

Fig. 2.2. Window; Barnsley, NB 3

Fig. 2.3. Window; Schultz, NB 3

Fig. 2.4. House; Barnsley, NB 3

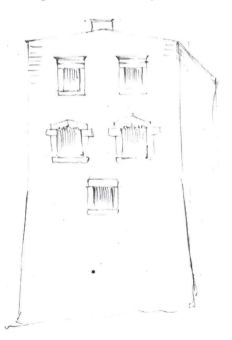

Fig. 2.5. House; Schultz, NB 3

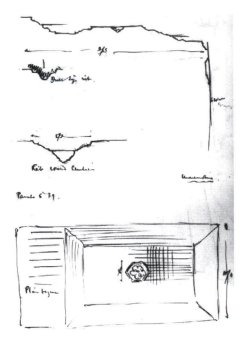

Fig. 2.6. Wooden ceiling; Barnsley, NB 3

Fig. 2.7. Stellakis house; Schultz, NB 3

Fig. 2.8. Stellakis house; Barnsley, NB 3

Fig. 2.9. A house; Schultz, NB 3

Fig. 2.10. A house; Barnsley, NB 3

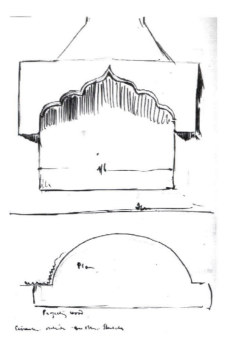

Fig. 2.11. Chimney; Barnsley, NB 3

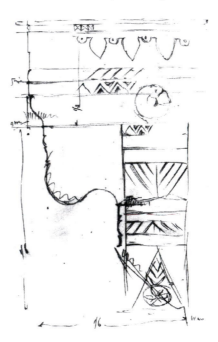

Fig. 2.12. Details of chimney; Barnsley, NB 3

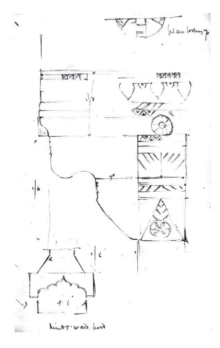

Fig. 2.13. Chimney and details; Schultz, NB 3

Fig. 2.14. Shop with double window; Barnsley, NB 3

Fig. 2.15. Twin shops; Barnsley, NB 3

Fig. 2.16. Photograph of twin shops

had similarities with the Stellakis – for example, a projecting chimney and lovely carved windows. It was approached by an external vaulted staircase (Figures 2.9 and 2.10). The house no longer exists and it has not been possible to identify its remains. A final subject common to both is the fireplace in the interior of this house which is of a kind found frequently in Monemvasia (Figures 2.11–2.13).

Barnsley did some more drawings. One is of a shop with a house on top in the main street near the main gate of the lower city (Figure 2.14). It had a rare element above the large opening of the shop: a double window which has been blocked after their visit. Another is of twin shops situated next to the previous one in the main street. He notes: 'Sunday June 8'. The sketch is very pale. In this case it is clear that Barnsley's technical skills failed him and he was not able to record the complex façade with the protruding elaborate semi-hexagonal twin fireplaces, and various cornices and arches. All these are shown in detail in the charming corresponding photograph, which also shows a crowd of people who gathered around the photographer (Figures 2.15 and 2.16).

It is possible that, in this and other cases, Barnsley sketched while Schultz photographed; another sketch by Barnsley has a corresponding photograph. It is of a house situated near the sea-wall, not far from the Stellakis house. It had three stories and impressive buttresses. Some of

Fig. 2.17. House with buttresses; Barnsley, NB 3

Fig. 2.18. Photograph of house with buttresses

the houses around it exist to this day, but there is one fundamental change, with the building in the first years of the twentieth century of a large house in neo-classical style a little higher up (Figures 2.17 and 2.18).

Two sketches by Barnsley show an eighteenth-century wooden icon-stand, inlaid with ivory and mother-of-pearl, which is still in the metro-politan church. He comments, 'see photo'; and indeed two of their photographs do show this object (Figure 2.19). In one of the photographs the late seventeenth-century wooden iconostasis of the metropolitan church can be seen still in place; a new marble one was installed at the turn of the century. Two more pages of notes and sketches from Elkomenos by Schultz are found among the Saint Sophia material; they include the central apse with the synthronon, information on the iconostasis and a transcription of an inscription, which was found on 'a slab in Elkomenos'. The inscription, which mentions large-scale works in Elkomenos in 1538, was published by the Greek scholar C. Zesiou a few years later and seems to have been lost since.[7] On the same page there are sketches from other churches of the lower town: a section and elevation of the dome of

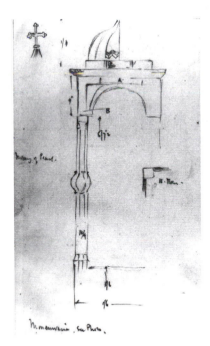

Fig. 2.19. Icon-stand in the church of Elkomenos; Barnsley, NB 3

---

[7] *Byzantis* 1 (1909), 114–25.

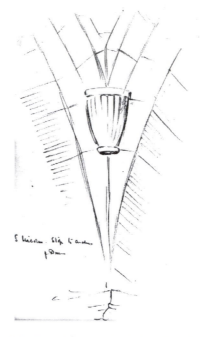

Fig. 2.20. Detail from St Nicholas; Barnsley, NB 3

Fig. 2.21. Chimney; Barnsley, NB 3

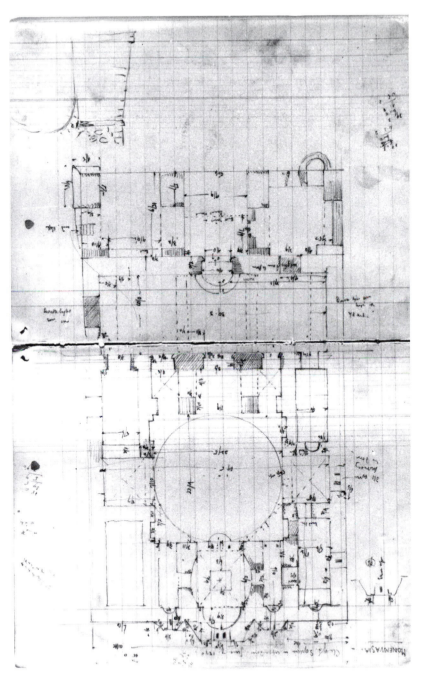

Fig. 2.22. Sketch of plan for the survey of St Sophia; Barnsley, NB 8

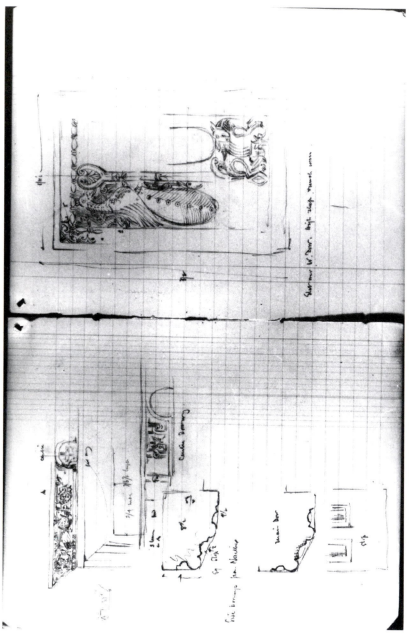

Fig. 2.23. Details for the survey of St Sophia; Barnsley, NB 8

Our Lady of Crete and a plan of Saint Nicholas. Barnsley also has a sketch of Saint Nicholas (Figure 2.20). An additional Saint Nicholas sketch by Schultz is found among material from Mantineia and Thebes. Next to it is the sketch of a projecting chimney, which is the twin of a sketch by Barnsley who, being more tidy, had it in the sequence of his Monemvasia drawings. It most probably represents a chimney of the Kalogeras house, and this brings us back to the twin reflections (Figure 2.21).

No other place in Greece caught the interest of the two architects as much as Monemvasia. They give occasional, often twin, drawings in Mistra, or Livadia, or Argos, but never as numerous. Their main task in Monemvasia was the survey of Saint Sophia. It is interesting to note that in the case of the survey of Saint Sophia the work has been divided and each one of the architects, as normally is the case, prepared their respective and distinctive sketches before collaborating for measuring (Figures 2.22 and 2.23). The unique intensity of the architecture of the lower town, however, must have been very impressive and kept them busy with sketching when not surveying. During their wanderings among the ruins, Barnsley was quick to sketch his friend drawing while under an umbrella (Figure 2.24).

The architects seem to have left Monemvasia on 9 June and the story should have ended there. However, there is a coda. The impression left by their travels before arriving in Monemvasia is that, after leaving Tripolis in late May 1890, they took the road, to Mistra, as they had done several times, and from there arrived, by road, in Monemvasia a few days later. However, such was not the case.

For an unknown reason some pages in Schultz Notebook no. 14 have been erased, but if the light comes from the right direction, one can read some of the original notes:

> 4th June Cab to Piraeus and boat: 7.40
> Fare and Dinner: 31
> Books to …
> … to Monemvasia: 2
> Church: 170
> Bath at Monemvasia: 20 …, etc

This means that from Tegea they returned to Piraeus and from there took the boat to Monemvasia. So it is not certain if the two quick and impressive views, one of the rock with the old bridge and one of the lower town, which Schultz's skilful hand was able to produce, were really made when they approached the rock on 4 June or when they left for Kythera some days later (Figures 2.25 and 2.26).

From Kythera they visited Methoni, Navarino and Christianoi, before arriving around the end of the month in Saint Nicholas at Kambia, visit-

Fig. 2.24. Schultz sketching in Monemvasia; Barnsley, NB 8

Fig. 2.25. The rock and the bridge; Schultz, NB 3

Fig. 2.26. The rock and the lower town; Schultz, NB 3

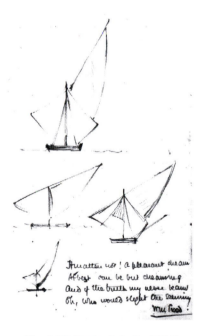

Fig. 2.27. Boats; Schultz, NB 1

ing Skripou and Hosios Loukas in July, then Thebes, Thessaloniki, Hosios Loukas again and Arta in October. Sometime in 1891 Schultz is found working in Megalopolis, Argos, Oropos and Athens. He had returned to the classical world.[8]

Schultz and Barnsley seem to have enjoyed every moment of their trips. It was an experience that went beyond the strict study of ancient or Byzantine monuments. Their sketches convey a special flavour of the Greek landscape, the blend of historical periods, of seasons, of hospitality, liturgy, herbs, architectural details and boats – such as the ones Schultz sketched when he was in poetic mood (Figure 2.27).

---

[8] The British School had by then ceded some rights for archaeological research to the French; cf. *JHS* 12 (1891), xlvii.

3. The Great Palace dig: the Scottish perspective

Mary Whitby

Introduction: the Great Palace mosaic

In 1997 a fifteen-year rescue, restoration and conservation project (1983–97) on the peristyle mosaic pavement of the Great Palace in Constantinople was completed.[1] Sixty years after its discovery, this work has at last established an archaeological basis for dating the mosaic: the restorers locate it in the reign of Justinian, and suggest that it formed part of his great rebuilding programme in the capital following the destructive fires of the Nika Riot (AD 532).[2] Its importance and interest remain undis-

---

[1] Organized jointly by the Austrian Academy of Sciences and the Directorate General of Monuments and Museums in Turkey. A preliminary report appeared in 1992: W. Jobst and Hermann Vetters, eds, *Mosaikforschung im Kaiserpalast von Konstantinopel*, Österreichische Akademie der Wissenschaften, philosophisch-historische Klasse, Denkschriften, 228 Band (Vienna, 1992). Illustrated updates for 1993–95: *Anzeige der phil.-hist. Klasse der Österreichischen Akademie der Wissenschaften* 131 (1994), 43–51; 132 (1995), 29–49; 133 (1996), 11–27. See further W. Jobst, 'Archäologie und Denkmalpflege im Bereich des "Grossen Palastes" von Konstantinopel', in A. Iacobini and E. Zanini, eds, *Arte profana e arte sacra a Bisanzio* (Rome, 1995), 227–36; W. Jobst, B. Erdal and C. Gurtner, *Istanbul. The Great Palace Mosaic. The story of its exploration, preservation and exhibition, 1983–1997* (Istanbul, 1997) [text in Turkish, German and English; many illustrations].

[2] Date: Jobst, Erdal and Gurtner, *Great Palace Mosaic*, 58–61. Among recent art-historical discussions, see especially James Trilling, 'The Soul of the Empire: style and meaning in the mosaic pavement of the Byzantine imperial palace in Constantinople', *DOP* 43 (1989), 27–72 (survey of earlier studies, 31–6); P. J. Nordhagen, 'The mosaics of the Great Palace of Constantinople: a note on an archaeological puzzle', in L. Rydén and J. O. Rosenqvist, eds, *Aspects of Late Antiquity and Early Byzantium*, Swedish Research Institute in Istanbul, Transactions, vol. 4 (Uppsala, 1993), 167–71; M. Mundell Mango, 'Imperial art in the seventh century', in P. Magdalino, ed., *New Constantines: the rhythm of imperial renewal in Byzantium, 4th–13th centuries* (Aldershot, 1994), 109–38, at 131–4, and L.-A. Hunt, 'The Byzantine Mosaics of Jordan in context: remarks on imagery, donors and mosaicists', *Palestine Exploration Quarterly* 126 (1994), 106–26, at 115–19. See further Addendum (p. 56).

---

puted, both as a major art-historical find crucial to the understanding of
the development of Byzantine art, and as the most spectacular part of the
Great Palace to have been revealed by archaeological excavation.

This chapter deals, however, not with scholarly or archaeological issues, but with personalities. It sketches the unusual background to the
first excavation, which was undertaken between 1935 and 1938 under
the auspices of the Walker Trust of the University of St Andrews, Scotland,[3] and focuses on three figures, two Scots and an Englishman, none a
professional archaeologist or Byzantinist, whose combined operations
brought them to an altogether unexpected discovery. At the centre is Sir
David Russell, Fife paper manufacurer, entrepreneur, philanthropist and
benefactor, who instigated and financed the enterprise and offered personal support over twenty years.[4] The 1930s dig was led by the Glaswegian James Houston Baxter, Professor of Ecclesiastical History at the
University of St Andrews, while driving force and inspiration was provided by Major Wellesley Tudor Pole, who came from a Bristol family of
flour, grain and cereal merchants and saw distinguished service in the
Middle East in the First World War.[5]

Wellesley Tudor Pole and the Quest

> *Now* we can hope and believe that the stars are fighting on our side & that
> a new spiritual & historical revelation is at hand.

This sentence from a letter of Tudor Pole (Figure 3.1) to Baxter in March
1933[6] describes his excitement and optimism that archaeological work
on the Great Palace site might soon begin. A letter written two months
earlier, on 3 January 1933, gives fuller details about the background to
the dig.[7] It followed a visit to Istanbul by Baxter in December 1932 in
which he had been able both to approach the Turkish authorities person-
ally with plans and the request for a permit to conduct a survey and

---

[3] Papers relating to the dig are preserved in two archives in St Andrews University
Library: the Russell Papers and the Baxter Papers; my essay is largely based upon the
Baxter correspondence. In working on these archives I have been greatly aided by Mr R.
N. Smart, until 1995 Archivist and Keeper of Muniments, who generously communicated
knowledge acquired over a long period and through personal acquaintance with the
participants; his assistants Mrs Christine Gascoigne and Mrs Cilla Jackson readily offered
cheerful practical help and his successor Dr Norman Reid has kindly resolved further
queries. I am grateful to Lady Jean Carroll and Mr David Tudor Pole, and to the Russell
Trust for permitting the publication of this material.

[4] See further Lorn Macintyre, *Sir David Russell: a biography* (Edinburgh, 1994). I am much
indebted to Dr Macintyre's work and to his ready assistance.

[5] Macintyre, *Russell*, 31, 34–7.

[6] St Andrews University Library, MS 36943/365.

[7] St Andrews University Library, MS 36943/316.

Fig. 3.1. Wellesley Tudor Pole in 1918 (photograph: Lady Jean Carroll)

Fig. 3.2. Baxter (left) and Russell inspecting one of the mosaic scenes uncovered
in 1935 (Baxter Papers, St Andrews University Library, MS 36966A)

limited digging (referred to in the letter as 'the Concession'), and to see for himself the sites in which he and his associates were interested.

> DR [David Russell] was extremely pleased with your report, indeed it could hardly have proved more satisfactory. We must now await further developments. If the time is ripe, then all will go forward smoothly. We have as you know various sources of information & guidance to draw upon, quite apart from the date, drawings and 'historical' details provided by BB. We cannot estimate the exact or proportionate values of the guidance received from these various sources. BB deals with practical matters, & in some ways his work can be likened to that of a water diviner, who can 'sense' where a well should be sunk.
>
> It is true that in 1908 (long before the BB work began) and using quite other methods of guidance, I visited the ruins of Justinian's house and felt sure that the remains of his Library could be found somewhere beneath these ruins. BB may quite likely save us time and expense, by indicating the exact spot where a shaft should be sunk and we cannot underestimate his part in Q[uest] work, or that of those through whom his 'directions' reach us. BB says he can mark the plan definitely now that you have visited the spot, as he was able to use your consciousness for 'seeing' conditions as they now are. In the past, under somewhat similar circumstances he has done the same, using me or another presence at certain spots for sensing the position there. But we have other sources. (i) Our individual inner vision or intuition. (ii) An intelligence called the Sage about whom DR will tell you more. His province is more with spiritual values than with material data. (iii) And of course the purely external history and traditions associated with these places and records found elsewhere. None of these avenues can be dismissed as without value. If they can all be unified, then we are in a strong position. It must be left to Destiny to decide who shall and who shall not be present on the spot when the actual excavations take place. To secure the Concession is the next step. The Russians have ceased all démarches in their efforts to secure French 'papers'. There will be no more danger there. You are very busy and this does not call for an answer, but I hope you will see DR again before long.

The initials BB refer to the spiritual 'control', later identified as Prince Oleg of Saxe-Altenburg, who had manifested himself in sessions conducted by Tudor Pole together with three Russian refugees (referred to at the end of the letter), whom he had adopted and supported after the Russian Revolution with the aid of friends, in particular his Quest collaborator, Frederick Leveaux, and David Russell. Although himself a psychic, Tudor Pole regarded his own powers as limited, and relied on the assistance of BB and other intermediaries like the 'Sage'.

The ruins of the House of Justinian with their striking arcaded loggia still stand close to the Sea of Marmara, although they were partially destroyed by the construction of the railway line in 1871. As the letter indicates, Tudor Pole's interest in this site went back to the first decade of this century,[8] when he had visited it for himself and become convinced that the library of the sixth-century emperor lay beneath. Superficial subterranean galleries had been revealed during work on the railway cutting, and in one of them was found a 'pagan marble statue of an angel', which had been appropriated by Tudor Pole's contact, Sir William Whittall.[9] The attempt to uncover the yet more precious material which Tudor Pole believed lay hidden intact in deeper chambers became 'the Quest' which occupied him until his death. In the course of the search the Great Palace pavement was discovered.

Tudor Pole explained to Baxter in a letter of 31 October 1932[10] (shortly before the latter's visit to Istanbul) that documents dating from the ninth to the eleventh century preserved in various Russian monasteries[11] provided evidence for the subterranean tunnel-system and the parchments and other treasures preserved in them. A gatehouse dated AD 273, built on a foundation of 650 BC, was believed to lie at a particular point beneath the gardens of the Sultan Ahmet (Blue) Mosque, and, in an adjacent oubliette, 'precious church vessels and parchments which have an association with St Paul'. Documents brought from Byzantium to Kiev by imperial ambassadors and patriarchal missionaries in the time of Prince (Saint) Vladimir had been carefully hidden by the abbot during the Revolution (information which presumably derived from the Russian monks in Tudor Pole's care). They included eight parchments dating from AD 872 which described the 'fight against the worship of Ikons and the last days of the Emperor Konstantin Kopronimos'. These recorded

---

[8] A letter of 1 May 1931 from Tudor Pole to David Russell suggests that it dated back as far as 1903: Macintyre, *Russell*, 125.

[9] St Andrews University Library, MS 36943/258, dated 19/10/32. The statue was perhaps a winged victory. Archaeological work has identified at least two stages in the development of the city walls in this area and various sculptural fragments are associated with the site. See E. Mamboury and T. Wiegand, *Die Kaiserpaläste von Konstantinopel* (Berlin and Leipzig, 1934), 1–25; D. Talbot Rice, ed., *The Great Palace of the Byzantine Emperors*, Second Report of the Walker Trust (Edinburgh, 1958), 168–93; C. Mango, 'Constantinopolitana', *Jahrbuch des Deutschen Archäologischen Instituts* 80 (1965), 305–36, at 317–23 (*Studies on Constantinople* [Aldershot, 1993], no. II). There is also literary evidence that the later terrace was built over a cistern: Theophanes Continuatus, 88.4–10 (Bonn ed.; I owe this reference to Professor Cyril Mango); the existence of subterranean passages and galleries is therefore unsurprising.

[10] St Andrews University Library, MS 36943/268d.

[11] Mentioned are the St Serge Monastery, Moscow, the Monastery of Ss Zozima and Zavaty (or Savvatij) on Solovky (or Solovetsky) island and the Kievo Pechevskaja Lavra. The documents from the Solovky monastery, now a prison, were believed to be preserved in the Rumiantzevsky Museum in Moscow, where Tudor Pole had a contact (MS 36948/263).

the burial in the cellars of the palace in Constantinople of the holy books and records of the library founded by 'Theodossian' and Justinian.

This letter accounts for Tudor Pole's interest in the vicinity of the Blue Mosque, which was to be the ultimate location of the 1935 excavation. It does not, however, make explicit that those engaged in the Quest expected to discover not only ancient documents and holy relics, but in addition a fabulous hoard of treasure. Tudor Pole had felt caution about revealing too much to Baxter at an early stage, lest the scholar be deterred by knowledge that the information was psychically received,[12] but correspondence during 1933 gradually enlightened him. A long letter of 26 March, which detailed 'Quest history', money so far outlaid, and a proposed schedule of excavation,[13] concluded on an optimistic note: 'However, immediately Chamber V is tapped and found *not* to be empty, money difficulties will disappear, even if no MSS are allowed to leave the country (even on loan).' Chamber V is prominently marked on scale plans which plotted the tunnel-system in minute detail (Figure 3.3), while a document marked 'Private and Confidential' and headed 'Supplemental Inventory: being List of Objects excluded from the Abridged Inventory'[14] itemizes the contents of twelve chests which were to be found in Chamber V. This three-page list includes ancient treasures such as 'the sword of the Emperor Arcadius (used as a sceptre at his coronation)', garments and artefacts adorned with jewels, and priceless gems such as 'an Indian sapphire, called "The Eye of God", (12 × 9 × 4.5 cms) XIX B.C., unset, wrapped in a brocade'.

It is easy to dismiss the combination of specious history, detailed plans and directions, and meticulous catalogue of treasure trove as mere dangerous fantasy, but there can be no doubt of the genuine and powerful sense of religious mission which inspired the Quest. In April 1933 Tudor Pole wrote to Baxter:[15]

> I hope MP [Michael Pojidaiev]'s descriptions etc. have not given you a too Arabian Nightish view of Quest activities! I have always known of the existence of these hoards secreted from the Treasury of Constantine and Justinian and was fairly sure that they were somewhere in the same series of underground chambers and not far from Ch. V. BB has given their location. In a way I am sorry for this, anyway at this juncture. The valu-

---

[12] Macintyre, *Russell*, 127.

[13] St Andrews University Library, MS 36943/385; cf. note 32 below.

[14] St Andrews University Library, MS 36943/435. This document was sent to Baxter in May 1933 by Tudor Pole's collaborator, Frederick Leveaux (MS 36943/434).

[15] St Andrews University Library, MS 36943/426. Michael Pojidaiev was one of the three Russians supported by Tudor Pole. Another, Dmitry Sissoeff, had died in 1930 (Macintyre, *Russell*, 125).

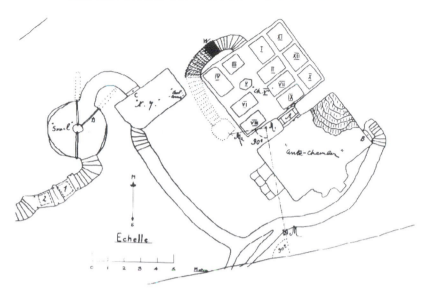

Fig. 3.3. Scale plan of subterranean passages, showing Chamber V with its twelve chests (one of four plans preserved in the Baxter Papers, St Andrews University Library, MS 36966A)

Fig. 3.4. Russell and Baxter in discussion with Turkish colleagues at the dig site (Russell Papers, St Andrews University Library, Box 16)

> ables in Ch. V (among the documents) are complication enough and will
> render our task more onerous and delicate. However, light will come step
> by step and we can but go forward along the allotted path.

In the letter of 13 March 1933 which provided the opening quotation[16]
Tudor Pole assured Baxter that he was about to succeed 'where the
Kaiser and the Austrian Emperor and others failed': attempts in 1906,
1908 and 1912 to secure a Concession to conduct archaeological work in
the area had been unsuccessful because 'the time was not ripe and the
people concerned were out for personal ends'. In November 1932 he
wrote, 'You will feel the call of this work more and more as each step is
taken, because the spiritual issues involved are far greater than either the
archaeological or the historical interests. I cannot explain what I mean by
letter, but the facts are as stated'.[17]

So, in December 1932 Baxter approached the Turkish authorities seeking permission for the Walker Trust of the University of St Andrews to
conduct a survey and to dig at specified points on the site of the House
of Justinian and in the gardens of the Sultan Ahmet mosque, which
certainly lies on top of part of the Great Palace. For Tudor Pole, Baxter's
visit to Istanbul marked the culmination of his twenty-five-year 'Quest'.

James Houston Baxter

Baxter appears to have become involved in the Quest late in 1931. By
then he was at the height of a distinguished academic career which
brought him the award of an honorary Doctorate of Divinity from Glas-
gow University in 1932 at the age of only 38. He had already held the
Chair of Ecclesiastical History at St Andrews for ten years.[18] He was a
Glaswegian of humble origins: interspersed amidst his extensive correspondence in several European languages with the most eminent scholars of the day are occasional letters from his father written on lined
exercise paper beginning 'Dear Son and Daughter', which describe everyday family affairs and, when appropriate, congratulate the son on his
academic achievements.

Baxter's chief interests were literary and focused on the Latin Fathers,
in particular St Augustine, although he also won high acclaim for his
edition of the letter-book of a fifteenth-century prior of St Andrews which

---

[16] See note 6 above.

[17] St Andrews University Library, MS 36943/286.

[18] In 1928 Mrs Burnet, widow of the former Professor of Greek, wrote in response to
Baxter's condolences, 'My husband had a great belief in your future, he had often said to
me that you would be one of those men the University of St Andrews would be very
proud of' (MS 36942/288).

he had discovered by accident in the ducal library at Wolfenbüttel in Germany.[19] But his main work was on the manuscript tradition and lexicography of early Christian texts and he was a leading figure in an international project to produce a new dictionary of medieval Latin, the 'New Du Cange'. He was clearly not the most obvious person to lead an archaeological investigation: his official remit to the Turkish authorities was a study of the Emperor Justinian and his times, but his notes and jottings indicate that he was a novice in this field.[20] Nevertheless, the promise held out by Tudor Pole of an unprecedented collection of ancient manuscripts is sufficient explanation for his interest in the enterprise.[21]

Although David Russell shared Baxter's enthusiasm for ancient texts, manifest in his plan to publish a reproduction of a Gospel Book of Queen Margaret of Scotland in 1930,[22] it seems to have been a common interest in spiritualism which brought the two men together. By 1928 Baxter had been persuaded by Russell to write an introduction to the third volume of *The Scripts of Cleophas*, an account of early Christian history dictated to the celebrated medium Geraldine Cummins by a group of 'Seven Messengers'. Baxter did, however, see fit to leave his introduction anonymous,[23] although he continued to collaborate in the publication of spiritualist texts over the next few years.[24] Russell arranged for Baxter to meet Tudor Pole in London in January 1932, in conjunction with plans to approach the Turkish authorities for permission to excavate in spring 1933.[25]

David Russell

David Russell first met Tudor Pole in 1912, also through his spiritualist interests. By then Russell had become president of the Leven Lodge of the Theosophical Society founded in New York in 1875, which described

---

[19] *Copiale Prioratus Sancti Andree* (Oxford, 1930). Russell was impressed by a lecture given by Baxter on this material in April 1925 (Macintyre, *Russell*, 123).

[20] MS 36943/294, the Walker Trust submission to the Turkish Minister for Public Instruction, dated 28 November 1932. Earlier the same month Blackwell's offered Baxter the French edition of Vasiliev's *History of the Byzantine Empire* (the English one being out of print), and explained that they were seeking second-hand copies of Ebersolt and Mordtmann, also out of print (MS 36943/267a).

[21] A secret report from Tudor Pole in December 1931 speaks of manuscripts from the Library of Justinian in 'Greek, Hebrew, Latin etc. and Indian tongues': Macintyre, *Russell*, 126.

[22] St Andrews University Library, MS 36942/486.

[23] Macintyre, *Russell*, 124.

[24] E.g., MS 36942/361 (17 April 1929); MS 36943/71 (27 July 1931).

[25] MS 36943/135, letter from Russell to Baxter dated 20 January 1932.

itself as 'an absolutely unsectarian body of seekers after Truth, striving to serve humanity on spiritual lines, and therefore endeavouring to check materialism and revive religious tendency'. In 1906 Tudor Pole's psychic vision had led to the discovery of a sapphire blue bowl at Chalice Well, Glastonbury, and when Russell later learned of this he went down to Bristol to meet him. The two became close friends and corresponded almost daily until Russell's death in 1956.[26]

But Russell was a cultured man of vision in a more practical sense, a genuine philanthropist with a wide range of interests and readiness to invest in new technology and innovative methods, for example in the field of alternative medicine. He was renowned as a humane factory-owner, who organized charabanc outings for his workers in the 1920s[27] and pioneered in his Fife factory new techniques for paper-making which included the import to Scotland on a massive scale of esparto grass from North Africa. He was always on the lookout for business: Baxter's remit for a visit to Istanbul in 1933 included negotiations with a Greek businessman, Georges Tektirides, concerning the possible opening of a new paper-mill in Turkey.[28] Russell was perhaps too humane to show the ruthlessness of true business acumen: a certain Clarence Hatry with whom he was in negotiation over the amalgamation of Scottish paper-mills in the 1920s was sentenced in 1930 to fourteen years' penal servitude for fraud with a concurrent sentence of two years' hard labour. Characteristically Russell sent him a gift of shortbread to Maidstone prison at Christmas 1933.[29]

Although his interest dated back to 1912, it was not until 1931 that David Russell became financially involved in the 'Quest'. In that year a survey expedition to Istanbul was conducted under the auspices of the Walker Trust,[30] which had been founded in 1883 in memory of Russell's great-uncle, the Reverend George Walker, a former student of St Andrews University. Protracted and careful negotiations for securing the necessary permit to work in Istanbul were supervised by him[31] and all subsequent fieldwork was paid for through the Walker Trust. When

---

[26] Macintyre, *Russell*, 31 f.

[27] Macintyre, *Russell*, 63.

[28] E.g. MS 36943/505–7 (all from August 1933).

[29] Macintyre, *Russell*, 49–57.

[30] MS 36943/385: letter of 26/6/33 from Tudor Pole to Baxter. 'The Walker Trust of the University of St Andrews' was little more than a pseudonym (adopted for publicity purposes in connection with the dig) for Sir David Russell, who was sole trustee with absolute control over funds.

[31] Including a politic grant in 1933 of £250 for restoration of the Yedikule or Golden Gate, at just the right moment to ease negotiations for an excavation permit, MSS 36943/347, 363; cf. Macintyre, *Russell*, 152.

digging in 1935 finally uncovered not a hoard of manuscripts and accompanying treasure trove, but a spectacular mosaic, Russell continued to take a keen interest, travelling out to the dig site whenever possible (Figures 3.2 and 3.4). Above all, he poured into the scheme unquantified sums of money, which included (unsuccessful) 'conservation' work on the mosaic[32] and two decades of legal negotiations and compensation claims to numerous 'landowners' who claimed that the dig encroached upon their property. Between 1951 and 1954 the Walker Trust financed a second series of seasons under the direction of David Talbot Rice which did what was possible to conserve the mosaic in a new museum and complete the work of the original excavators, as well as undertaking archaeological work at Tudor Pole's original target, the House of Justinian.[33] All this was done with tireless attention and an unassuming profile. Baxter became the hero of the first dig, a celebrity to whom the future Edward VIII sent a formal apology for failure to visit the site in 1936,[34] but it was Russell who, after ultimately breaking with Baxter, and following the disruption of the Second World War, finally supervised the assembly of archaeological material in the First Report of the Walker Trust, which was published anonymously in 1947.

The Great Palace dig was only one among many archaeological enterprises which Russell helped to fund, in places as far-flung as Turkish Harran and Scottish Iona. The work of aspiring young archaeologists such as Michael Gough in Cilicia and Bruce-Mitford in Cyprus was supported. It was not inappropriate that in January 1957 his obituary in the mill magazine, the *Rothmill Quarterly*, dubbed him an 'archaeological Maecenas'.[35]

---

[32] In March 1933, Tudor Pole estimated that about £2,000 had been spent by Frederick Leveaux between 1922 and 1930 (including living expenses for the three Russians); about £2,000 was currently available from David Russell (and Tudor Pole could if necessary find another £2,000 himself). Total Quest expenditure to date was estimated at £5,000 (MS 36943/385).

In 1936 the Walker Trust signed a contract with Bernard Gauer for conservation of the mosaic, agreeing to pay a total of £3,400 (Baxter papers, MS 36966A).

[33] Published in the Second Report of the Walker Trust, see note 9 above; cf. also Macintyre, *Russell*, 233–40.

[34] Russell Papers, Box 39.

[35] *The Rothmill Quarterly* 27 (4) (1957), 208; pp. 208–17 provide a convenient survey of Russell's archaeological interests and his work on Iona. Macintyre, *Russell*, 105–17 and 193–203 discusses the latter in more detail.

Addendum

The building which contains the peristyle mosaic has recently been identified as the Augusteus and a post-Justinianic date proposed by Jonathan
Bardill, 'The Great Palace of the Byzantine emperors and the Walker
Trust excavations', *Journal of Roman Archaeology* 12 (1999), 217–30, especially 217, 227–29.

4. The British contribution to fieldwork in Byzantine studies in the twentieth century: an introductory survey

David Winfield

Fieldwork in the present century is neatly divided by the two world wars, although it will be seen that there are interesting threads of continuity running through the three periods.[1]

Before 1914 fieldwork was not widespread, but it did take off in style with the publications of Schultz and Barnsley on Hosios Loukas in 1901;[2] that of Ramsay and Bell on the *Thousand and One Churches* in 1909;[3] and W. S. George's study of St Eirene in 1912.[4] The particular value of George's careful recording techniques has been shown in Robin Cormack's use of his watercolours of the mosaics at St Demetrios in Salonica, made before the disastrous fire of 1917.[5]

The first period also saw the beginning of some institutional support in the formation of the Byzantine Research and Publication Fund in 1908. The money for this venture and indeed its inspiration came largely from Edwin Freshfield.[6] He provides a family link to another fund which

---

[1] Scant bibliography is given here. Further details on most of the authors cited in this chapter can be found in the Dumbarton Oaks bibliographies of Byzantine Art (*Literature on Byzantine Art, 1892–1967*, 3 vols [Washington, D.C., 1973–76]) or in the *Byzantinische Zeitschrift* bibliographies (also accessible in microfiche: J. S. Allen, ed., *Author Index of Byzantine Studies*, 2 vols [Washington, D.C., 1986–96]). A full treatment of this subject with a comprehensive bibliography would make a useful thesis.

[2] R. W. Schultz and S. H. Barnsley, *The Monastery of Saint Luke of Stiris in Phocis, and the dependent monastery of Saint Nicolas in the Fields, near Skripou, in Boeotia* (London, 1901). See too the chapter by H. Kalligas elsewhere in this volume (Chapter 2).

[3] W. M. Ramsay and G. L. Bell, *The Thousand and One Churches* (London, 1909).

[4] W. S. George, *The Church of Saint Eirene in Constantinople* (London, 1912).

[5] R. Cormack, 'The mosaic decoration of S. Demetrios, Thessaloniki: a re-examination in the light of the drawings of W. S. George', *ABSA* 64 (1969), 17–52.

[6] Best known, perhaps, for his work on Roman law: E. H. Freshfield, *A Manual of Roman Law. The Ecloga published by the emperors Leo III and Constantine V* (Cambridge, 1926).

From *Through the Looking Glass: Byzantium Through British Eyes*, eds Robin Cormack and Elizabeth Jeffreys. Copyright © 2000 by the Society for the Promotion of Byzantine Studies. Published by Ashgate Publishing Ltd, Gower House, Croft Road, Aldershot, Hampshire, GU11 3HR, Great Britain.

supported field research in Byzantine subjects. This was the Asia Minor Exploration Fund. Among the institutions that supported this fund were the Royal Geographical Society, of which Douglas Freshfield was the President, and the Society for the Promotion of Hellenic Studies. Although the bias was towards classical archaeology, early beneficiaries, like Ramsay and his pupil D. G. Hogarth, constantly found their work spilling over into the Byzantine period.

The composition of the committee running the Byzantine Research and Publication Fund is a useful indication of some of the future strands of field research. Four of the committee members were practising architects and illustrate the particular interest in Byzantine architecture around the turn of the nineteenth century. That architectural interest runs strongly through our three periods of field research. Lethaby and Swainson wrote on St Sophia.[7] Gertrude Bell proved excellent at recording and photographing architecture as can be seen from the book on the *Thousand and One Churches* and from her account of the Churches of the Tur Abdin.[8] George Jeffrey was another architect already publishing valuable work on the Byzantine churches of Cyprus.[9] And the many topological and functional studies of individual Byzantine buildings that appeared up to the 1970s were capped by Cyril Mango's fine historical study in 1976.[10] It built on and used earlier field studies, but its great value lies in his own field observations of the buildings.

Two further committee members were Directors of the British Schools in Athens and Rome. Dawkins, although he is better known for his linguistic work, produced early articles on cruciform fonts in the Aegean area and on Byzantine pottery from Sparta.[11] The British Schools at Athens and Rome, and the Schools subsequently founded abroad, provided an essential foundation for Byzantine field research.

Four more committee members were departmental curators or directors of our national museums, and one of these was O. M. Dalton.[12] They provided essential financial support for field research.

---

[7] W. R. Lethaby and H. Swainson, *The Church of Sancta Sophia, Constantinople. A study of Byzantine building* (London and New York, 1894).

[8] G. L. Bell, *Churches and Monasteries of the Tur Abdin and Neighbouring Districts*. Zeitschrift für die Geschichte der Architektur, Beiheft 9 (Heidelberg, 1913). Now reprinted with annotations and illustrations as G. M. L. Bell and M. M. Mango, *The Churches and Monasteries of the Tur Abdin* (London, 1982).

[9] G. Jeffrey, *A Brief Description of the Holy Sepulchre, Jerusalem, and other Christian churches in the Holy City* (Cambridge, 1919).

[10] C. Mango, *Byzantine Architecture* (New York, 1976).

[11] R. M. Dawkins, 'Byzantine pottery from Sparta', *ABSA* 17 (1910–11), 23–8 (with J. P. Droop); and 'Cruciform fonts in the Aegean area', *ABSA* 19 (1912–13), 123–32. See too P. Mackridge's chapter elsewhere in this volume (Chapter 14).

[12] Dalton's career is discussed by C. Entwistle elsewhere in this volume (Chapter 13).

Two of the remaining committee members were distinguished historians. William Miller appears to have stuck to his historical last, although he travelled widely. But J. L. Myres made at least one excursion into field researches with an article on Byzantine jewellery in Cyprus.[13] The remaining members, the Treasurer and the President, were gentlemen amateurs who have also played a not undistinguished part in Byzantine field research.

Thus the committee of the Byzantine Research and Publication Fund well represents the inspiration and directions in which British field workers started out. The one important exception not directly represented on the committee was the impulse given by Christianity. It was but a short step from biblical archaeology to the archaeology of the Early Church, and from patristic studies to an interest in the places from whence the Fathers came and where they worked. The first fruits of these lines of research were in epigraphical studies and topographical research. Sir William Ramsay was once again the British forerunner with his works on St Paul the Traveller, *St Luke the Physician*, and the *Cities and Bishoprics of Phrygia*.[14] Ramsay would have been pleased that it was a British scholar, Michael Ballance, who was finally able to identify the site of the Pauline city of Derbe in the 1950s.[15]

For continuity between the first period and the second period from 1919 to 1939 the best link is John Crowfoot. He began his academic career with articles on Christian antiquities in Turkey and Syria and, as an assistant to Strzygowski, he contributed to *Kleinasien, ein Neuland der Kunstgeschichte*.[16] But his major work was done between the wars.[17]

The British Mandate was a fruitful period for the archaeology of Palestine. A Department of Antiquities was set up, and the British School of Archaeology in Jerusalem was founded by Professor John Garstang in 1919. For good measure Garstang directed the Antiquities Service as well, and Crowfoot joined him there. Crowfoot himself became a director of the School in the 1930s and throughout the twenties and thirties he and many other British scholars produced articles on early Christian and Byzantine churches.

---

[13] J. L. Myres, 'Byzantine jewellery in Cyprus', *Reliquary and Illustrated Archaeologist* (1898), 109–12.

[14] E.g. W. M. Ramsay, *The Historical Geography of Asia Minor* (London, 1890); *The Cities and Bishoprics of Phrygia* (Oxford, 1895); *Luke the Physician and other studies in the history of religion* (London, 1908).

[15] M. H. Ballance, 'Derbe and Faustinopolis', *Anatolian Studies* 14 (1964), 139–45.

[16] J. Strzygowski, *Kleinasien, ein Neuland der Kunstgeschichte*. Kirchenaufnahmen von I. W. Crowfoot und J. L. Smirnov (Leipzig, 1903).

[17] See, e.g., J. Crowfoot, 'The churches of Gerasa 1928, 1929', *Palestine Exploration Fund Quarterly Statement for 1930*, 32–43; 'The cathedral at Bosra', ibid., 1936, 7–13; and many articles in the *Quarterly of the Department of Antiquities of Palestine* from 1931 onwards.

Kathleen Kenyon first worked with Crowfoot on the dig at Samaria where in 1932 they identified the Church of the Invention of the Head of St John the Baptist described by John Phocas in 1185.[18] Dame Kathleen Kenyon was of course better known as a prehistorian and for her excavations at Jericho, but she contributed her share to Byzantine subjects, and became a director of the re-founded School of Jerusalem in the 1950s.[19] K. A. C. Cresswell, later an eminent authority on Islamic architecture, investigated the Byzantine origin of the Dome of the Rock in the 1920s.[20] Another archaeologist who did a great deal of work on early Christian and Byzantine churches was R. W. Hamilton. He also began his career under John Crowfoot[21] and his work takes us into the third period after the Second World War when he in turn became Director of the Jerusalem School.

The Palestine Department of Antiquities began conservation work on churches in the 1930s and published the reports of William Harvey on the Church of the Nativity at Bethlehem and on the Holy Sepulchre.[22] There is a follow-up to these in Canon John Wilkinson's field researches since the Second World War. As Director of the Jerusalem School he carried out the most detailed study until then of the structural history of the Aedicule over the Tomb of Christ.[23] This in turn is being continued by Martin Biddle.[24]

The Church of England has given unwitting encouragement to Byzantine research through its Philip Usher Scholarship. The purpose of this is to allow young priests to spend a year studying the Orthodox Church and promote an understanding of it. The Reverend Derwas Chitty was a holder of it and he wrote a number of papers on excavations of Palestinian churches as well as his book on monasticism *The Desert, a City*.[25]

In Turkey the tradition of Ramsay's field researches was continued by Sir William Calder, who carried out survey work in the 1920s. He was a founder of the *Monumenta Asiae Minoris Antiqua* project, the first volume of which appeared in 1932.

---

[18] J. W. Crowfoot, K. M. Kenyon and E. L. Subenik, *The Buildings at Samaria I* (London, 1942).

[19] See, e.g., her *Digging up Jerusalem* (London and Tonbridge, 1974).

[20] K. A. C. Cresswell, *The Origin of the Plan of the Dome of the Rock*. British School of Archaeology in Jerusalem, Supplementary Papers 2 (London, 1924).

[21] See, e.g., J. W. Crowfoot and R. W. Hamilton, 'The discovery of the synagogue at Jerash', *Palestine Exploration Fund Quarterly Statement for 1929*, 211–19; and many further reports.

[22] W. Harvey, *Church of the Holy Sepulchre, Jerusalem: structural survey, final report* (Oxford, 1935).

[23] J. Wilkinson, 'The tomb of Christ: an outline of its structural history', *Levant* 4 (1972), 83–97.

[24] See, most recently, M. Biddle, *The Tomb of Christ* (Stroud, 1999).

[25] Derwas J. Chitty, *The Desert, a City* (Oxford, 1966).

The first conservation work on Byzantine mosaics began in the 1930s. It was an American initiative financed by the Byzantine Institute of America, but Thomas Whittemore looked to British craftsmen to carry out the work. He began with the Gregory brothers who were stonemasons, and then took on Ernest Hawkins. Many Byzantinists have benefited from the late Ernest Hawkins's immense practical knowledge of mosaic work.

It was in the twenties that the first British fieldwork specifically in the subject of Byzantine wall-painting and mosaic was undertaken. This was the period when Talbot Rice began work, and his early visits to Athos produced the important book *The Birth of Western Painting*, written with the traveller and gentleman-amateur Robert Byron as co-author.[26] Talbot Rice followed an active career in Byzantine field research. He produced a steady stream of pioneering articles and books, among them the work on the Great Palace excavations, and a book on the icons of Cyprus. His work at Trebizond in the 1920s was followed up in the 1950s and 1960s with the book on Hagia Sophia, Trebizond.[27]

In the inter-war years, the spheres of influence of the European Powers heavily influenced their areas of scholastic research and so it is not surprising that abundant British work was produced in Palestine and Cyprus. Rupert Gunnis, another gentleman-amateur, produced *Historic Cyprus* in the 1930s and this is still the most useful village-by-village inventory of the churches on the island, many of which go back to the Byzantine period.[28] The Bucklers wrote on inscriptions in the painted churches of Cyprus and on the frescoes at Galata and at Asinou.[29] Indianos and Thomson produced the first account of the twelfth-century paintings in the monastery of St Neophytos at Paphos.[30] These high-quality

---

[26] R. Byron and D. Talbot Rice, *The Birth of Western Painting: a history of colour, form and iconography* (London, 1930).

[27] Great Palace: S. Casson, D. Talbot Rice, F. F. Hudson and A. H. M. Jones, *Preliminary Report upon the Excavations carried out in the Hippodrome of Constantinople in 1927* (London, 1928); D. Talbot Rice, ed., *The Great Palace of the Byzantine Emperors*, Second Report of the Walker Trust (Edinburgh, 1958); on the activities of the Walker Trust see also the chapter by Mary Whitby elsewhere in this volume (Chapter 3). Cyprus: D. Talbot Rice, *The Icons of Cyprus* (London, 1937). Trebizond: G. Millet and T. Rice, *Byzantine Painting at Trebizond* (London, 1936); D. Talbot Rice, *The Church of Hagia Sophia at Trebizond* (Edinburgh, 1968).

[28] R. Gunnis, *Historic Cyprus: a guide to towns and villages, monasteries and castles* (London, 1936).

[29] W. H. Buckler, 'Frescoes at Galata, Cyprus', *JHS* 53 (1935), 105–10; W. H. and Georgina Buckler, 'Dated wallpaintings in Cyprus', *Annuaire Inst. Hist. et Phil. Orient. et Slav.* 7 (1939/44), 47–70; V. Seymer, W. H. Buckler and Mrs Buckler, 'The Church of Asinou, Cyprus and its frescoes', *Archaeologia* 83 (1933), 327–50.

[30] A. C. Indianos and G. H. Thomson, 'Wallpaintings at St Neophytos Monastery', *Kypriakai Spoudai* 3 (1939), 155–224.

paintings received a more scholarly treatment by Mango and Hawkins in the 1960s.[31]

In Egypt, Sir Flinders Petrie dug up a church or two in the pre-1914 period; and Margaret Murray, more famous for her work *The Splendour that was Egypt*, produced a study of St Menas of Alexandria and his monastery.[32] Ward-Perkins produced a study of the Monastery of Taposiris Magna and his name may serve to bring us into the period since the Second World War.[33] That now comprises half a century of Byzantine field research, and the quantity of work is too large for a comprehensive survey to be made.

The British Institute at Ankara, founded in 1948, and the British Institute at Amman, founded in 1978, have both provided valuable bases for Byzantinists. Michael Gough took over the directorship of the Ankara School in 1961. Originally a classical scholar and Romanist with a profoundly Catholic Christian background, he had already shown a marked interest in Byzantine subjects with his researches in southern Turkey. These included the later history of the city of Anazarbus,[34] and the iconoclast decoration of Al Oda.[35] His major work which only appeared posthumously was the excavation of Alahan,[36] but he also excavated at Dağ Pazarı, and he pioneered work in the cleaning and preservation of wall-paintings at Eski Gümüş,[37] and encouraged epigraphical work such as that by Richard Harper, who is now Director of the British School in Jerusalem.[38]

Various other bodies, notably the Society of Antiquaries of London, encourage fieldwork, and Professor Frend, who has himself made some

---

[31] C. Mango and E. J. W. Hawkins, 'The Hermitage of St Neophytos and its wall-paintings', *DOP* 20 (1966), 119–216.

[32] M. Murray, 'St Menas of Alexandria', *Proceedings of the Society of Biblical Archaeology* 29 (1907), 25–30, 51–60, 112–22.

[33] J. B. Ward-Perkins, 'The monastery of Taposiris Magna', *Bulletin de la Société Royale d'Archéologie d'Alexandrie* 36 (1943–44), 48–53.

[34] M. Gough, 'Anazarbus', *Anatolian Studies* 2 (1952), 85–150.

[35] M. Gough, 'A church of the (?) iconoclast period in Byzantine Isauria', *Anatolian Studies* 7 (1957), 154–61.

[36] Mary Gough, ed., *Alahan: an early Christian monastery in Southern Turkey* (Toronto, 1985).

[37] M. Gough, 'Dağ Pazarı. The basilical church "extra muros"', in G. Robertson and G. Henderson, eds, *Studies in memory of Talbot Rice* (Edinburgh, 1975), 147–63; idem, 'The monastery of Eski Gümüş: a preliminary report', *Anatolian Studies* 14 (1964), 147–61 and 15 (1965) 157–64; idem, 'Byzantine painting at Eski Gümüş', *Türk Arkeoloji Dergisi* 12, 1963 (1965), 37–42.

[38] E.g., R. P. Harper, 'Tituli Comanorum Cappadociae', *Anatolian Studies* 18 (1968), 93–147; idem, 'Inscriptiones Comanis Cappadociae in A.D. 1967 effossae', *Anatolian Studies* 19 (1969), 27–40.

notable contributions to field research,[39] has instituted the Society's Frend Medal as an annual encouragement to workers in the early Christian field.

Libya was occupied by the British after the Second World War and the British supported the newly established Kingdom of Libya which provided a fertile base for Richard Goodchild, who was briefly in charge of antiquities there. He published a number of surveys of early Byzantine churches and fortifications in Tripolitania,[40] and Martin Harrison and Elizabeth Rosenbaum were among the Byzantinists who started their field work with him.[41]

Cyprus continued as a British colony until 1960 and A. H. S. Megaw was appointed Director of Antiquities just before the war and continued in that post until 1959. His contributions to Byzantine fieldwork began with churches in Mani in 1930.[42] He directed excavations in Egypt and Cyprus at Byzantine sites. His contribution to conservation work on Byzantine churches in Cyprus has been outstanding.[43]

Among institutions in the UK pride of place must go to Birmingham University where the enthusiasm of Anthony Bryer has created a Department of Byzantine Studies. He himself is a keen field worker, and he has inspired and helped many young Byzantinists to undertake field researches. At a conference in 1994 James Crow rightly referred to him as the Grand Old Man of Pontic Studies, and many of his students first tried out their skills in Byzantine Pontus. In our Pontic studies both Anthony and I felt that we were carrying on a historic link with Talbot Rice's work of the 1930s.[44] Anthony's pupil Margaret Mullet has in her turn set up Byzantine Studies at the University of Belfast.

---

[39] E.g., W. H. C. Frend, 'The Byzantine basilica church at Knossos', *ABSA* 57 (1962), 186–238; 'The Podium site at Qasr Ibrim', *Journal of Egyptian Archaeology* 60 (1974), 30–59; 'Recently discovered material for the writing of the history of Christian Nubia', *Studies in Church History* 11 (1975), 19–30; and the collected papers in *Archaeology and History in the Study of Early Christianity* (Aldershot, 1988).

[40] E.g., R. G. Goodchild, 'Roman sites in the Tarhum Plateau of Tripolitania', *Papers of the British School at Rome* 19 (1951), 42–77; idem, 'The Roman and Byzantine limes in Cyrenaica', *JRS* 43 (1953), 65–76; R. G. Goodchild and J. B. Ward-Perkins, 'The Roman and Byzantine defence of Leptis Magna', *Papers of the British School at Rome* 21 (1953), 42–73. See, too, Goodchild's contributions to *Apollonia, the Port of Cyrene. Excavations by the University of Michigan, 1965–1967* (Tripolis, 1976).

[41] See, e.g., E. Alföldi-Rosenbaum and J. B. Ward-Perkins, *Justinianic mosaic pavements in Cyrenaican churches* (Rome, 1980).

[42] A. H. S. Megaw, 'Byzantine architecture in Mani', *ABSA* 33 (1935), 137–62; see also 'The chronology of some middle-byzantine churches', *ABSA* 32 (1931/2–1934), 90–130.

[43] To single out but two publications: A. H. S. Megaw and E. J. W. Hawkins, 'The Church of the Holy Apostles at Perachorio, Cyprus and its frescoes', *DOP* 16 (1962), 277–368; idem, *The Church of the Panagia Kanakaria at Lythrankomi in Cyprus* (Washington, D.C., 1977).

[44] A. Bryer and D. Winfield, *The Byzantine Monuments and Topography of the Pontos*, 2 vols (Washington, D.C., 1985).

At the University of Newcastle, Martin Harrison gave the Chair of Classical Archaeology a strong Byzantine bias. He himself was a keen field worker with important Byzantine discoveries in Lycia, and excavations at St Polyeuktos and Amorion.[45] He also encouraged other young Byzantinists. His pupil, Stephen Hill, has set up Byzantine Studies at the University of Warwick with strong encouragement to field research by the example of his own discoveries in Turkey.[46] James Crow, another Newcastle graduate, is doing important work on Byzantine fortifications and in Pontic studies,[47] apart from continuing the Newcastle tradition of work on Hadrian's wall.

Fortifications are perhaps one area where British fieldwork is continuing an active original line of research. F. W. Hasluck produced an early description of Bithynian churches and fortifications in 1906.[48] The brothers T. E. and A. W. Lawrence both produced studies of fortifications,[49] and Clive Foss and myself produced the first general introduction to the subject.[50] Foss initiated the Anatolian Castles survey which is being actively continued by Mark Whittow, and in a different aspect of fortification Denys Pringle has produced new work on Byzantine fortification in North Africa, and currently in the Holy Land.[51]

The tradition of British conservation work that began in the thirties has been honourably carried on at Trebizond and at Eski Gümüş. The Courtauld Institute, in a new initiative, has engaged in wall-painting conservation in Cyprus.

In one particular area, Byzantine pottery, we can reasonably claim that John Hayes's work puts Britain in the forefront of Byzantine field research.[52]

---

[45] Lycia: R. M. Harrison, 'Churches and chapels of Central Lycia', *Anatolian Studies* 13 (1963), 117–51. St Polyeuktos: R. M. Harrison, *Excavations at Saraçhane in Istanbul*, 2 vols (Washington, D.C., 1986) and *A Temple for Byzantium: the discovery and excavation of Anicia Juliana's palace church in Istanbul* (London, 1989).

[46] Now brought together in S. Hill, *The Early Byzantine Churches of Cilicia and Isauria* (Aldershot, 1996).

[47] See, e.g., the report of fieldwork for 1997–98: *Bulletin for British Byzantine Studies* 25 (1999), 32–3.

[48] F. W. Hasluck, 'Bithynica', *ABSA* 13 (1906/7), 285–308.

[49] T. E. Lawrence, *Crusader Castles* (London, 1936); A. W. Lawrence, *Greek Aims in Fortification* (Oxford, 1979).

[50] D. C. Winfield and C. Foss, *Byzantine Fortifications: an introduction* (Pretoria, 1986).

[51] D. Pringle, *The Defence of Byzantine Africa from Justinian to the Arab Conquest. An account of the military history of the African provinces in the sixth and seventh centuries* (Oxford, 1981); idem, *The Red Tower (al-Burj at Ahmar). Settlement in the Plain of Sharon at the time of the Crusaders and Mamluks, A.D. 1099–1516* (London, 1986).

[52] Amongst his publications, see J. Hayes, *Late Roman Pottery* (London, 1972) and his contributions to excavations and their reports at Carthage, and Saraçhane and the Myrelaion in Istanbul.

The British contribution thus forms a solid body of factual work on Byzantine topography, epigraphy, architecture, fortification and mural decoration. Its value to Byzantine studies is already considerable since many of the monuments that have been recorded have now disappeared. Its value in the future will be ensured by reassessment in the light of new perspectives and of greater knowledge than was available to the original researchers.

Section II

Encounters with books

5. The distorting mirror: reflections on the Queen Melisende Psalter (London, B.L., Egerton 1139)[1]

Barbara Zeitler

An illuminated psalter (London, B.L., Egerton 1139) in Latin, commonly known as the Queen Melisende Psalter, ranks among the most famous artefacts from the Latin East. It is a manuscript *de grand luxe* made, with the likely exception of its calendar, in Jerusalem in the middle of the twelfth century. The lavishness of its decoration indicates that the codex was made for a person of high social standing. The use of the term *peccatrix*, e.g. on fols 21 and 198, and the recurrence of adjectives with feminine endings in the prayers, e.g. 'Visita me infirmam' (fol. 199v) show that its first owner was a woman.

The recent exhibition of Byzantine art from British Collections at the British Museum afforded us the rare opportunity to see two of the twenty-four full-page Christological miniatures that preface the calendar and the psalms, as well as the two delicately carved ivory covers studded with semi-precious stones, now separate from the manuscript.[2] The juxtaposition in the exhibition of the double page showing the Anastasis and the Marys at the Tomb (fols 9v–10r) with miniatures from Byzantine manuscripts demonstrated the former's profound debt to Byzantine art. At the same time, however, illuminations from Constantinople and elsewhere in the eastern Mediterranean in the show only highlighted the unusual character of the miniatures in Egerton 1139.[3] The same observation applies in equal measure to the ivory covers which, at least with

---

[1] It is my pleasure to acknowledge Elizabeth Teviotdale's constructive comments.

[2] Entries by J. Lowden in D. Buckton, ed., *Byzantium: Treasures of Byzantine Art and Culture from British Collections* (London [British Museum], 1994), 164–6.

[3] See, e.g., the miniatures in the Codex Ebnerianus (Oxford, Bodleian Library, Auct. T. inf. 1.10), dated *c.* 1125 to 1150 from Constantinople, or those in a late twelfth-century Gospel (London, B.L., Harley 1810), in Buckton, *Byzantium*, 162–3, 179–80.

From *Through the Looking Glass: Byzantium Through British Eyes*, eds Robin Cormack and Elizabeth Jeffreys. Copyright © 2000 by the Society for the Promotion of Byzantine Studies. Published by Ashgate Publishing Ltd, Gower House, Croft Road, Aldershot, Hampshire, GU11 3HR, Great Britain.

regard to their format and decorative vocabulary, owe more to Islamic than to Byzantine art.[4] Clearly, the inclusion of Egerton 1139 in an exhibition of Byzantine art raises fundamental questions about how this enigmatic artefact can be understood. The recent display of the manuscript might also encourage us to think more critically about widely accepted assumptions concerning its date, patronage and ownership.

Of all the miniatures in Egerton 1139, the New Testament cycle, which precedes the calendar and the psalms, is the most widely known. The last miniature of the cycle, the Deesis (fol. 12v), bears the signature of the artist responsible for these images: 'BASILIUS ME FECIT'. In his magisterial study of manuscript illumination from the Latin Kingdom of Jerusalem, Hugo Buchthal argued that Basilius, despite his Greek name, was a Western artist who painted in a Byzantine style.[5] More recently, the suggestion has been made that he was an Eastern Christian artist, probably an Armenian.[6] The lavish New Testament cycle has perhaps detracted attention from other parts of the codex. It is only very recently, for instance, that the ivory covers, showing, respectively, scenes from the life of David accompanied by depictions of episodes from the Battle of the Virtues and Vices from Prudentius's *Psychomachia*, and the Six Works of Mercy (Matthew 25:35–6) performed by a male figure wearing mostly Byzantine imperial garb, have received a fuller treatment.[7] The silk embroidery once attached to the spine of the codex has only recently been given its first mention in print.[8] Slowly, Egerton 1139 is beginning to be regarded as a composite artefact combining a variety of artistic media and pictorial imagery. Jaroslav Folda, for instance, has referred to the formal relationship among the parts of the binding, suggesting that the design of the silk embroidery is echoed in the 'textile pattern' of the ivory covers. At the same time, ivories studded with turquoise and other semi-precious stones provide a colouristic contrast to the red, blue and green crosses stitched on a silver background.[9]

The careful execution and precious adornment of the manuscript's exterior is mirrored in the quality and wealth of its internal decoration.

---

[4] See note 56.

[5] H. Buchthal, *Miniature Painting in the Latin Kingdom of Jerusalem* (Oxford, 1957), 2–9.

[6] W. Grape, *Grenzprobleme der byzantinischen Malerei* (University of Vienna Ph.D., 1973), 103–4, 113. See also Lowden, in Buckton, *Byzantium*, 164, who suggests that Basilius may well not have worked within the immediate artistic orbit of Constantinople.

[7] B. Kühnel, *Crusader Art of the Twelfth Century: a geographical, and historical, or an art-historical notion* (Berlin, 1994), 67–125.

[8] J. Folda, *The Art of the Crusaders in the Holy Land, 1098–1187* (Cambridge, 1995), 156–7, pl. 6.11 and colour plate 13. The embroidery has been examined by H. Granger-Taylor, *British Library Pamphlet* no. 3338 (London, 1989).

[9] Folda, *Art of the Crusaders*, 157–8.

Perhaps the most remarkable miniature in the manuscript is the double-page *Beatus Vir* initial (fols 23v–24r), showing King David playing the harp. The image is executed in fine-pen drawing on a background of highly burnished gold leaf. Pen drawing, burnished gold and gold letters on purple are also used for the seven full-page initials that mark the liturgical divisions of the psalter.[10] As we shall see in more detail later, some of the designs found in the initials are rooted in Islamic art. Conversely, the depictions of the signs of the zodiac in the calendar (fols 13–21), which follow the Basilius miniatures, find, as will be discussed presently, close parallels in Romanesque illumination from Northern France and England. The last set of miniatures occurs among the prayers at the end of the manuscript dedicated to the Virgin and certain saints (fols 197v–211v). Some of these are preceded by small miniatures showing the holy figure to whom the prayer is addressed.

Even though many of the miniatures in Egerton 1139 are rooted in the visual traditions of the Eastern Christian Church, it is, in several respects, a remarkably English manuscript. The calendar pages of the psalter, for instance, would not have been out of place in an exhibition of English Romanesque art.[11] They are very similar to those in a mid-twelfth-century psalter from the cathedral priory of St Swithun in Winchester (Madrid, Biblioteca Nacional, MS vitr. 23–8).[12] As Francis Wormald pointed out, all the English saints in the calendar of Egerton 1139 also occur in the Madrid codex, the only concessions to the specific circumstances of the Latin East in the former being the reference to the capture of Jerusalem (15 July) and the obits of Baldwin II (1118–31), third king of Jerusalem, on 21 August, and that of his wife Morphia (d. 1126–27) on 1 October (Figure 5.1). The fact that Egerton 1139 appears to abbreviate the calendar of the manuscript from St Swithun's indicates that it was possibly composed in southern England.[13] The similar scripts and the virtually identical page lay-outs in the calendars of Egerton 1139 and the Madrid psalter, the zodiac miniatures in both being placed half-way down the page, would certainly support the

---

[10] Psalms 26:1 (fol. 46v), 38:2 (60v), 52:2 (74v), 68:2 (89v), 80:2 (106v), 97:1 (123r) and 109:1 (139v) of the Vulgate.

[11] Such as the show at the Hayward Gallery in London in 1984: The Arts Council of Great Britain, *English Romanesque Art, 1066–1200* (London, 1984).

[12] C. M. Kauffmann, *Romanesque Manuscripts, 1066–1190* (London, 1975), 104–5; N. Morgan, 'Notes on the post-conquest calendar and litany and martyrology of the Cathedral Priory of Winchester with a consideration of Winchester diocese calendars of the pre-Sarum period', in A. Borg and A. Martindale, eds, *The Vanishing Past. Studies Presented to Christopher Hohler* (Oxford, 1981), 133–72.

[13] F. Wormald, 'The Calendar of Queen Melisende's Psalter', in Buchthal, *Miniature Painting*, 123.

suggestion that the calendar of Egerton 1139 is an English import into the Holy Land.

Connections with English art have also been identified in the ivory covers. The closest iconographic parallels for the depiction of the Virtues and Vices on what was probably the upper cover of the manuscript can be found on an enamel crosier (Florence, Museo nazionale del Bargello) and an enamel casket (Troyes, Cathedral). Both are of English origin, dating from about 1170.[14] On the Bargello crosier, as on the ivory cover, scenes from the life of King David are combined with depictions of the Virtues and Vices. Twelfth-century ivories from England also provide technical parallels to the covers of Egerton 1139. For instance, the rendering of the eyes of figures and animals by means of small beads of jet or other coloured stone set into tiny holes drilled into the ivory can also be found on English ivories from the eleventh and twelfth centuries.[15]

The first owner of the psalter would not necessarily have been aware of these connections with English art. On opening the manuscript – should she have run the risk of opening such an exceedingly precious manuscript adorned with delicately carved ivory covers – the owner would have found a calendar replete with English saints. She would also have engaged with a manuscript that, as regards the relationship of text and image, is identical to illuminated psalters from twelfth-century England. Buchthal has already referred to the fact that the prefacing of the psalms with a New Testament cycle is a Western concept. In the Byzantine sphere, by contrast, New Testament imagery, even though it does occur in psalters, is distributed throughout the text.[16] This type is especially common in English manuscript illumination of the twelfth century. Continental examples of this type often originate from areas with close links to England.[17] The earliest surviving example of a psalter with prefatory illustrations, in this case coloured outline drawings, is a mid-eleventh-century Anglo-Saxon manuscript (London, B.L., MS Cotton Tiberius C. VI) from Winchester.[18] The first extant manuscript with full-page, mainly New Testament illuminations is the St Albans Psalter (Hildesheim, Basilika St Godehard), made for the anchoress Christina of Markyate

---

[14] Kühnel, *Crusader Art*, 107–8.

[15] Kühnel, *Crusader Art*, 112.

[16] Buchthal, *Miniature Painting*, 2; A. Cutler, *Aristocratic Psalters in Byzantium* (Paris, 1984).

[17] O. Pächt, C. R. Dodwell, F. Wormald, *The St. Albans Psalter* (London, 1960), 52. An example is the Ingeborg Psalter (Chantilly, Musée Condé. MS 1695) of *c.* 1200. See F. Deuchler, *The Ingeborg Psalter* (London, 1967).

[18] Arts Council of Great Britain, *English Romanesque*, 85–6.

between *c.* 1120 and 1130.[19] Such a structural resemblance, however, should not detract from the fact that the New Testament cycle in Egerton 1139 has a much less pronounced narrative character than its English parallels. By contrast, its images are firmly rooted within the celebration of the Eastern Christian liturgy.[20]

The English characteristics of Egerton 1139 have been explained by drawing attention to the presence of Englishmen in the Latin kingdom, among whom were William, one of the priors of the Holy Sepulchre and later archbishop of Tyre (1127–32), and Ralph, the chancellor of King Baldwin III.[21] An English presence, however, has also been discerned among the people most closely associated with the manuscript. Two entries in the calendar of Egerton 1139 indicate that the woman for whom the psalter was destined must have been connected with the ruling dynasty of the Latin kingdom of Jerusalem. These are the aforementioned obits of King Baldwin II and of his wife Morphia. It is widely thought that the female owner was the eldest child of Baldwin and Morphia, Melisende, who married Fulk of Anjou (1131–43) and became Queen of Jerusalem (1131–62).[22] Melisende was not only one of the most powerful figures of the Latin East in the twelfth century, but also an important patron of the arts.[23] She gave endowments to churches and religious foundations. As the offspring of a mixed marriage, her mother being the daughter of Gabriel of Melitene, an Armenian Orthodox-rite Christian, it is not surprising that Melisende's patronage was directed towards both Latin-rite and Orthodox-rite churches.[24] Her most important foundation was the Benedictine nunnery of St Lazarus at Bethany, which she established in 1143 for her sister Iveta, later to become abbess of the convent. Melisende donated magnificent gifts to the convent, including church furnishings, liturgical vessels and manuscripts, in keeping with a royal foundation.[25]

---

[19] Arts Council of Great Britain, *English Romanesque*, 93. Other English twelfth-century examples include the Shaftesbury Psalter (London, B.L., MS Lansdowne 383), dated *c.* 1130–40: ibid., 99; and the Winchester Psalter (London, B.L., MS Cotton Nero C.IV), dated *c.* 1150: see K. Haney, *The Winchester Psalter* (Trowbridge, 1986).

[20] Folda, *Art of the Crusaders*, 155.

[21] Wormald, 'Calendar', in Buchthal, *Miniature Painting*, 123.

[22] On this identification see most recently Folda, *Art of the Crusaders*, 137, 151, 154–5.

[23] H. E. Mayer, 'Studies in the history of Queen Melisende of Jerusalem', *DOP* 26 (1972), 93–182; idem, 'The succession of Baldwin II: English impact on the East', *DOP* 39 (1985), 139–47.

[24] B. Hamilton, 'Women in the Crusader states: the Queens of Jerusalem (1100–1190)', in D. Baker, ed., *Medieval Women*, Studies in Church History, Subsidia 1 (Oxford, 1978), 143–74, especially 147 and 156; H. E. Mayer, *Bistümer, Klöster und Stifte im Königreich Jerusalem* (Stuttgart, 1977), 372–402.

[25] Mayer, *Bistümer*, 372–402; Hamilton, 'Women in Crusader States', 156; D. Pringle, *The Churches in the Crusader Kingdom of Jerusalem: A Corpus*, vol. 1 (Cambridge, 1993), 122–37.

Although there is only circumstantial evidence to suggest that the manuscript was made for Melisende, her status and role within the Latin kingdom indicate that she would have made a very appropriate first owner.

Despite her documented activities as a patron, however, Melisende need not have commissioned Egerton 1139. It has been argued recently that the manuscript was commissioned by Fulk of Anjou for his wife, the English characteristics of the codex being seen as reflecting the wishes of Fulk, whose family was closely connected with the Plantagenet dynasty of England.[26] Together with this, a more precise date has been suggested for the manufacture of the codex. Buchthal dated the manuscript to between 1131 and 1143 on account of the fact that the calendar contained an obit for Baldwin II, but none for Fulk.[27] Within this timespan, the year 1136 has recently been suggested as the most likely date, the ivory covers being seen as 'one of the expressions of the reconciliatory atmosphere dominating the relations between Fulk and Melisende'[28] who, prior to 1136, had been at loggerheads with one another over Fulk's attempts to reduce the power of the queen.

Both the date of Egerton 1139 and its close association with Fulk, however, are open to doubt. Certainly, Baldwin's death in 1131 provides a firm *terminus post quem* for the manuscript. Its *terminus ante quem*, however, is less easily identifiable. Any endeavour to date the manuscript must include a consideration of how much weight ought to be given to the evidence provided by the calendar.[29] Such a consideration must apply to any manuscript, but is perhaps particularly necessary in the case of Egerton 1139, the calendar of which, as we saw earlier, appears to have been an English import into Jerusalem.[30] Even though the evidence provided by the calendar has been used to date the manuscript before 1143, a palaeographical analysis of the scripts employed would easily support a date in the later 1140s, even the 1150s.[31]

---

[26] Folda, *Art of the Crusaders*, 154. J. K. Golden, *The Melisende Psalter Reconsidered: a reassessment of its patron and its miniaturist*, M.A. dissertation (The University of Pittsburgh, 1993), argues that Egerton 1139 was intended as a gift for one of Fulk's English relatives.

[27] Buchthal, *Miniature Painting*, 1.

[28] Kühnel, *Crusader Art*, 82. The same date is also suggested by Folda, *Art of the Crusaders*, 154.

[29] On this point see A. Borg, 'The lost apse mosaic of the Holy Sepulchre in Jerusalem', in Borg and Martindale, *Vanishing Past*, 7–12. His suggestion that the manuscript must date from before 1149 because the dedication of the Holy Sepulchre is not mentioned is equally problematic.

[30] Wormald, 'Calendar', in Buchthal, *Miniature Painting*, 123.

[31] There are no notable palaeographical differences between the script of Egerton 1139 and that of a Gospel book from Jerusalem (Paris, B.N., MS lat. 276), dated to the third quarter of the twelfth century. See Buchthal, *Miniature Painting*, 25, pls 17 and 35. See also

The close stylistic similarities that exist between the saints' miniatures in Egerton 1139 and the miniatures in a missal (Paris, Bibliothèque nationale, MS lat. 12056) also raise concerns about the commonly accepted dating of the psalter and the manuscripts related to it. Like Egerton 1139, the Paris Missal is thought to have come from a scriptorium attached to the Holy Sepulchre. It is extensively decorated with historiated initials and other miniatures. They have been interpreted either as using the saints' miniatures in Egerton 1139 as their prototype or as being derived from a putative model closely related to the saints' miniatures in the psalter.[32] The assumption that Egerton 1139 must be the prototype of the Paris Missal, or closely related to the latter's model, has perhaps obscured the very close relationship that exists between the saints' miniatures in the psalter and the historiated medallions in the missal. Stylistic comparisons are certainly not objectively verifiable, but even a cursory glance at the two sets of miniatures suggests that they could well be by the same artist. The missal has been dated to just before the middle of the twelfth century, presumably because the consecration of the Holy Sepulchre on 15 July is not included in its calendar.[33] Again, however, the absence of such an entry does not necessarily provide us with a *terminus ante quem*, bearing in mind also that the only Jerusalem manuscripts containing this particular entry date from the thirteenth century.[34] The close similarities between the saints' miniatures in the psalter and the illuminations of the missal of course do not in themselves undermine their commonly accepted dating, but the possibility that an artist, presumably of Western origin, whose work shows a careful engagement with Byzantine art, worked on both these manuscripts might suggest that their chronological sequence may have to be understood differently.

Apart from the calendar, two pictorial motifs of the Works of Mercy ivory cover have been used to strengthen the association of the codex with Fulk of Anjou. The first is the fact that the Works of Mercy are performed by a male royal figure. Taken on its own, however, the presence of this figure merely emphasises the high-status character of the codex. The second motif is the large, stout bird shown at the top of the same cover which is accompanied by an inscription reading HERODIUS. In the first publication to deal extensively with the ivory covers, Cahier argued that the bird

---

the redating of another Jerusalem Gospel book (Rome, Bibl. vat. lat. 5974) from the third quarter of the twelfth century to the last quarter of the twelfth century by V. Pace, in Erzbischöfliches Diözesanmuseum Köln, *Vaticana*, exhibition catalogue (Stuttgart, 1992), 154–5.

[32] Buchthal, *Miniature Painting*, 17–20; Folda, *Art of the Crusaders*, 159–63.

[33] Buchthal, *Miniature Painting*, 14, 116.

[34] These are a psalter (Florence, Biblioteca Riccardiana, MS 323) and a sacramentary (London, B.L., MS Egerton 2902). See Buchthal, *Miniature Painting*, 116.

was a rebus of the name Fulk and, thus, a direct reference to the royal couple with whom the codex is generally associated.[35] Whilst it is not a figment of a romantic nineteenth-century imagination that an animal could function as a rebus for an individual's name, Cahier's interpretation of the bird accompanied by the inscription HERODIUS is problematic.[36] Cahier was right to argue that in medieval bestiaries, the bird 'herodius' (Gr., heron) was often used synonymously with the word 'fulica' (Lat., coot).[37] His view, however, that this constitutes an indirect reference to Fulk, whose name in the French vernacular was identical to the French for coot ('foulque'), is difficult to accept.[38] Long ago it was pointed out that none of the other animals depicted on the cover appears to have any association with medieval bestiaries.[39] More seriously, perhaps, the fact that the bird is accompanied by an inscription runs counter to an interpretation of this motif as a riddle in which pictures substitute for words.[40] Cahier was indeed aware of this problem and argued that the motif was added some time after the manufacture of the cover.[41] There can be little doubt, however, that the inscription HERODIUS is contemporaneous with the cover and the other inscriptions. The complications inherent in Cahier's interpretation of the stout bird as a rebus for Fulk suggest that the hypothesis, advanced in the nineteenth century and summarily dismissed by Cahier, that HERODIUS might be the name of the carver should be reconsidered.[42] Admittedly, Herodius is a somewhat unusual name, and ivory-carvers do not appear often to have left their signatures on their works.[43] Considering, though, that the New Testament images in Egerton 1139 bear an artist's signature, it would not be surprising if the ivory-carver were to leave a record of his name.[44]

---

[35] P. Ch. Cahier, *Nouveaux mélanges d'archéologie, d'histoire et de littérature*, vol. 2 (Paris, 1874), 10–12.

[36] Rebuses often occur in heraldry. On fol. 341 of John of Salisbury's *Life of St. Thomas Becket* (London, B.L., MS Cotton Claudius B. II), dated to *c.* 1180, depicting the murder of St Thomas, Reginald Fitzurse is distinguished by his armorial bearings, a bear rampant. See Kauffmann, *Romanesque Manuscripts*, 116, no. 93.

[37] F. McCulloch, *Mediaeval Latin and French Bestiaries* (Chapel Hill, 1960), 125; N. Henkel, *Studien zum Physiologus im Mittelalter* (Tübingen, 1976), 197.

[38] Linguistically, this argument applies to Modern and Old French usage. Compare 'fouque' in A. Tobler and E. Lommatzsch, *Altfranzösisches Wörterbuch* (Berlin, 1925) with 'Fouque' in the Old French translation of William of Tyre.

[39] O. M. Dalton, *Catalogue of the Ivory Carvings of the Christian Era* (London, 1909), 26.

[40] E.-M. Schenk, *Das Bilderrätsel* (Hildesheim/New York, 1973); J. Céard and J.-C. Margolis, *Rébus de la Renaissance* (Paris, 1986).

[41] Cahier, *Mélanges*, 11.

[42] Cahier, *Mélanges*, 10, note 3, and 11.

[43] Dalton, *Catalogue*, 26.

[44] Admittedly, a complication is presented here by the fact that, unlike Basilius, Herodius did not sign as 'Herodius me fecit'.

The preceding discussion has emphasized that the attribution of the codex to the joint reign of Fulk and Melisende rests on not altogether firm foundations. The difficulties of pinpointing a precise date at which Egerton 1139 was made and of identifying its patron and first owner with certainty suggests that different questions might have to be addressed to this enigmatic artefact. Certainly, an examination of the English characteristics in the manuscript is a corrective to the preoccupation with its 'Byzantineness', serving as a salutary reminder that Egerton 1139 is essentially a Western manuscript that happens to commence with a set of very Byzantine-looking miniatures. It might be tempting to regard the Byzantine frontispiece miniatures in Egerton 1139 as an exoticism in an English manuscript similar to the two icon-like images of the Dormition of the Virgin (fol. 29) and the Virgin Enthroned (fol. 30) in the Winchester Psalter (London, B.L., MS Cotton Nero C.IV).[45] Such a perspective, like the emphasis on the Byzantine elements in the manuscripts, however, is unlikely to contribute substantially to our understanding of the codex, the highly composite decoration of which speaks so eloquently of the encounter of different cultural and artistic traditions in the Latin kingdom of Jerusalem in the middle of the twelfth century.

Our perceptions of Egerton 1139 have been profoundly shaped by the prefatory New Testament cycle signed by Basilius. This has sometimes been to the detriment of the other miniatures in the manuscript, most notably the small miniatures showing various saints. Basilius, assuming he was a Western artist, has been credited with producing a competent emulation of Byzantine art, even though his work has also been described as 'a laboured and literal translation of western concepts into a foreign idiom'.[46] By contrast, the artist of the saints' miniatures has been seen as producing a 'Byzantinism' which is 'not even skin-deep', but merely a 'surface decoration'.[47] Or it has been emphasized that a Byzantine style, authentic or otherwise, was considered the most appropriate style, or mode of representation, for the main images in the codex, the New Testament cycle.[48] There can be little doubt that the full-page miniatures fulfilled an important devotional function, but the saints' images in the prayer section probably served a similar purpose. This suggests that the stylistic discrepancies between the various sets of miniatures might have to be explained differently, not least because we cannot be

---

[45] Haney, *Winchester Psalter* (as in note 19), 43–5, 125; H. A. Klein, 'The so-called Byzantine Diptych in the Winchester Psalter, British Library, MS Cotton Nero C.IV', *Gesta* 37 (1998), 26–43.

[46] Buchthal, *Miniature Painting*, 8.

[47] Buchthal, *Miniature Painting*, 11.

[48] Lowden, in *Byzantium* (as in note 2), 164.

certain that the first owner of the manuscript would necessarily have considered the stylistic differences existing, for instance, between the New Testament and the saints' images to be as noteworthy as they are to the trained eyes of modern art historians.

Given the stylistic differences between the various sets of miniatures in Egerton 1139, a crucial question is whether modern perceptions of these differences would have coincided with medieval ones. It would be dangerous to argue that stylistic differences did not matter to medieval viewers. The German pilgrim Theoderic, who visited the Holy Sepulchre in the 1170s, noted, for instance, that the mosaic of Christ Emmanuel on the triumphal arch linking the eleventh-century building of the Anastasis rotunda with the twelfth-century Crusader choir looked to be 'in the same style of work but old'.[49] If anything, however, Theoderic's account suggests that he did not consider the twelfth-century Crusader decoration to differ substantially from the eleventh-century Byzantine one. It may be possible, therefore, that, to its first owner, the saints' miniatures in Egerton 1139 looked as 'Byzantine' as did the New Testament scenes by Basilius. Furthermore, even if we assume that medieval viewers perceived stylistic differences in the same way as art historians have done in the modern period, these differences may not have been evaluated in the same way. If, for the sake of the argument, we consider the manuscript to have been made for Melisende, it is not inconceivable that to her, who was half Orthodox, the New Testament images may have been less striking than the images of saints which betray such a thorough knowledge of Western medieval art. This statement might also be applicable to second- or third-generation Westerners in the Levant, for whom the visual traditions of Eastern Christianity were perhaps already more familiar than those of Latin-rite Christianity.

A further area of enquiry may be a renewed consideration of the miniatures for which Egerton 1139 is best known. As we saw earlier, it has been central to the study of the New Testament cycle to elucidate the ethnic background of the illuminator Basilius. Buchthal adduced a number of iconographic clues to strengthen his case that Basilius was a Western artist. He argued, for instance, that Basilius was Western because the scene of the Three Marys at the Tomb (fol. 10) included three, rather than two Marys, as is customary in Byzantine art.[50] Counting the number of Marys present, however, is not a satisfactory way of establishing the miniaturist's ethnic origin. Supporters of the view that Basilius was of Armenian origin might use the three Marys in support of their argu-

---

[49] J. Wilkinson, *Jerusalem Pilgrimage* (London, 1988), 281.

[50] Buchthal, *Miniature Painting*, 5–6.

ment.[51] Two Marys, however, can be found in both Western and Armenian art.[52] Such evidence adds a cautionary note to the assumption that an artist's ethnic background can be determined by an analysis of a few isolated iconographic clues.

More seriously, perhaps, attempts to establish Basilius's ethnic background rarely acknowledge the difficulty of determining ethnicity in an area with complex cultural dynamics, such as the Latin East. Assuming, for the sake of argument, that Basilius was Western, in the sense of belonging to the Western segment of the population in the Crusader Levant, the question arises to what extent his 'Westernness' is quantifiable and how it would have affected his artistic output. These questions are particularly relevant to the Latin East, the Western population of which was of great complexity, ranging from permanent settlers to pilgrims. If, for the sake of argument, we assume that Basilius was a second-generation Levantine Westerner, he was probably familiar largely with imagery rooted in the traditions of the Eastern Christian churches. It needs to be examined to what extent certain modes of representation would have been linked to a particular ethnic group in the Latin East. There are indeed artefacts which suggest that stylistic differentiation served to articulate different ethnic identities. The architecture of the Holy Sepulchre, or of the cathedrals in Nicosia and Famagusta in Cyprus, might, for instance, be interpreted as prominent markers of a French presence, distinguishing a largely francophone, European settler society from the indigenous population in the Levant.[53] Equally, however, some eastern Mediterranean artefacts suggest that neither subject-matter nor style was necessarily the prerogative of a particular ethnic group. Among these are certain examples of thirteenth-century Islamic metalwork from Syria on which Christian subject-matter is shown. Inscriptions on at least some of the objects indicate that they were made for Muslim patrons,

---

[51] An example is in an eleventh-century Armenian Gospel book (Yerevan, Matenadaran 2743). See T. Mathews and A. K. Sanjian, *Armenian Gospel Iconography* (Washington, D.C., 1991), 115, fig. 179b.

[52] P. Bloch, 'Das Reichenauer Einzelblatt mit den Frauen am Grabe im Hessischen Landesmuseum Darmstadt', *Kunst in Hessen und am Mittelrhein* 3 (1963), 25–43. And see fol. 77 in a twelfth-century Gospel book (Vienna, Mekhitharist Library 141/120) from Cilicia, reproduced in S. der Nersessian, *Miniature Painting from the Armenian Kingdom of Cilicia* (Washington, D.C., 1993), vol. 2, pl. 72.

[53] C. Coüasnon, *The Church of the Holy Sepulchre in Jerusalem* (London, 1981); C. Enlart, *Gothic Art and the Renaissance in Cyprus*, trans. D. Hunt (London, 1987). For a discussion of this issue with regard to Mesoamerican art, see E. Pasztory, 'Identity and difference: the uses and meanings of ethnic styles', in S. J. Barnes and W. S. Melion, eds, *Cultural Differentiation and Cultural Identity in the Visual Arts* (Hanover, New Hampshire and London, 1989), 15–38, esp. 27–31.

who appear to have had no objections to this type of imagery.[54] Another instance is a triptych from Ethiopia showing St George and scenes from his martyrdom, dated between 1480 and 1526. It is steeped in the iconographic and stylistic conventions of Ethiopian art. Yet an inscription on the icon states that it was made by a Venetian artist.[55] These examples suggest that the quest for an artist's ethnic identity may be a dangerous game to play within the specific cultural and social dynamics of the Latin East.

The imagery and decoration of Egerton 1139 pose another difficult issue, namely how the presence of the visual traditions of the three main cultures present in the Crusader East in the twelfth century can be interpreted in a manuscript, the text of which follows the conventions of the Latin-rite church and which appears to have been made for a high-ranking female owner associated with the ruling dynasty of the Jerusalem kingdom. This question is particularly resonant in the case of those parts of the book's decoration that are rooted in Islamic art. The decoration of the ivory covers and some of the formal devices used on them, such as the frames of the medallions, find close parallels not only among Islamic ivories, but also in bookbindings and metalwork.[56] A similar observation can be made about the illuminations that mark the liturgical divisions of the psalms. Some of their geometric ornament is paralleled in Islamic art, an example being two squares placed at a 45-degree angle over one another in two initials of the letter 'D' (fols 46v and 74v [Figure 5.2]). One need not look to southern Italy to find their sources of inspiration.[57] A more likely source is provided by Islamic metalwork from the Levant, which would have been easily accessible to the illuminator of these initials. It is not irrelevant in this respect that the Crusaders are known to have placed a high value on Islamic metalwork, which they had appropriated from mosques after the conquest of Jerusalem.[58]

The quest for such parallels, however, is rarely enlightening in itself. It is far more difficult, yet central to an understanding of Egerton 1139, to establish why high-status objects from the Islamic world should have been used as an inspiration for the manuscript's decoration and what conclusions can be drawn from this. An obvious answer would be that the decoration of Egerton reflects the availability of Islamic artefacts at the royal court or in the bazaars of Jerusalem. But is it possible to estab-

---

[54] E. Baer, *Ayyubid Metalwork with Christian Images* (Leiden, 1989).

[55] M. Heldman, *African Zion* (New Haven and London, 1993), exhibition catalogue, 188–9, no. 88; R. Cormack, *Painting the Soul* (London, 1997), 211–13.

[56] Kühnel, *Crusader Art*, 115–24.

[57] Buchthal, *Miniature Painting*, 12–13.

[58] Kühnel, *Crusader Art*, 123–4.

lish links between the decoration of the codex and the political and social circumstances of the Crusader territories in the twelfth century? The almost equal representation of the visual traditions of the three main cultures present in the Levant in the manuscript is all the more surprising in the light of relations between Crusaders and Muslims in the Latin East. The lot of Muslims in the Crusader territories was generally an unhappy one, being subject to stringent apartheid-style policies.[59] At the same time, hostile Muslim neighbours posed an almost constant threat to the Crusader domains. None of these historical circumstances appears to have found any resonance in the decoration of Egerton 1139. These points, however briefly put here, highlight the limitations of using an artefact in interpreting a society which was culturally heterogeneous and in contact with other societies. Egerton 1139 is a clear example of the aesthetic appeal of Eastern Christian and Islamic art among the Western population of the Levant, but it tells a story that is largely separate from, if not contradictory to, that enshrined in other source material.

---

[59] B. Z. Kedar, 'The subjected Muslims of the Frankish Levant', in J. M. Powell, ed., *Muslims under Frankish Rule, 1100–1300* (Princeton, 1990), 135–74.

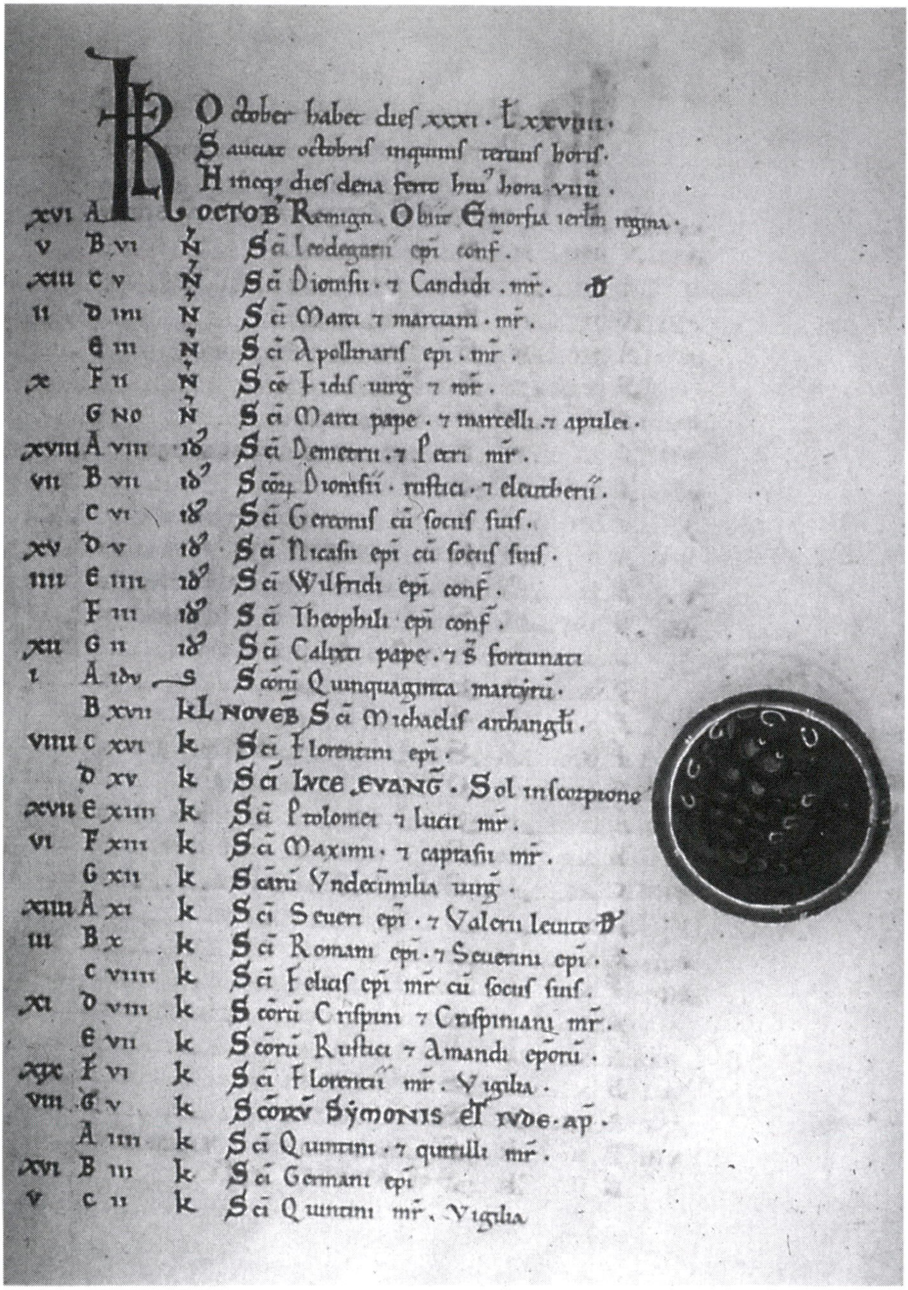

*Fig. 5.1. The Queen Melisende Psalter (London, B.L., Egerton 1139, fol. 18r)
(photograph: British Library)*

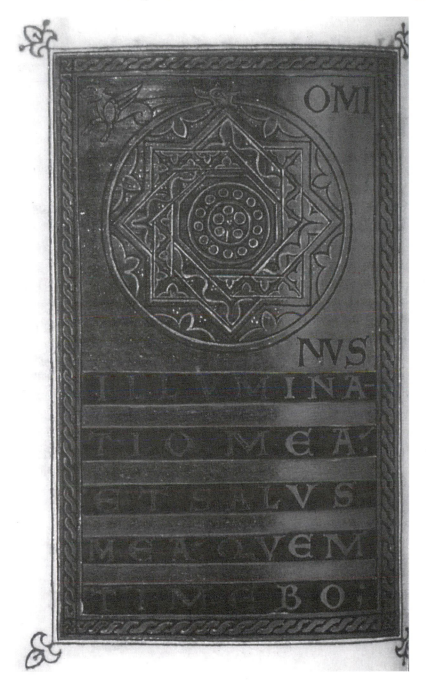

Fig. 5.2. The Queen Melisende Psalter (London, B.L., Egerton 1139, fol. 46v)
(photography: British Library)

6. Byzantium perceived through illuminated manuscripts: now and then

John Lowden

Images from manuscripts now play an important role in forming perceptions of Byzantium.[1] Emperor Basil II (976–1025), for example (Figure 6.1), is frequently brought before us in the form of reproductions of the full-page frontispiece in the Psalter in the Marciana Library in Venice (MS Marc. gr. Z. 17).[2] The illustrated Chronicle of Skylitzes in Madrid (Biblioteca Nacional, MS vitr. 26–2), to take another example, is becoming a favoured source for present-day authors, editors or picture researchers who want to enliven a book's narrative or cover, since it includes many pictures of historical events and 'personalities'.[3] Manuscripts in general are able to provide innumerable images of biblical scenes and figures, of saints and martyrdoms, of aristocrats or ascetics, even of agrarian tools or methods of bandaging, many executed with superlative craftsmanship in the costly materials and elegant styles that we readily recognize and term 'Byzantine'.

To exemplify how preponderant images from manuscripts now are, we need look no further than the three volumes of the indispensable *Oxford*

---

[1] Because this paper was written for the symposium linked to the exhibition *Byzantium: Treasures of Byzantine Art and Culture from British Collections* (London [British Museum], 1994), it draws particular attention to works that were exhibited at that time. In revising it for publication (in 1995 and again in 1999) I have made only minor changes in the text, and at the editors' request have kept annotation to a minimum. I am particularly grateful to the institutions that have permitted photographs to be reproduced, to Patricia Easterling, and to the library of the Warburg Institute.

[2] Anthony Cutler, *The Aristocratic Psalters in Byzantium* (Bibliothèque des Cahiers Archéologiques 13; Paris, 1984), cat. no. 58, figs 412–13.

[3] André Grabar and M. Manoussacas, *L'illustration du manuscrit de Skylitzès de la Bibliothèque Nationale de Madrid* (Bibliothèque de l'Institut Hellénique d'Etudes Byzantines et Post-Byzantines de Venise 10; Venice, 1979).

From *Through the Looking Glass: Byzantium Through British Eyes*, eds Robin Cormack and Elizabeth Jeffreys. Copyright © 2000 by the Society for the Promotion of Byzantine Studies. Published by Ashgate Publishing Ltd, Gower House, Croft Road, Aldershot, Hampshire, GU11 3HR, Great Britain.

† τὸ θᾶχμα καινὸν ὦδε τῶν ὁρωμένων·
χριστὸς προτίνει δεξιᾷ ζωηφόρω
ἐξ οὐρανοῦ τὸ τέμμα σύμβολον κράτους,
πιστῶ κραταιῶ δις πότη βασιλείω
κάτωθεν οἱ πρώτιστοι τῶν ἀσωμάτων·
ὁ μὲν λαβὼν ἤνιγκε καὶ χαίρων στέφει·
ὁ δὲ προσάπτων τῶ κράτει καὶ τὰς νίκας·
ρομφαίαν ὅπλον ἐκ φόβου νέμαν τίους.
φέρων δι' ἄω σιχειρὶ τῆ τοῦ δεσπότου·
οἱ μάρτυρες δὲ συμμαχοῦσιν ὡς φίλω,
ρίπτοντες ἐχθρὸυς τοὺς ἐπ' οἷ σι προσμενημένους·

Fig. 6.1. continued

Dictionary of Byzantium (1991). Its 120 illustrations can be subdivided into categories on the basis of their subject-matter in the following manner:

Manuscripts	39
Architecture and sculpture (including distant and/or aerial views)	23
Metalwork (including enamel)	14
Mosaics	13
Wall-paintings	9
Icons (including miniature mosaics)	9
Ivories	7
Ceramics	2
Coins and seals	2
Textiles	2
(Total	120)

From this table it can be seen that only if we add together all the images of the interiors and exteriors of Byzantine buildings (architecture and sculpture [23], mosaics [13], and wall-paintings [9]) does the subtotal pass that for Byzantine manuscript images.

Once images from manuscripts are reproduced on the pages of a book – whether intended primarily for a scholarly or a popular audience – alongside images of mosaics, wall-paintings, enamels, ivories, icons, textiles and so forth, it requires a major effort for a modern viewer/reader to recall the very different purposes that differing Byzantine works were made to serve, and the enormously varied circumstances that conditioned their visibility and surrounded their use. The main theme of this chapter is therefore to question the validity of an aspect of our modern perception of Byzantium, and to contrast it with older perceptions, using the illuminated Byzantine manuscript as a case that merits special attention.

My first point is a simple one in three parts, and concerns modern viewing conditions of Byzantine art. We can begin with scale. When reproduced in a book, an image from a manuscript some 10–30 cm tall may well be found alongside a wall-painting perhaps some 100–300 cm tall (and quite possibly an enamel just 1–3 cm tall). The implication seems to be – and here I exaggerate somewhat for effect – that the relative or absolute dimensions of the originals can be ignored, and that each image should help to mould our perceptions of Byzantium to a similar degree. The proposal that vast differences in scale should be irrelevant in looking at art is patently ridiculous.

The second issue concerns the physical context of the object reproduced. Illustrations in books often seriously mislead by masking the surroundings of an image. Even in the interior of a Byzantine church in its current state a modern viewer is unlikely to perceive only a single image at a time. In a Byzantine manuscript, even the modern viewer looking into a display case will see an opening of two pages, not just the miniature that is usually reproduced. The implication of masking images for reproduction, or in the case of manuscripts of reproducing only one page or a detail instead of an entire opening, seems to be that 'extraneous' material may be distracting, and could adversely affect our perceptions.[4] All those who visit Byzantine sites will be familiar with the realization that preconceptions derived from reproductions in books need to be abandoned as the importance of topography, scale, lighting, condition and many other factors become apparent. Physical context is literally essential to the image.

The third issue concerns accessibility. Because it is less immediately obvious than the first two points, it is perhaps more in need of emphasis. An image from a manuscript when reproduced in a book is viewed by exactly the same number of readers as the adjacent reproduction of an image from a church. But originally the image in the church – assuming the building was relatively large – could have been viewed by hundreds of people at the same time and by literally thousands, even tens of thousands, every year. The image in the manuscript, on the other hand, is unlikely ever to have been clearly visible to more than one or two people at a time, and may well have gone completely unseen by all but a few individuals for most of its history.[5] Perceptions are formed largely (if not quite exclusively) by what is perceptible. Most images in most Byzantine manuscripts were virtually invisible until very recently.

My proposition, therefore, is that whereas illuminated manuscripts will undoubtedly continue to be of great importance in creating a modern perception of Byzantium because they are such a rich source of images, the situation in Byzantine and post-Byzantine times in the East, and in medieval or post-medieval times in the West was utterly different. Byzantine illuminations, I suggest, were rarely seen. In view of the British focus of this collection of papers the proposition will be tested by looking at the evidence (either direct or in the form of 'reflections') for

---

[4] I considered the need to reproduce openings of manuscripts in 'The royal imperial book and the image or self-image of the medieval ruler', in Anne J. Duggan, ed., *Kings and Kingship in Medieval Europe* (King's College London Medieval Studies 10; London, 1993), 213–40, especially 217–22. All the illuminated manuscripts in the *Byzantium* catalogue were reproduced as openings although in some cases it was necessary to publish two photographs side by side, and these sometimes differ markedly in colour balance (e.g., cat. no. 180).

[5] See also John Lowden, *Early Christian and Byzantine Art* (London, 1997), 8.

the presence in Britain of illuminated Byzantine manuscripts in all centuries before the eighteenth, but more especially before *c.* 1500.[6]

There are now, by my reckoning, approximately 3,230 Greek manuscripts in Britain (excluding papyri and modern scholarly transcriptions of Greek texts). The figure is calculated from Jean-Marie Olivier's *Répertoire des bibliothèques et des catalogues de manuscrits grecs de Marcel Richard* (Turnhout, 1995). Although the figure is certainly not entirely accurate, I doubt if it is more than about ±1 per cent adrift, giving a total in the range of 3,200–3,260 manuscripts. It should be borne in mind that some of these manuscripts are merely fragments consisting of one or more leaves or parts of leaves, and a significant proportion are of post-Byzantine manufacture. Thus the 'Byzantine' manuscripts form a subset of as yet unquantified magnitude within the set defined as manuscripts written in Greek. For comparative purposes it can be noted that according to Olivier's *Répertoire* the Bibliothèque nationale de France is home to some 4,900 manuscripts, and the Biblioteca Apostolica Vaticana to some 4,700.

From an art-historical perspective it would be particularly interesting to know exactly how many of the 3,230 (±1 per cent) Greek manuscripts in Britain contain some form of 'art'. Since the sort of systematic investigation that would be required to produce a reliable figure has yet to be undertaken, it is necessary to resort to an estimate provided by a theoretical model. This model can be derived from Irmgard Hutter's exhaustive work on Oxford libraries, specifically the Bodleian, published in the first three volumes of the *Corpus der byzantinischen Miniaturenhandschriften* (hereafter *CBM*; Stuttgart, 1977–82).[7] Her inclusive definition of 'art' as not merely figurative or scenic representations, but all types of ornamental decoration,[8] provides satisfactory criteria, and manuscripts in this category will here be termed 'illuminated'. Not surprisingly, Hutter established that some of the collections within the Bodleian proved to have a much higher proportion of illuminated manuscripts than others: among the twenty-six Greek manuscripts from the D'Orville collection (which now have shelfmarks beginning 'Auct.X.') there is not a single one that she considered worth including in her survey, whereas the twenty-seven Greek manuscripts with Cromwell shelfmarks include seventeen that she catalogued as illuminated. A variation between 0 per cent and 63 per cent in the proportion of illuminated to non-illuminated manuscripts seems to suggest a most unpromising basis for analysis, but I think the

---

[6] Contrast now the situation revealed by Robert S. Nelson, 'The Italian appreciation and appropriation of illuminated Byzantine manuscripts, *c.* 1200–1450', *DOP* 49 (1995), 209–35.

[7] Note the lengthy addenda and corrigenda in Hutter, *CBM* III, 315–52.

[8] Hutter, *CBM* I, ix, and especially the discussion in *CBM* III, ix–x.

final totals that are reached as further collections are added are large enough for the discussion to have some statistical validity.[9] The total number of Greek manuscripts in the Bodleian is 1,567; the total number with some form of illumination is 279 (according to Hutter's figures), or 17.8 per cent. In round figures this means that there is very roughly one illuminated Byzantine or post-Byzantine manuscript in the Bodleian for every four without illumination. The total for all British collections ought according to this calculation to be around 575 illuminated manuscripts (17.8 per cent of 3,230), but this is an estimate that should be recognized as containing a significant margin of error.

For present purposes it is appropriate, or at least necessary, to define a further subset, namely those Byzantine manuscripts that contain not merely some form of decoration, but also images of human figures. I will call these 'illustrated' as distinct from 'illuminated' manuscripts, although this does beg various important questions about the way that images were used in the books, questions which it will not be possible to explore here. My justification for this narrowing of the focus of enquiry – and it undoubtedly could be bogus – is the hypothesis that illustrated Byzantine manuscripts (which will in any case also contain examples of Byzantine decoration) can be assumed to have been more likely to have affected British perceptions over the centuries than Byzantine manuscripts containing decoration alone.[10]

A preliminary survey of the 3,230 Greek manuscripts in all British collections which I carried out reveals that there are approximately 120 illustrated examples, amounting to 3.7 per cent of the total. This is in line with Hutter's work on the Bodleian, which also indicated that 3.7 per cent (58 out of 1567) of the Greek manuscripts in that collection were illustrated (but bear in mind that the Bodleian manuscripts represent more than 48.5 per cent of the total sample). Thus in Britain one illustrated Greek manuscript survives for every twenty-six or so without illustration, in sharp contrast to the relatively high proportion containing some form of illumination.

To pursue the question of how these 120 illustrated manuscripts might have affected British perceptions of Byzantium we need first to establish when they arrived in Britain. For some we know the precise date and circumstances, although not necessarily the motivation for their acquisi-

---

[9] The distortions possible in a small sample are evident in Hutter's recent work on Christ Church: 55 illuminated manuscripts were catalogued out of a total of 86 (64 per cent). See I. Hutter, *CBM* IV, 1–2, *Oxford, Christ Church* (Stuttgart, 1993).

[10] Contrast Robert Nelson's observations on the Greek Gospels (London, B.L., Harley 5790) made in 1478 for Cardinal Francesco Gonzaga: cited in D. Chambers and J. Martineau, eds, *Splendours of the Gonzaga* (London, 1981), cat. no. 26.

tion. For example, William Wake (the last Archbishop of Canterbury to travel by boat between Lambeth Palace and the Houses of Parliament – he was rowed in state across the Thames in the former royal barge) acquired the two illustrated Gospel books that were displayed in the *Byzantium* exhibition from the shadowy Greek dealer Antonios Triphilis in 1735 (Wake left them on his death to Christ Church, Oxford).[11] The two Greek Canonici manuscripts from the Bodleian Library in the *Byzantium* exhibition were purchased along with 2,045 other manuscripts in various languages for £5,444 5s. 1d. in Venice in 1817.[12] (Allowing for monetary inflation, the Canonici Collection represents the single most costly purchase ever made by the Bodleian.) The wonderful Theodore Psalter, dated 1066 (a year of more consequence in the history of Britain than of Byzantium) ,was purchased by the British Museum in 1853 at the sale in London of the collection of the Smyrna-based trader and numismatist Henry Borrell.[13]

It is generally more difficult to establish the precise details surrounding the pre-eighteenth-century acquisition of those illustrated Byzantine manuscripts now in Britain. Yet the general pattern in chronological terms seems to be clear. So far as I can discover, among the 120 or so illustrated Byzantine manuscripts now in Britain only a single one was certainly in this country before 1453. This is the Gospel book which was presented to Gonville and Caius College, Cambridge (now MS 403/412), by Thomas Hatcher in 1567, having been lent to the Cambridge Franciscan Richard Brinkley in the early sixteenth century (Figure 6.2).[14] Prior to that period it had been in the Franciscan house in Oxford, to which it had been left by Robert Grosseteste, Bishop of Lincoln and *Lector* to the Oxford Franciscans, who died in 1253.

Historically, this manuscript is of the greatest interest. Grosseteste is a figure of enormous importance in the study and knowledge of Greek in England (in Europe, indeed) on account of his translations and biblical exegesis.[15] Five other Byzantine manuscripts that 'belonged' to him have

---

[11] *Byzantium*, cat. nos 177, 203. On Wake see Hutter, *CBM* IV.1, xxvii–xliv, with further references. On the role of Triphilis see Hutter, *CBM* IV.1, xxxvi–xxxviii. Patricia Easterling generously supplied me with a list of ten further manuscripts, mostly in Cambridge University Library, which have a certain or probable connection with Triphilis. Most of these passed through the collections of Richard Mead (d. 1754) and/or Anthony Askew (d. 1774).

[12] *Byzantium*, cat. nos 148, 170.

[13] *Byzantium*, cat. no. 168. A facsimile publication of the Theodore Psalter on CD-ROM by Charles Barber, with a contribution by John Lowden, is in preparation by University of Illinois Press.

[14] *Byzantium*, cat. no. 197.

[15] A. C. Dionisotti, 'On the Greek studies of Robert Grosseteste', in A. C. Dionisotti, A. Grafton and J. Kraye, eds, *Uses of Greek and Latin; Historical Essays* (London, 1988), 19–39.

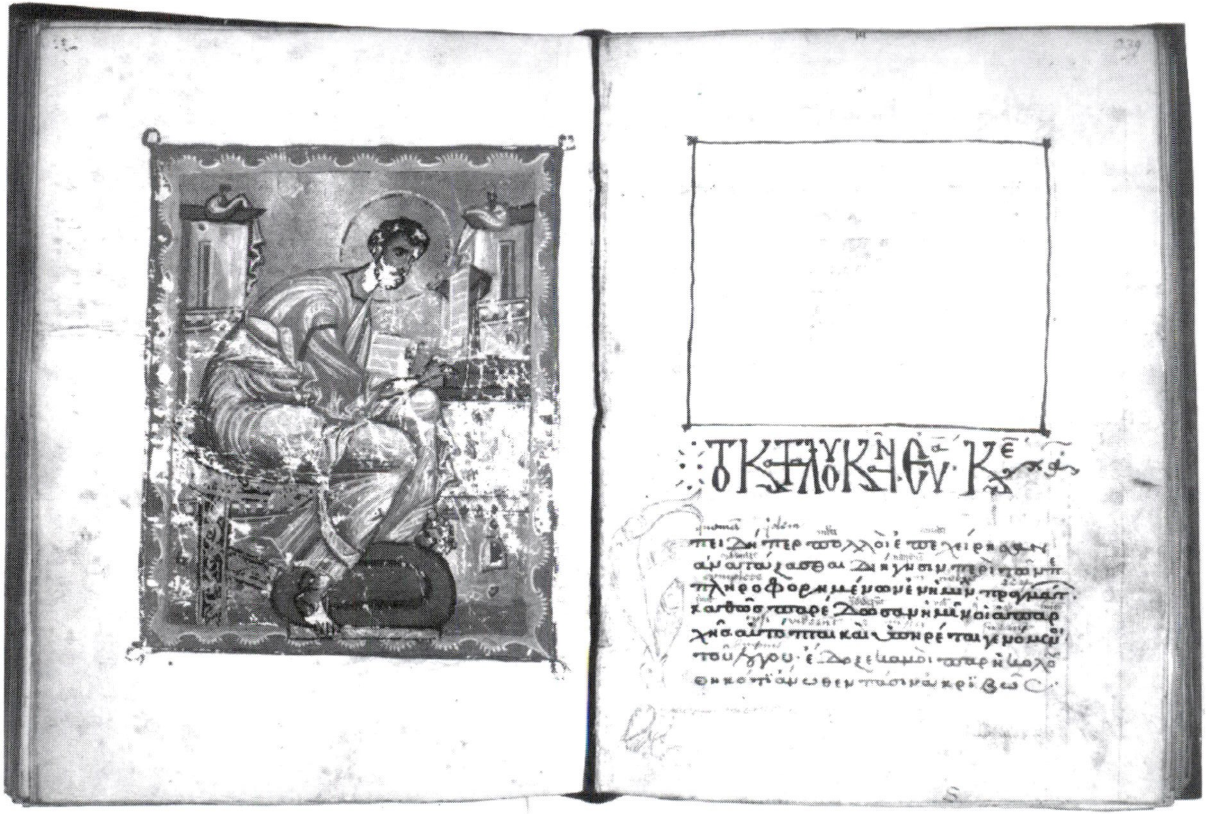

Fig. 6.2. Cambridge, Gonville and Caius College, MS 403/412, pp. 238–9: St Luke and the opening of his Gospel (photograph: library)

survived, although none is illustrated. He had a small twelfth-century
Psalter, now Cambridge, Corpus Christi College MS 480; a ninth-century
Aristotle, now Oxford, Corpus Christi College MS 108; a copy of the *Suda
Lexikon*, made in Southern Italy before 1205, and now MS Voss.gr.F.2 in
the Library of the Rijksuniversiteit at Leiden (of which there is a single
leaf in Canterbury);[16] a copy of the complete works of Pseudo-Dionysius,
probably made for him at Saint-Denis, and now MS Canonici gr. 97 in the
Bodleian (it went from Oxford to Italy before returning); and a tenth-
century manuscript containing the Testaments of the Twelve Patriarchs
and other texts, now Cambridge University Library MS Ff.I.24. This last
had been discovered in Athens by John of Basingstoke – about whose
exploits there the chronicler Matthew Paris wove a net of fantasy[17] – and
was acquired by Grosseteste in 1242.

Grosseteste annotated his Gospel book with a few variant readings,
indicating that he must have had access to at least one other Byzantine
Gospel manuscript. The book's illustration takes the standard form for a
Byzantine Gospel book: it has images of Mark and Luke (Figure 6.2) on
single leaves from an original set of four evangelist portraits.[18] They face
the openings of their Gospels, which have large blank spaces for decorated headpieces that were never completed. The precise circumstances
of manufacture of the Gonville and Caius Gospels are not known, but
Annemarie Carr has suggested a date in the 1220s or 1230s, and she
raises the possibility that the book was produced in southern Greece.[19]

Did Grosseteste, we may ask, particularly want an *illustrated* Gospel
book? We have no way of knowing, but I doubt it. What is not in doubt,
however, is that he appears to have paid no special attention to the
book's images once he had acquired it. Nor do we find any shred of
evidence for a sudden interest in Byzantine art in Oxford (or anywhere
else in England) in the mid-thirteenth century.[20]

If the result of looking at the one illustrated Byzantine manuscript that
we know to have been in England since the Middle Ages for signs of
changed perceptions is negative, the answer may be that we are looking

---

[16] N. G. Wilson, 'Two Greek fragments in Canterbury', *Scriptorium* 30 (1976), 46–7. The
leaf had already been removed in the late fifteenth-century.

[17] Matthew Paris, *Chronica Maiora* (Rolls Series; H. R. Luard, ed.; London, 1880), vol. 5,
284–7, esp. 286–7 on the 'wonderful Athenian girl'.

[18] The Mark opening is reproduced (in colour) in *Byzantium*, cat. no. 197.

[19] Annemarie Weyl Carr, *Byzantine Illumination, 1150–1250* (Chicago, 1987), 117–20, and
cat. no. 36.

[20] To judge from N. Morgan, *Early Gothic Manuscripts* [I] *1190–1250* (Survey of Manu-
scripts Illuminated in the British Isles 4.1; London, 1982); and N. Morgan, *Early Gothic
Manuscripts* [II] *1250–1285* (Survey of Manuscripts Illuminated in the British Isles 4.2;
London, 1988).

in the wrong direction. (Of course I am not saying that the Byzantine manuscripts that Grosseteste acquired were unimportant; his translation of the Testaments of the Twelve Patriarchs, for example, was a sensational success;[21] but the subject at issue is the specifically visual aspects of these manuscripts.) Perhaps, or so it could be argued, the illustrated Byzantine manuscripts in question did once exist but were subsequently lost, like so much medieval material. Let us then approach the issue from this alternative direction and look for evidence in 'British' art for a knowledge of Byzantine art. At the same time we shall need to ask whether this knowledge, if we find it, was acquired specifically through looking at Byzantine manuscripts. Parts of this path are well worn, for under the misleading label 'Byzantine influence' art historians have frequently sought an explanation for aspects of change in English art, notably in the twelfth century, in precisely such connections.[22] The field of enquiry is vast, so it will only be possible here to look at three varied examples, and only the first of these can be treated at length.

The first case is provided by one of the greatest products of these islands of any period, namely the Lindisfarne Gospels (London, B.L., MS Cotton Nero D. IV).[23] For present purposes we can accept that the book was made at Lindisfarne to honour God and St Cuthbert and completed before 721, perhaps around the year 698. It was later in Durham Cathedral, was acquired by Sir Robert Cotton in the early seventeenth century, and eventually reached the British Museum with the rest of the Cotton collection. In addition to its extraordinary wealth of decoration, the Lindisfarne Gospels contains a set of four full-page evangelist portraits. Each figure is conspicuously named within the image in a curious mixture of Greek and Latin, written in one of the characteristic display scripts of the book: O AGIOS MATTHEUS (Figure 6.3), O AGIUS MARCUS, O AGIOS LUCAS (Figure 6.4), and O AGIOS IOHANNES. We can note that in the first three cases the scribe placed a small sloping

---

[21] Dionisotti, 'Grosseteste', 29.

[22] E.g., remarks in C.M. Kauffmann, *Romanesque Manuscripts, 1066–1190* (Survey of Manuscripts Illuminated in the British Isles 3; London, 1975), 18–28; Otto Pächt speaks frequently in terms of 'Byzantine influence' in England, as in his *Book Illumination in the Middle Ages* (London, 1986), 138–41; see also O. Demus, *Byzantine Art and the West* (New York, 1970); A. Grabar, 'L'asymétrie des relations de Byzance et de l'Occident dans les domaines des arts du moyen âge', in I. Hutter, ed., *Byzanz und der Westen. Studien zur Kunst des europäischen Mittelalters* (Vienna, 1984), 9–24; G. Cavallo, 'La circolazione dei testi greci nell'Europa dell'alto medioevo', in J. Hamesse and M. Fattori, eds, *Rencontres de cultures dans la philosophie médiévale: traductions et traducteurs de l'antiquité tardive au XIVe siècle* (Louvain-la-Neuve and Cassino, 1990), 47–64.

[23] T. D. Kendrick and others, *Evangeliorum Quattuor Codex Lindisfarnensis ...* (Olten and Lausanne, 1956–60), 142–57; J. J. G. Alexander, *Insular Manuscripts, 6th to the 9th Century* (Survey of Manuscripts Illuminated in the British Isles 1; London, 1978), 35–40.

Fig. 6.3. London, B.L., MS Cotton Nero D. IV, fol. 25v, St Matthew (photograph: library)

Fig. 6.4. London, B.L., MS Cotton Nero D. IV, fol. 137v, St Luke (photograph: library)

stroke above the O that approximates to the rough breathing. And whereas in three of the images he wrote OAGIOS (or OAGIUS) without spacing, for Luke the words are correctly split O and AGIOS (Figure 6.4).

The use of the formula O AGIOS instead of SANCTUS in these images was explained by Bruce-Mitford in the massive publication that accompanied the facsimile edition of the Lindisfarne Gospels (1960) as follows. It was evidence to support his theory that the model for the Lindisfarne Gospels was Volume VII of the nine-volume set of biblical manuscripts (called the *Novem Codices*) made for Cassiodorus at Vivarium in the deep south of Italy before 553. Behind this lost model, he suggested, lay a further lost model in the form of a Greek or 'Greco-Latin' (his term) illustrated Gospel book of the sort Cassiodorus could have encountered in his long service at Ravenna.[24] Bruce-Mitford, however, argued himself into a tight corner by asserting at the same time that the Matthew image of the Lindisfarne Gospels was adapted from the Ezra frontispiece in Cassiodorus's lost one-volume Bible, the *Codex Grandior*, which was, he proposed, also in Northumbria around 700, and which was the model for the Codex Amiatinus (now Florence, Biblioteca Laurenziana, MS Amiat. 1).[25] The controversy that these hypotheses raised about the possible influence of putative lost models continues unresolved (and is by its nature unresolvable).[26] For present purposes we can note that the O AGIOS formula has been considered evidence not for the presence of an illuminated Byzantine Gospel book in late seventh-century Northumbria, but for the existence of a book of similar type in mid-sixth-century Italy.

It would be wise to leave the question of the source of the Lindisfarne O AGIOS considerably more open than did Bruce-Mitford for a variety of reasons. We do not have any pre-iconoclast Byzantine Gospel book, or contemporary Latin book, with evangelist portraits containing inscriptions like these.[27] For the most part, in sixth-century Byzantine art inscriptions, if present, provide the name of the figure alone, omitting O AGIOS entirely. O AGIOS does seem to become increasingly common, however, from the late sixth century onward (hence closer to the date of

---

[24] R. Bruce-Mitford, 'The Art of the Codex Amiatinus', *Journal of the British Archaeological Association* 32 (1969), 1–25.

[25] *Codex Lindisfarnensis*, 146–9.

[26] K. Corsano, 'The first quire of the Codex Amiatinus and the *Institutiones* of Cassiodorus', *Scriptorium* 41 (1987), 3–34; G. Henderson, 'Cassiodorus and Eadfrith once again', in R. Spearman and J. Higgitt, eds, *Age of Migrating Ideas. Early Medieval Art in Northern Britain and Ireland* (Edinburgh and Stroud, 1993), 82–91; R. Marsden, 'Job in his place: the Ezra miniature of the Codex Amiatinus', *Scriptorium* 49 (1995), 3–15.

[27] I have considered this further in 'The beginnings of biblical illustration', in J. Williams, ed., *Imaging the Early Medieval Bible* (University Park, 1999), 10–59.

the Lindisfarne Gospels than to that of the supposed Cassiodoran model).[28] Indeed, the idea for the wording of the inscriptions in the Lindisfarne Gospels need not have come from a manuscript source at all.[29] The fragments surviving from the contemporary silver cover of the portable altar of St Cuthbert show a seated figure of St Peter identified as S[ANCTUS] [PETR]OS [APOSTOLO]S or [APOSTOLU]S with a similar angular three-stroke 'S', and a similar mixture of Greek and Latin words as in the Lindisfarne Gospels (although the amount of reconstruction required to complete the inscription should be noted).[30] Other types of Byzantine objects with inscriptions – such as metalwork, painted panels or textiles – if imported to Northumbria, could equally well have provided a model. Whatever the source of the O AGIOS formula, however, one thing is clear. No tradition for its use sprang up in England, whether in the period of the Lindisfarne Gospels or later, despite its conspicuous presence in this remarkable exemplar.

Recent work by Bischoff and Lapidge on the 'Byzantine' Archbishop Theodore of Canterbury (d. 690) and his close colleague Abbot Hadrian (d. *c.* 709) has opened up new perspectives on this period, and specifically on the presence of Byzantine manuscripts in England.[31] The unusual Neapolitan pericopes and lists in the Lindisfarne Gospels, for example, could have been brought to Canterbury by Hadrian (who came from Naples) and thence to Northumbria, rather than from Rome directly to Northumbria, as Bruce-Mitford argued.[32] The Greek-speaking Theodore and Hadrian also produced biblical commentaries at Canterbury that demonstrate a knowledge of a wide range of patristic Greek authors, and imply the presence of a considerable number of Greek (i.e. Byzantine) manuscripts.[33] Among these the most intriguing for present

---

[28] For reproductions see, e.g., K. Weitzmann, ed., *Age of Spirituality; Late Antique and Early Christian Art, Third to Seventh Century* (New York, 1979); K. Weitzmann, *The Monastery of Saint Catherine at Mount Sinai; The Icons* I (Princeton, 1976); V. Lazarev, *Storia della pittura bizantina* (Biblioteca di storia dell'arte 7; Turin, 1967); for a specific case see R. Cormack, 'The mosaic decoration of S. Demetrios, Thessaloniki: a re-examination in the light of the drawings of W. S. George', and 'The Church of Saint Demetrios: the watercolours and drawings of W. S. George', reprinted in his *The Byzantine Eye: Studies in Art and Patronage* (London, 1989), studies I–II.

[29] As suggested by David Wright: for references and further bibliography see Alexander, *Insular Manuscripts*, 35–40.

[30] C. F. Battiscombe, ed., *The Relics of Saint Cuthbert* (Oxford, 1956), 330, fig. 2.

[31] B. Bischoff and M. Lapidge, *Biblical Commentaries from the Canterbury School of Theodore and Hadrian* (Cambridge Studies in Anglo-Saxon England 10; Cambridge, 1994).

[32] Bischoff and Lapidge, *Biblical Commentaries*, 155–60.

[33] If the excerpts were pre-selected, so to speak, in biblical manuscripts with *catenae*, these have no parallel in surviving Byzantine *catena* manuscripts: Bischoff and Lapidge, *Biblical Commentaries*, 229–32.

purposes is the text now generally referred to as 'Cosmas Indicopleustes', but known to Theodore and Hadrian as *Christianus historiographus*. This mid-sixth-century work requires images, and the earliest surviving manuscript (the late-ninth-century *Vaticanus gr.* 699) is a magnificent illustrated book.[34] Lapidge raises the intriguing possibility that when Bede records how Benedict Biscop purchased a *Cosmographiorum codex* at Rome, and subsequently presented it to King Aldfrith of Northumbria (685–705) in exchange for an estate valued at eight hides (a huge sum), not only was this manuscript an illustrated 'Cosmas', but it could have come via Canterbury, for Benedict was in the retinue that brought Theodore from Rome to England in 669.[35] That having been said, we search in vain for even a single image in Insular (or later British) art that appears to show a knowledge of an illustrated Byzantine 'Cosmas' manuscript.

Our two further cases must be treated more briefly. One comes from the twelfth century and involves a second manuscript from the Cotton collection, made, it is thought, in Winchester around 1150, and seemingly kept at the Benedictine nunnery of Shaftesbury Abbey from at least the mid-thirteenth century.[36] This Psalter (London, B.L., Cotton MS Nero C. IV) has a long cycle of frontispiece images amongst which two immediately stand out as completely different from anything else in the book. According to the French inscriptions above the top border, which may be a slightly later addition, they represent the Assumption of the Virgin (ICI EST LA SUMTION DE NOSTRE DAME), and the Virgin as Queen of Heaven (ICI EST FAITE REINE DEL CIEL) (Figure 6.5). Basing himself on their style, and the deduction that they originally faced one another as the book lay open (the folios were remounted in the nineteenth century), Wormald termed the pages 'the Byzantine Diptych'.[37] They are probably the most familiar case of what has been perceived as 'Byzantine influence' on English art.

A recent M.A. thesis at the Courtauld Institute by Holger Klein considered at length the possible sources for the so-called Byzantine Diptych of

---

[34] C. Stornajolo, *Le miniature della Topografia Cristiana di Cosma Indicopleuste codice Vaticano greco 699* (Codices e Vaticanis Selecti … 10; Milan, 1908).

[35] Bischoff and Lapidge, *Biblical Commentaries*, 208–11. Note that there is no consideration of Greek manuscripts in David N. Dumville, 'The importation of Mediterranean manuscripts into Theodore's England', in Michael Lapidge, ed., *Archbishop Theodore: commemorative studies on his life and influence* (Cambridge Studies in Anglo-Saxon England 11; Cambridge, 1995), 96–119.

[36] See first, Kristine Edmondson Haney, *The Winchester Psalter, An Iconographic Study* (Leicester, 1986).

[37] Francis Wormald, *The Winchester Psalter* (London, 1973), 87–91; see also figs 4, 88 (in colour).

the Winchester Psalter.[38] Klein concluded that no Byzantine manuscript or icon has or is likely to have had a diptych of images of precisely this sort. Whatever the artists of the Winchester Psalter had in mind, there is thus no evidence that it was an illustrated Byzantine manuscript, which was in England in the mid-twelfth century, but subsequently disappeared. And as with the Lindisfarne O AGIOS formula, the two images that form the 'Byzantine Diptych', unusual and readily recognizable as they are, had no known followers.[39]

Sir Robert Cotton is also the link to our final case, the manuscript known as the Cotton Genesis (Figure 6.6), which was all but totally destroyed in a fire at Ashburnham House in London, where the Cotton Library was deposited, in 1731.[40] I include this manuscript to provide a contrast to the other cases we have been able to consider: not because it was enormously influential on people's visual perception of Byzantium in England – it was not – but because it certainly did have this effect before it reached England.

The Cotton Genesis, a manuscript which originally contained the text of Genesis alone, accompanied by some 339 miniatures, was in England by 1575. In the thirteenth century, however, it was in Venice. Weitzmann and Kessler propose that prior to that it had remained in Egypt, where they believe it was made,[41] although it remains more likely, in my view, that it was looted from Constantinople by the Venetians after 1204, whatever its place of manufacture. Once in Venice, the manuscript received the most extraordinary compliment. Its images were taken as the models for more than one hundred scenes in mosaic that were set up in the domical vaults and adjacent spaces of the atrium of San Marco in around the 1220s–1230s.[42]

There can be no doubt that in thirteenth-century Venice this Genesis manuscript was perceived as very unusual and very old. In some way

---

[38] Now published: Holger Klein, 'The so-called Byzantine Diptych in the Winchester Psalter, British Library, MS Cotton Nero C.IV', *Gesta* 37 (1998), 26–43.

[39] Richard Gameson has drawn attention to an unusual initial with scenes from the life of St Demetrius in a Passional from St Augustine's, Canterbury of the end of the eleventh century (London, B.L., Arundel 91. See his 'English manuscript art in the late eleventh century: Canterbury and its context', in R. Eales and R. Sharpe, eds, *Canterbury and the Norman Conquest* (London, 1995), 95–144, esp. pp. 128, 137–8, and pl. 9b. He suggests 'pictorial sources of Byzantine origin' (p. 138), although the image is un-Byzantine in appearance.

[40] *Byzantium*, cat. nos. 66–67.

[41] K. Weitzmann and H. L. Kessler, *The Cotton Genesis, British Library Codex Cotton Otho B. VI* (The Illustrations in the Manuscripts of the Septuagint 1; Princeton, 1986), 6, 30–34.

[42] K. Weitzmann, 'The Genesis Mosaics of San Marco and the Cotton Genesis Miniatures', in Otto Demus, *The Mosaics of San Marco in Venice*, vol. 2 (Chicago, 1984), 105–42.

*Fig. 6.5. London, B.L., MS Cotton Nero C. IV, pp. 29–30: Assumption of the
Virgin, Virgin as Queen of Heaven (photographs: Conway Library, Courtau
Institute of Art)*

Fig. 6.5. continued

Fig. 6.6. London, B.L., MS Cotton Otho B. VI: author's reconstruction of an opening (photograph: Conway Library, Courtauld Institute of Art)

its presence added to the prestige of the city and of St Mark. The decision to reproduce the manuscript's images at monumental scale made these points as public as they could possibly be. Here we do have a case in which literally thousands of people saw and still do see at least a version of the images of a manuscript. That having been said, the Genesis mosaics convey a much less 'Byzantine' impression than do most of the other twelfth- or thirteenth-century mosaics in San Marco, and even making due allowance for losses this is likely always to have been the case. It is thus reasonable, if seemingly paradoxical, to assert that in the thirteenth century the images derived from the Cotton Genesis would probably have been perceived in Venice as 'un-Byzantine'. They were valued by the Venetians, in part at least, because they looked so 'Early Christian'.

The Cotton Genesis, and the use to which it was put in San Marco, far from providing a paradigm for the wider perception and use of illuminated Byzantine manuscripts, as has often been claimed, needs to be recognized as a case without close parallel.[43] No other city had a relationship with Byzantium and Byzantine art quite like that of Venice. No other Byzantine manuscript was quite like the Cotton Genesis, or is known to have been treated in quite the same way. And before concluding I wish to make just two more observations about this manuscript. First, it is a puzzle why the Cotton Genesis did not end up in the treasury of San Marco, but somehow was brought to England between the second and third quarters of the sixteenth century. And second, when the Cotton Genesis was intensively studied through the seventeenth and eighteenth centuries – before the fire of 1731 – it was a Frenchman, Nicholas-Claude Fabri de Peiresc, who was the only scholar to take a serious interest in its images.[44]

My conclusion can be brief. I suggest that it is only in recent times that British perceptions of Byzantium have been strongly influenced by the images in Byzantine manuscripts. The pendulum has indeed swung so far that we now risk losing a historical understanding of the material we look at, especially when it is reproduced selectively. The image in the Psalter of Basil II (Figure 6.1), for example, was always intended to be seen (by those fortunate few permitted to view it) juxtaposed with the verses written in gold that still face it. The verses explain and justify the image in various ways, and are present to guide and instruct the Byzan-

---

[43] J. Lowden, 'Concerning the Cotton Genesis and other illustrated manuscripts of Genesis', *Gesta* 31 (1992), 40–53. The nearest parallel is that considered by A. Grabar, 'Fresques romanes copiées sur les miniatures du Pentateuque de Tours', *Cahiers archéologiques* 9 (1957), 329–41.

[44] Weitzmann and Kessler, *Cotton Genesis*, 3–7.

tine viewer.[45] But how often is the image of the emperor reproduced together with the verses today? The miniature, and the opening on which it is located, were planned and executed to do much more than present a casual viewer with a picture to be captioned 'Emperor Basil II'. Images, especially those derived from manuscripts, need to be treated with respect as complex historical documents. The alternatives, an image of Byzantium without history, or a history of Byzantium without images, are both unthinkable.

---

[45] The verses are translated as follows by I. Sevcenko, 'The illuminators of the Menologium of Basil II', *DOP* 16 (1962), 272: 'A strange marvel is to be seen here: from heaven, Christ, in his life-bringing right, extends the crown, the symbol of power, to Basil, the pious and mighty ruler. Below are the foremost [two] of the incorporeal beings: one of them has taken [the crown], brought it down, and is joyfully crowning [the emperor]; the other, adding victories to the [symbol of] power, is placing the sword, a weapon that frightens the enemy away, in the ruler's hand. The martyrs are his allies, for he is their friend. They smite [his enemies] who are lying at his feet.'

7. From Britain to Byzantium: the study of Greek manuscripts

Patricia Easterling

My choice of title calls for a word of explanation – perhaps of apology. When I opted to discuss the study of Greek manuscripts I was thinking particularly about the pioneering days of the eighteenth and early nineteenth centuries, and I hoped to find out what sort of imaginative impression was made on classical scholars of the time by Byzantine culture in the shape of its books.

What I have found is plenty of evidence to reinforce my sense that this was indeed an exciting and even heroic period, when scholars attached enormous importance to tracking down manuscripts, and lavished a great deal of money and effort on travelling to find them and make collations or to acquire them for their own collections. But for all this excitement and energy they turn out to have very little indeed to say about the culture that produced the books, and their model of the Byzantine world has proved to be quite elusive.

It is odd in a way that of all the items on show in the 'Byzantium' exhibition[1] it was probably Byzantine books that were more easily accessible to eighteenth-century Englishmen than anything else. Anyone with the right credentials for access to a university or college library or private collection could have direct and intimate contact with extraordinarily well-preserved primary evidence for Byzantine education, learning and culture, both religious and secular. But it is not the Byzantine world that seems to have aroused interest, and I think we should look for reasons why.

This may sound rather like the dog that didn't bark in the night, but I do have a story to tell, although it involves making a rather roundabout

---

[1] I refer to the exhibition *Byzantium: Treasures of Byzantine Art and Culture from British Collections* (London [British Museum], 1994) associated with the symposium.

From *Through the Looking Glass: Byzantium Through British Eyes*, eds Robin Cormack and Elizabeth Jeffreys. Copyright © 2000 by the Society for the Promotion of Byzantine Studies. Published by Ashgate Publishing Ltd, Gower House, Croft Road, Aldershot, Hampshire, GU11 3HR, Great Britain.

approach to my topic. I have picked out three remarkable men to be the focus of my chapter – three passionate enthusiasts for the study of Greek manuscripts, who conveniently cover the period I want to evoke.

My chosen three are Humphry Wanley, Anthony Askew and Richard Porson; Wanley, the oldest, was born in 1671, and Porson died last, in 1808. I will try to use them to illustrate some of the things that seem to be important about British contact with the Byzantine world at the time.

There are several reasons for choosing the eighteenth century. First, the science of palaeography was not properly established until the early years of that century, and indeed Wanley was one of its great pioneers. Manuscripts had of course been greatly valued, sought after and collected in earlier times, but until around the end of the seventeenth century no one had worked out a systematic way of dealing with them. So unless a book happened to be explicitly dated – and more often than not they were not – arriving at its age was a matter of guesswork.[2] There were some rough indications, such as the general expectation that capital script meant 'more ancient' than minuscule, but the lack of methodology could lead to some extremely bizarre notions (as discussed below). There was certainly a growing interest, which had first manifested itself for doctrinal reasons in the field of biblical scholarship, in establishing authoritative texts – and this must have created the incentive for more systematic study. Whereas most of the makers of the first printed editions in the fifteenth and sixteenth centuries had been content to use as copy whatever manuscripts were conveniently to hand, the notion had been developing that better texts could be produced if one compared a range of different witnesses or identified some particularly venerable one. What was needed was a new system of study skills, and when Montfaucon in France and Wanley in England came up with one, the new expertise spread quickly (like photography or computer technology in more recent times).

Another reason for choosing the eighteenth century is that there was still a great deal of material to be found, whether on the European market or in libraries in the West, or from the Greek-speaking world. Many collections in Europe were uncatalogued or unknown to scholars (in Spain, for example, or Hungary); manuscripts were more likely to be in private collections, and thus more mobile, than they are nowadays; and there were still unexplored monastic libraries in Greece and elsewhere (this was a long time before the travels of E. D. Clarke, Robert Curzon and Constantin Tischendorf). Even though the drift of Greek books westward had been very strong from the fifteenth century on-

---

[2] See my article 'Before palaeography: notes on early descriptions and datings of Greek manuscripts', *Texte und Untersuchungen* 124 (1977), 179–87, with further bibliography.

wards – first brought by émigrés for humanist patrons, then sought out by travellers, dealers and collectors – it is clear that there were still plenty to be located in the East Mediterranean. A glance at Montfaucon's list published in 1708 of British libraries owning Greek manuscripts, where in some cases he gives rough estimates of their numbers, shows how many were still to come.[3] Many of the books on display in the 'Byzantium' exhibition were brought to England in the eighteenth century. This is where Anthony Askew fits into my story: a collector on a heroic scale whose posthumous sale of books in 1785 was one of the great events in the history of British book collecting.[4]

Lastly, from the point of view of historical perceptions, our period pre-dates the influence of Gibbon until 1776, the date of the publication of the first volume of *The Decline and Fall of the Roman Empire*. So of my three only Porson was exposed to the Gibbonian analysis of the Byzantine world.

Humphry Wanley

Born in 1672 in Coventry, Humphry Wanley was apprenticed to a draper and worked at that trade till he was twenty-two, but he was an amazing autodidact: we are told he spent whatever spare time he had 'in the turning over old manuscripts, and copying the various hands, by which he acquired an uncommon faculty of distinguishing their dates'[5] (this does not mean Greek in the first instance). He was recognized as a potential scholar by the Bishop of Lichfield, who got him admitted to St Edmund Hall in Oxford; he then moved to University College after a year. The Principal of St Edmund Hall, John Mill, the friend of Bentley, was a great biblical scholar, and Wanley worked for him on collections of New Testament manuscripts. He was appointed to the staff of the Bodleian and eventually attracted the interest of Lord Harley; he became librarian of the great collection of the Earls of Oxford and in due course made the catalogue of the Harley MSS now in the British Library. The crucial influence on Wanley in his early days was the *De Re Diplomatica* of the Benedictine scholar Jean Mabillon (1681), which did not deal with Greek hands, but pointed the way to the kind of work that was needed on any tradition of manuscripts, whether books or documents. The essence of this new approach was the recognition that handwriting has an historical

---

[3] Bernard de Montfaucon, *Palaeographia Graeca* (Paris, 1708), xxviii.

[4] Copies of the sale catalogue (*Bibliotheca Askeviana*, 7 March 1785) were on sale in London, Paris and Leiden. (The printed books had been sold separately in 1775.) For a copy, with notes on various purchasers and the sums paid, see Cambridge University Library, Adv.c.75.8.

[5] John Nichols, *Literary Anecdotes of the Eighteenth Century*, vol. 1 (London, 1812), 84.

development and that evidence for dates and provenance can be studied systematically. As Wanley himself put it in a letter written in 1701 and published in the *Philosophical Transactions* of the Royal Society for 1705:

> What Methods Learned Men have taken in order to inform themselves of the different Ages of MSS, I know not, but my own has been this. I have been careful to get all the Dates I could, wherein 'twas said that such an individual MS was written, at such a time, or by such a particular person; every Book with a Date, being as a Standard whereby to know the Age of these Books of the same or a like Hand, and of those that are not very much older or newer.[6]

Wanley's work was exactly contemporary with that of a pupil of Mabillon, another Benedictine from St Maur, Bernard de Montfaucon, whose *Palaeographia Graeca* (1708) gave us the term palaeography and remains the definitive book that established the methodology of the subject (and took in inscriptions and diplomatic for good measure).

Let me quote an instance of the effectiveness of Wanley's method. There is a group of manuscripts now in Cambridge – one Latin, one Arabic and eight Greek, which was long associated with Theodore of Tarsus, the Archbishop of Canterbury famous for bringing Greek books to England in the 660s. The manuscripts, divided between the University Library, Corpus Christi and Trinity Colleges,[7] bear notes that make this ascription, though any modern palaeographer would know at first glance that none could be dated as early as the seventh century. Several are Renaissance manuscripts written on paper, and the Greek hands range in date from the tenth to the sixteenth centuries. Even so, the supposed connection with Theodore was taken seriously until the beginning of the eighteenth century. The ascription was evidently made by no less a scholar and bookman than Matthew Parker, Archbishop of Canterbury in the reign of Elizabeth, famous for his magnificent collection of Anglo-Saxon manuscripts. He was influenced by the happy discovery by a baker at Canterbury of one of the books in a pile of rubbish after the dissolution of St Augustine's monastery. This is a fine fifteenth-century illuminated Homer with the name ΘΕΟΔΩΡΟC on the title page, which may have caused the initial confusion.[8] When Wanley visited Cambridge in 1699 he was able both to give the book its correct date on palaeographical

---

[6] *Philosophical Transactions* 24 (1704–5), 1996.

[7] University Library: Ff.1.24 (*Chronicles*, etc.); Ff.1.26 (Euthymius on the Psalms); Ff.1.30 (Pauline Epistles); Ii.3.25 (Chrysostom). Corpus Christi College: 81 (Homer); 158 (Cicero); 401 (Arabic text); 403 (Euripides); 480 (Greek Psalter). Trinity College: B.10.11 (Greek Psalter).

[8] See M. R. James, *The Sources of Archbishop Parker's Collection of MSS at Corpus Christi College, Cambridge* (Cambridge, 1899), 9.

grounds and to account for the muddle: the Theodoros in question was no doubt Theodore Gaza, the fifteenth-century scholar, scribe and grammarian whom Wanley knew to have owned a Homer that exactly fitted this description. After a while scholars were willing to give up the cherished link with Theodore of Tarsus; it did not take long for the skills pioneered by Mabillon, Montfaucon and Wanley to be generally taken for granted.[9] What is important is that they made possible the properly historical study of the primary evidence – the basic stage needed before any other kind of research could be systematically conducted.

Wanley's interests, like those of Montfaucon, ranged very widely. His particular specialism was Anglo-Saxon manuscripts, but he also had projects for writing on the history of paper-making and printing; he studied abbreviations and different scripts in different languages, and he was always extremely interested in the search for new texts both biblical and classical. Here is part of a project for collecting materials abroad, quoted by Nichols:[10]

> Harl. MS 5911, also contains another of Mr. Wanley's projects for the advancement of learning, well worth consideration. 'We are almost positive that the old Italic Version of the Bible, which the Latin Church used before St. Hierome's Translation, as also that a good part of Origen's Hexapla and Octapla, in short, that many noble authors are still extant in foreign libraries, that are by us supposed to be utterly lost, and perhaps may soon be so, through the ignorance or carelessness of their present possessors; on the other hand, we know in what particular libraries some most valuable books are now to be found, which were never printed, nor are known to be extant any where else.
>
> [Examples follow]
>
> And many more which are suspected by us to be untruly represented in print, by corrupting, interpolating, and suppressing, divers material passages; as many foreign editions of the Fathers, not to mention other antient or modern authors. – It is humbly conceived, therefore, that it will conduce very much to the benefit of Learning in this kingdom, if some fit person or persons were sent abroad, who might make it his or their business:
>
> 1. To view the Libraries of France, Italy, and Germany, and to give a good account of their present state, and of the most valuable MSS therein.
>
> 2. To collate with printed editions the most remarkable and precious copies of the works of the Antients, now remaining amongst them, written in capital letters; whereby we may reasonably hope to have a true text restored to many places now unintelligible.
>
> 3. To transcribe some particular books in Greek or Latin, which we have no copies of in England, and have not been yet printed; by which means,

---

[9] Easterling, 'Before palaeography', 184–7.
[10] Nichols, *Literary Anecdotes*, 100–101.

there will be an accession of more learning to the kingdom than it has at this present. And the Papists are communicative enough, for love or money, of any book that does not immediately concern their controversies with Protestants ...

Wanley's energy and enterprise seem to have been limitless, hampered only by lack of opportunity to travel. But even he does not seem to have thought the Byzantine world an important field of research in itself. What he says, for example, about theological texts, suggests that he and his contemporaries were more likely to be interested in the contribution these could make to the debate between Protestants and Catholics than for the insights they might offer into Orthodox doctrine or spirituality.

It should not surprise us that Wanley lays great stress on the whole range of antiquarian studies and on collecting in general: marbles, inscriptions, seals were as much to be sought out as books, and books for their illuminations as well as for their texts. This was typical of the times: Montfaucon, for example, wrote on ancient sculpture as well as on manuscripts. This is the context in which we must set the activities of Anthony Askew.

Anthony Askew

Of our three Anthony Askew is the only one who was born into a well-off family; his father Adam was a highly regarded physician to the gentry of the Newcastle area, and Anthony too was destined for medicine, like many of his relatives. He belonged to the sort of social group that could afford serious collecting – people like noblemen who went on the grand tour, learned divines who got lucrative preferment in the hierarchy (John Moore, William Wake), or successful doctors like his friend and mentor Richard Mead, who formed an outstanding collection of books and antiquities.[11] Askew took his M.B. at Emmanuel College Cambridge and then went to Leiden, as medical students often did. But he seems to have been at least as interested in seeking out and collating manuscripts of Aeschylus, and while he was there, at the age of twenty-four, he published a pamphlet which he called a specimen of a new edition of the tragedies of Aeschylus, giving his text of thirty-three lines of the *Eumenides*.[12] This was all he ever did publish, but he spent the rest of his life gathering materials in an extraordinarily serious way.

---

[11] The surviving sale catalogues of Mead's pictures, prints, drawings, books, gems, bronzes and other antiquities give an impression of the scale on which he collected.

[12] *Novae editionis Tragoediarum Aeschyli specimen, curante Antonio Askew* (Leiden, 1746). Dr Mead was the dedicatee.

Before he settled down to practise medicine (he ended up as physician at St Bartholomew's Hospital, Registrar of the Royal College of Physicians, and father of twelve children), he travelled around Europe, and one way and another made the acquaintance of learned men, including Montfaucon, through whom he was able to commission collations of manuscripts of Aeschylus. He succeeded too in arranging for Professor Salvini in Florence to send him a copy of his collation of the great Mediceus (the tenth-century manuscript now known as M, then called the Victorianus). He collected manuscripts, early printed books and inscriptions on a prodigious scale, and no doubt could pay lavishly for collations. But he was far from being a rich dilettante and nothing more. He was taken seriously by scholars – by John Taylor, for example, who edited Demosthenes, was University Librarian and then Registrary at Cambridge, and left him his books and *adversaria*. He bought books on Greek medicine and mathematics (now in the Wellcome Library)[13] and patristic and liturgical texts, some of these magnificently illuminated (e.g. no. 69 in the 'Byzantium' exhibition). Although he never fulfilled his main project, the edition of Aeschylus, he did a lot of collating, and his work on manuscripts was good enough to be paid serious attention by Porson. His notes suggest he had absorbed the new methodology on dating; though he was wrong, no doubt, to think of himself as a textual critic.[14]

What from our point of view is the main interest of a man like Askew? We know he had contacts with the Greek world – more than Wanley or Porson, who could not afford travel. In 1746 and 1747 he went on an extensive tour which took him as far as Constantinople; he studied inscriptions at Athens, Paros and Smyrna, and visited Mount Athos. The *Liber Amicorum*, or album of autographs that he kept as a souvenir of his meetings with scholars on these travels, is preserved in the library of Emmanuel College (MS 47); Frank Stubbings has published an account of this album which throws fascinating light on what it meant to 'do research' at the time.[15] As Stubbings points out, it was rare for English travellers to visit Greece at all in the 1740s, and the expedition of Stuart and Revett did not begin till 1751.[16] So even if Askew was playing the role of scholar rather than as yet having much to show for himself, he certainly

---

[13] See Warren R. Dawson, *Manuscripta Medica, a descriptive catalogue of the manuscripts in the Library of the Medical Society of London* (London, 1932).

[14] Some of his collations survive, e.g. Cambridge University Library Nn.1.17, Nn.3.17 and Adv.a.51.1. See Frank Stubbings, 'Anthony Askew's *Liber amicorum*', *Transactions of the Cambridge Bibliographical Society* 6 (5) (1976), 306–21 (see 307–8 for Askew's work on Aeschylus). I am grateful to Dr. Stubbings for further advice on Askew.

[15] Stubbings, 'Askew's *Liber amicorum*'.

[16] Stubbings, 'Askew's *Liber amicorum*', 319.

displayed unusual enterprise. He started off by visiting German classical scholars, fifteen of whose autographs appear in the *Liber Amicorum*; he also collated at least one manuscript of Aeschylus while he was in Germany, but his main purpose seems to have been to prepare for his travels in the Levant. Some of the entries suggest that he had discussed with the German experts his hopes of collecting manuscripts there: J. M. Gesner of Göttingen, for example, wishing him success on his travels, bids him return 'laden with Greek treasures', to be published to the learned world.[17]

Askew travelled by way of Vienna to Constantinople, where he stayed some months under the protection of the Ambassador to the Porte, but his main objective was Mount Athos. The only entry in the album from Athos records that he spent three days as a guest at the monastery of Vatopedi, and includes the names of six of its dignitaries; the author, the ex-abbot Ambrosios Casanova, writes in an elegant and practised hand. At Thessaloniki he visited a learned priest, John Moschopoulos, who composed elegiacs in his honour and conversed with him in ancient Greek, and there is another set of verses from one Bessarion Byphos, 'teacher among the monks of Athens'.[18] So he had an opportunity to meet people who were as well equipped as any in Greece at the time to give him a sense of Greek culture as perceived by native speakers. But to judge from their verses, decorated with references to the Muses and the Graces, Apollo and Pallas, their aspirations, like Askew's, were directed towards the classical past.

Askew must have had a strong interest in buying books when he visited Athos;[19] some of the manuscripts listed in the catalogue of his sale clearly came from there, though it is not certain that he bought any of them direct. The most likely is no. 540 in the catalogue (now Wellcome MS 52), a collection of Greek medical texts from the monastery of Stavronikita, brought to England in 1749. There are four others, all religious books, listed as 'brought from Mt Athos',[20] and Stubbings has suggested that Emmanuel College MSS 12–15 (Chrysostom), identified as from the monastery of Kastamoniti, could have been bought by Askew on his visit. None of these books bears any relation to his Aeschylean project, but he did acquire some classical texts from Athos from Dr Mead, and the history of these is worth exploring.

---

[17] Stubbings, 'Askew's *Liber amicorum*', 309.

[18] Stubbings, 'Askew's *Liber amicorum*', 312–15.

[19] Books had been moving west from Athos since the seventeenth century, but there was good reason to hope for more purchases; Stubbings, 'Askew's *Liber amicorum*', 315–17.

[20] The only one whose whereabouts are still known is a Gospel book in Cambridge University Library, Nn.2.36. For Emmanuel MSS 12–15 see Stubbings, 'Askew's *Liber amicorum*', 318.

Some have class-marks from the monastery of Dionysiou, and there are distinctive notes on provenance written in a mixture of Greek and Italian which link them with books now in the library of Christ Church, Oxford, left to the college by William Wake, Archbishop of Canterbury.[21] Several of the books carrying these notes are associated with one Antonios Triphilis, who was active in the first part of the eighteenth century and may (as Irmgard Hutter has suggested)[22] have been a dealer with access to monasteries on Athos and elsewhere. Alternatively he may have been a collector, whose books were bought up by a dealer and sold abroad; at all events a batch seems to have arrived in London in or before 1735. Where did Antonios Triphilis come from? He has a rather elegant seal (1713).[23] Could he have been an educated Greek of the diaspora, someone of the same sort as the doctor from Bucharest, Joannes Comnenos, who wrote an account of Mount Athos which was republished with Latin translation by Montfaucon?[24] Whoever was getting books out of Athos was interested in poetic texts (Aeschylus, Euripides, Aristophanes, for example) as well as illuminated Gospel books and lectionaries: it would be interesting to know what these *Greek* collectors/dealers thought about the books they were after. Clearly we are not dealing here with a specialised 'art history' market. Perhaps the general principles expressed by Robert Curzon a century later in relation to the search for manuscripts were already strongly operative: content, antiquity, illumination.[25] But it would be interesting to know how they defined these criteria and how they felt about persuading the monks to part with their sacred texts.

As well as visiting Athos and making the acquaintance of educated clergy, Askew had another remarkable link with the contemporary Greek world through his contact with a Greek from Arta called Ioannes Caravella (or Caravalla), evidently himself a priest, who prepared a large number

---

[21] Two of these were exhibited in the 'Byzantium' exhibition, nos 177 and 209; see the catalogue entries in David Buckton, ed., *Byzantium: Treasures of Byzantine Art and Culture from British Collections* (London [British Museum], 1994). The Cambridge manuscripts in question are Ff.4.47, Nn.3.3, Nn.3.14, Nn.3.15, Nn.3.16, Nn.3.17, and Add. MS 2603, on which see note 23 below.

[22] Irmgard Hutter, *CBM* IV, xxxvi–xxxvii.

[23] Cambridge University Library, Add. MS 2603, another manuscript from Dionysiou (works of Lucian), but not listed in the Askew catalogue, has the seal, as does Leiden BPG 74G (Nicomachus Gerasinus).

[24] Montfaucon, *Palaeographia*, 433–99.

[25] Robert Curzon, *Visits to Monasteries in the Levant* (London, 1849), 299 (on his visit to the Great Lavra): 'I went into the library several times and looked over all the vellum manuscripts very carefully, and I believe that I did not pass by unnoticed anything which was particularly interesting in point of subject, antiquity, or illumination.' In Greece Curzon visited the monasteries of Mount Athos and Meteora. See too the chapter by Robin Cormack elsewhere in this volume (Chapter 11).

of indices to classical authors. Caravella's index to Aristophanes, bought by the Bodleian from Askew's sale, was actually published at Oxford by the University Press in 1822 on the initiative of Peter Elmsley, who gives him the credit on the title page but deeply disapproves of Caravella's ignorance of ancient Greek and lack of scholarly grip.[26] It was through Askew that Caravella came to England and was employed for a year (1773–74) as bedell and library keeper at the Royal College of Physicians; he may also have worked for Askew as librarian.[27] One would very much like to know what an English collector and scholar was able to learn about his possessions from someone like Caravella. How historical was the contemporary Greeks' own sense of their past? It is perhaps a pity that Askew hankered after textual work on the pattern set by Bentley or Hermann rather than after the gathering of lore about the world of his Byzantine manuscripts.

Richard Porson

Richard Porson was the most famous of the three and certainly the most influential as a scholar, one of the greatest critics of texts of the Greek dramatists. He came from an even more modest social background than Wanley, but he was tutored by a local clergyman and sent to Eton with the aid of a patron and his friends.[28] When he was at Trinity as a Fellow he

---

[26] 'Fuit autem, si quis alius in media barbaria natus, veteris linguae Graecae ignarissimus; quippe qui scripturae suae menda quam plurima, quae neminem paullo doctiorem fallere potuissent, pro legitimis verborum Graecorum formis et ipse acceperit et nobis obtulerit' ('Moreover, he was completely ignorant of classical Greek, as you might expect of someone of his uncultivated origins. This is clear from the fact that he treats countless mistakes in his own transcription as genuine forms of Greek and presents them as such to his readers, though no one with a modicum of scholarship could have been taken in by them'); P. Elmsley, *Joannis Caravallae Epirotae Index Aristophanicus ex codice Bodleiano ... nunc primum editus* (Oxford, 1822), iv. For this adverse comment on Greek scholarship, cf. Montfaucon's remarks about the credulity of the Greeks (*Palaeographia*, 433–4).

[27] See Stubbings, 'Askew's *Liber amicorum*', 317, who quotes George Dyer's account of their relationship: 'Dr A. brought home little besides MSS and scarce printed books, except we may mention a curious native of Greek [*sic*], remarkable for his beautiful style of writing the language. Some specimens of it are in the British Museum. Dr A. procured for him a place as Librarian to the College of Physicians. His name was Ἰωάννης Καραουαλλᾶ – John Caravalla'. Two books in Cambridge University Library are associated with him: Nn.4.8, a miscellany, which he seems to have owned at some time, and Nn.2.21 and 22, an index to Aeschylus, which he probably compiled and copied. See also Oxford, Bodleian Library, Auct. V.2.

[28] For biographical details see J. S. Watson, *Life of Richard Porson* (London, 1861); on Porson's scholarly activities see J. E. Sandys, *History of Classical Scholarship*, vol. 2 (Cambridge, 1908), 424–30 and R. D. Dawe, 'Richard Porson' in Warren W. Briggs and William M. Calder III, eds, *Classical Scholarship: a biographical encyclopaedia* (New York and London, 1990), 376–88 with further bibliography.

never managed to do what he would have loved to do, which was to travel abroad to collate manuscripts. As a young man he put a scheme for a new edition of Aeschylus to the Syndics of the Cambridge Press; but he was untried, and they refused to back him. He particularly wanted to go to Florence to see the so-called Victorianus of which Askew had been able to get a collation. The Cambridge notables were not impressed: 'Mr Porson may *collect* his manuscripts at home' said the vice-chancellor.[29]

All his life Porson was an avid reader of manuscripts – many still in Cambridge show signs of his careful annotation[30] – and he seems to have been interested in them for themselves as books as well as for the texts they carried. He was certainly interested in scripts: his own was and is particularly admired, and it was his designs that led to a major change in the printing of Greek. 'Porsonian' types have dominated the nineteenth century and most of the twentieth century, particularly through the style of the Oxford Classical Texts.[31] The best-known story about his devotion to manuscripts is his work on the twelfth-century copy of Photius's *Lexicon* in Trinity which had belonged to Thomas Gale.[32] He spent nearly a year making a corrected transcription of the entire text to be the basis of a printed edition, but this was destroyed by fire along with many of his working papers – collations, emendations. 'Twenty years of my life', he said when he heard the news.[33] But he began again, and his *second* transcription was ultimately printed by P. P. Dobree in 1822 at Trinity's expense. Porson was often transported with excitement to find his conjectures confirmed: in 1794, when the Ravennas was first used for Aristophanes, he 'talked about it at home and abroad; dwelt upon its intrinsic value day and night', saying things like 'I am furious with the Ravennas which has taken away so many of my readings',[34] and he tried but failed to get it bought for an English library. The same happened when the Townley Homer and Clarke's Plato from Patmos made their appearance.

Porson's admirers and younger colleagues have written much about him and his interests, but they tell us nothing about the historical framework in which he placed the texts that he studied with such intensity. It would be wrong to try to except him from the scholarly preoccupations

---

[29] See F. Norgate, *The Athenaeum*, 9 May 1896, 38–9 with earlier references.

[30] Examples in Cambridge University Library: Nn.1.23, Nn.2.34, Nn.3.18.

[31] In Trinity Library there are Porson's transcriptions of the Codex Galeanus of Photius (note 32 below) and of his texts of *Medea* and *Phoenissae* (Porson No.4, R.4.62 and R.4.62a respectively).

[32] Trinity College, Cambridge, MS O.3.9.

[33] Thomas Kidd, ed., *Richard Porson ... Tracts and miscellaneous criticisms* (London, 1815), xxxix.

[34] Kidd, *Porson*, lxvii.

of his age, one of which was to recapture the Attic purity of the classical
authors and to remove the accretions and deformations of later times
when scribes let non-classical forms slip into their texts. Despite the
range and depth of his learning Porson seems to have had a very similar
objective. We can get a sense of how people looked at a Byzantine source
of such importance as Photius from a review by Bishop Blomfield of a
rival (German) edition of Photius's *Lexicon*.[35] He gives a potted and
tendentiously satirical account of Photius's career and a resumé of his
works, including the *Bibliotheca* or *Myriobiblon*, on which he has two
main comments to make – that 'the good and pious Patriarch' was very
rude about heretics, and that half of it was written by somebody else
anyway. The real point, though, comes at the end of the paragraph: our
present business, he says, is with the celebrated *Lexicon* 'which, imper-
fect and mutilated as it is, is more valuable to the critical scholar, than ten
Myriobibla'.[36] 'The critical scholar', he implies, should be concerning himself with later works largely for the light that they will throw on the
linguistic usage of classical Athens; and there is no doubt that the whole
style of eighteenth- and early nineteenth-century education and scholarship was supportive of the unquestioned priority of that aim.

But surely, one would think, the publication of Gibbon's *Decline and
Fall* (1776–88) must have made a difference to perceptions of Byzantine
history and culture? Porson's review is worth our attention:[37]

> An impartial judge, I think, must allow that Mr Gibbon's History is one of
> the ablest performances of its kind that has ever appeared. His industry is
> indefatigable; his accuracy scrupulous; his reading, which indeed is some-
> times ostentatiously displayed, immense; his attention always awake; his
> style emphatic and expressive; his periods harmonious. His reflections are
> often just and profound; he pleads eloquently for the rights of mankind,
> and the duty of toleration; nor does his humanity ever slumber except
> when women are ravished, or the Christians persecuted.
>
> Though his style is in general correct and elegant, he sometimes *draws
> out the thread of his verbosity finer than the staple of his argument*. In endeav-
> ouring to avoid vulgar terms he too frequently dignifies trifles, and clothes
> common thoughts in a splendid dress that would be rich enough for the
> noblest ideas. In short, we are too often reminded of that *great man*, Mr
> Prig, *the auctioneer, whose manner was so inimitably fine that he had as much to
> say upon a ribbon as a Raphael.*
>
> Sometimes, in his anxiety to vary his phrase, he becomes obscure, and
> instead of calling his personages by their names, defines them by their

---

[35] *Edinburgh Review* 21 (February – July 1813), 329–40. The editor was Gottfried Hermann.

[36] *Edinburgh Review*, 329.

[37] Originally printed in the preface to Porson's *Letters to Travis*, reproduced here from
Watson, *Life*, 85–6.

birth, alliance, office, or other circumstances of their history. Thus an honest gentleman is often described by a circumlocution, lest the same word should be twice repeated in the same page. Sometimes epithets are added which the tenor of the sentence renders unnecessary. Sometimes, in his attempts at elegance, he loses sight of English, and sometimes of sense.

A less pardonable fault is the rage for indecency which pervades the whole work, but especially the last volumes. And, to the honour of his consistency, this is the same man who is so prudish that he dares not call Belisarius a cuckold, because it is too bad a word for a *decent* historian to use. If the history were anonymous, I should guess these disgraceful obscenities were written by some *débauché*, who, having from age, or accident, or excess, survived the practice of lust, still indulged himself in the luxury of speculation; and *exposed the impotent imbecility, after he had lost the vigour of the passions*.

But these few faults make no considerable abatement in my general esteem. Notwithstanding all its particular defects, I greatly admire the whole; as I should admire a beautiful face in the author, though it were tarnished with a few freckles; or as I should admire an elegant person and address, though they were blemished with a little affectation.

It is interesting that Gibbon liked this enough to invite Porson to call on him, and asked him for detailed comments if he should ever read through the History again, while for his part Porson thought the *Decline and Fall* 'beyond all comparison the greatest literary production of the eighteenth century, and was in the habit of repeating long passages from it. Yet I have heard him say that there could not be a better exercise for a school-boy than to turn a page of it into *English*'.[38] What is at issue here is essentially a stylistic and literary matter, not a historical one, and Gibbon himself seems to have taken that in his stride. Nor, to be fair, did Gibbon's analysis of Byzantine culture challenge the prevailing values of Augustan classicism, and however intensely Porson engaged with the *Decline and Fall* he need not have found the experience threatening his own scholarly agenda.[39]

Each of these three men, the librarian, the collector, and the textual critic, did pioneering service in the scholarly study of Greek manuscripts, but all three were strongly influenced by a complex of factors that prevented

---

[38] Watson is quoting Thomas Maltby, *Recollections of the Table-Talk of Samuel Rogers. To which is added Porsoniana* (London, 1856), 302–3. Porson would have been amused to note how often passages from Gibbon were set as Latin and Greek prose composition exercises in the nineteenth century and later.

[39] See James Howard-Johnston, 'Gibbon and the middle period of the Byzantine empire', in Rosamond McKitterick and Roland Quinault, eds, *Edward Gibbon and Empire* (Cambridge, 1997), 53–77.

them from taking an interest in the Byzantine context of the books they so much valued. They belonged to a time when what mattered was first the sheer business of locating and identifying the primary materials and next the systematic application of the latest methods of dating and textual analysis, and when the consistent objective was the recovery of the 'authentic' texts of antiquity. The notion that the culture for which the books were produced was worth studying for itself was still far in the future. The practice of extracting cultural history from the manuscripts is a fairly recent one, though cataloguers over the years have contributed to its feasibility in crucially important ways: without the work of scholars like Robert Devreesse, Paul Canart, or Alexander Turyn and their predecessors the task would have been immeasurably harder. Studies such as those of Robert Browning and Nigel Wilson in this country, Paul Lemerle in France, and Costas Constantinides in Greece has put the emphasis strongly on what manuscripts can tell us about contemporary literacy, education, scholarship and culture,[40] recognizing that they do not have to be old, beautiful or textually important in order to be extraordinarily interesting.

---

[40] E.g., R. Browning, 'Recentiores non Deteriores', *BICS* 7 (1960), 11–21; idem, 'Literacy in the Byzantine world', *BMGS* 4 (1978) 39–54. N. G. Wilson, 'The libraries of the Byzantine world', *GRBS* 8 (1967), 53–80; idem, *Scholars of Byzantium* (London, 1983); idem, *From Byzantium to Italy* (London, 1992). P. Lemerle, *Le premier humanisme byzantin* (Paris, 1971). C. Constantinides, *Higher Education in Byzantium in the thirteenth and early fourteenth centuries* (Texts and Studies of the History of Cyprus XI; Nicosia, 1982).

8. Greek scribes in England: the evidence of episcopal registers

Jonathan Harris

In the library of Trinity College, Dublin, there exists a manuscript of the Grammar of Theodore Gaza, copied in 1484 by John Servopoulos of Constantinople. There is nothing particularly remarkable about this: Gaza's Grammar was in great demand in the later fifteenth century as more and more Western scholars resolved to learn Greek. What is striking about this particular example is that in the colophon the scribe stated that he copied it, not in Constantinople or one of the centres of the Italian Renaissance, but in what he called 'the island of the Britons'.[1]

The Trinity College manuscript does not stand alone. It is the earliest in a series of at least sixteen copied by Servopoulos, most of them at Reading Abbey where he was working until at least 1500.[2] Nor was he the only Greek scribe working in England in the later fifteenth century. M. R. James demonstrated that a number of manuscripts were probably copied there by an individual known only as 'Emmanuel of Constantinople'.[3] Henri Omont drew attention to a collection of extracts from Herodotus, copied in London by Demetrius Cantacuzenus, and more recently a Ph.D. thesis has been devoted to the activity of George Hermonymos, who was in England in 1476.[4]

---

[1] J. G. Smyly, 'Notes on the Greek mss in the library of Trinity College', *Hermathena* 48 (1933), 174.

[2] R. Weiss, *Humanism in England during the Fifteenth Century* (Oxford, 1957, 2nd edn), 148.

[3] M. R. James, 'The scribe of the Leicester Codex', *JThS* 5 (1904), 445–7; Weiss, *Humanism*, 145.

[4] H. Omont, *Fac-similés de manuscrits grecs des XVe et XVIe siècles* (Paris, 1887), no. 15; Maria Kalazi, *Georgios Hermonymos, a fifteenth-century scribe and scholar: an examination of his life, activities and manuscripts* (Ph.D. thesis, University of London, 1998).

From *Through the Looking Glass: Byzantium Through British Eyes*, eds Robin Cormack and Elizabeth Jeffreys. Copyright © 2000 by the Society for the Promotion of Byzantine Studies. Published by Ashgate Publishing Ltd, Gower House, Croft Road, Aldershot, Hampshire, GU11 3HR, Great Britain.

Yet in spite of these discoveries, the presence of Greek scribes in a country so far removed from their own remains slightly puzzling. At first sight, there seems to be no good reason why they should have left the more congenial climate of Italy, where so many of their compatriots had found refuge, and travelled hundreds of miles to a land in the grip of a protracted civil war. One wonders who would have been interested in the manuscripts they produced of the works of Plato or the commentaries of Eustratius of Nicaea on Aristotle. According to one disgruntled Italian visitor, the only books which appealed to the English were cookbooks.[5]

Yet if nobody was interested in Greek, how can we account for the scribes? The difficulty has been partly resolved by Roberto Weiss and others who have shown that there was a small but growing coterie of scholars in fifteenth-century England who had at least an interest in classical Greek.[6] However, this still does not provide a satisfactory explanation of why the scribes should risk travelling so far in search of employment, in preference to remaining in Italy where there was a known market for their wares.

The difficulty is partly lack of information. Most of what is known about these scribes is derived from the short colophons with which they sometimes, but by no means always, ended their manuscripts. These give us very little clue as to the reasons for their transplantation to England. This short chapter will seek to offer an explanation by supplementing the evidence of the colophons with that of English episcopal registers. On this basis it will be suggested that the key to the presence of Greek scribes in England lies in the personal contacts that existed between certain prominent churchmen in England and the Greek Cardinal Bessarion and the members of his so-called 'Academy' in Rome.

Bessarion was one of the foremost figures in the revival of Greek learning. During his long residence in Italy between c. 1440 and 1472 he expended a great deal of effort and money in an attempt to preserve what remained of Hellenic literature, employing a small army of scribes to copy books, and seeking out Greek manuscripts in monastic libraries. One by-product of this activity was that Bessarion's house in Rome became a meeting-place for Italian scholars who wished to enhance their

---

[5] Poggio Bracciolini, *Lettere*, ed. H. Harth, vol. 1 (Florence, 1984), 35.

[6] Weiss, *Humanism*, 71–5, 141–54; H. L. Gray, 'Greek visitors to England in 1455–6', in C. H. Taylor, ed., *Anniversary Essays in Medieval History by Students of Charles Homer Haskins* (Boston, 1929), 94–104; D. Hay, 'England and the humanities in the fifteenth century', in *Itinerarium Italicum – The Profile of the Italian Renaissance in the Mirror of its European Transformations: dedicated to Paul Osker Kristeller on the occasion of his 70th birthday* (Leiden, 1975), 328–33.

knowledge of Greek and discuss their interest with the Greeks in his household.[7]

This erudite world of classical scholarship may seem very remote from the rather more basic conditions then prevailing in England. A link between the two is provided by a number of indulgences recorded in episcopal registers.

Episcopal registers contained an official record of letters and acts issued by the bishops in their dioceses. These frequently included letters of indulgence in which a stated number of days' immunity from penance was promised to those who would bestow money on a particular charitable cause. After the fall of Constantinople to the Ottoman Turks in 1453, several such indulgences were recorded on behalf of Byzantine refugees.

The earliest of these appear in the register of the Archbishop of York for 20 February 1455. As in the case of the scribes, the obvious question is how and why these refugees were in England at all. The register provides part of the answer, informing us that two of them, Thomas Eparchos and George Diplovatatzes, bore letters of recommendation from 'B. Cardinalis Tusculani'.[8] The Cardinal of Tusculum at this time was, of course, their compatriot Bessarion.

The sudden appearance of Bessarion in the York register raises the question of whether his letters were directed to some specific individual in England. Unfortunately, the York register gives little clue as to who this individual might have been. The archbishop who issued the indulgence, William Booth, is not known to have had any contacts with Bessarion or with humanist circles in Italy. There were, however, four other English bishops who issued indulgences for Greek refugees and who had had some contact with Bessarion and the members of his Academy.

One of these was the Bishop of Ely, William Grey. In September 1455 he issued a letter of indulgence for Michael Charsianites of Constantinople to help him to raise enough money to ransom eleven members of his family.[9] The indulgence makes no mention of any letters carried by Charsianites but in view of the evidence of the York register there are

---

[7] Baptista Platina, *Panegyricus in Laudem Amplissimi Patris Domini Bessarionis*, PG 161, cvii, cxv; G. Mercati, *Per la cronologia della vita e degli scritti di Niccolò Perotti* (Rome, 1925), 77–81; K. M. Setton, 'The Byzantine background to the Italian Renaissance', *Proceedings of the American Philosophical Society* 100 (1956), 73–4; D. J. Geanakoplos, *Greek Scholars in Venice* (Cambridge, Mass., 1962), 81–5, 89–92.

[8] Borthwick Institute of Historical Research, York, Reg. 20, fols 167v–168; J. Harris, *Greek Emigrés in the West, 1400–1520* (Camberley, 1995), 193–4.

[9] Cambridge, University Library, EDR G/1/5, fols 10v–11; J. Harris, 'Publicising the Crusade: English bishops and the Jubilee Indulgence of 1455', *JEH* 50 (1999), 33–4.

grounds for supposing that he may have been sent to England by Bessarion.

If so, he may have carried letters specifically addressed to the Bishop of Ely. Grey had travelled widely earlier in his career and had spent a good deal of time in Italy, where he had studied under Guarino da Verona. Bessarion was among the many contacts he had made in humanist circles during his stay in Rome. Grey had secured a place for his secretary, Niccolò Perotti, in Bessarion's household so that he could learn Greek.[10] Bessarion may, therefore, have sought a repayment of the favour by asking Grey to assist Charsianites.

Another English bishop known to at least one Italian associated with Bessarion in Rome was Thomas Bekynton, Bishop of Bath and Wells. At the outset of his career Bekynton had become acquainted with the Roman antiquarian, Flavio Biondo. Biondo was one of the select group in Rome who shared two of Bessarion's passionate interests: the preservation of the classical Greek language and the projected crusade to reconquer Constantinople, and he is generally included in the list of those who frequented the Academy.[11] A number of letters exchanged between the English bishop and the Italian historian have survived and it would seem that Biondo was impressed enough with Bekynton to present him with a manuscript of his work, the *Decades*.[12]

Like that of Grey, Bekynton's register also contains an indulgence on behalf of a Greek. Dated October 1459, it appeals for assistance for John Stauracios, who had fought in the final siege of Constantinople. The indulgence specifically states that his plight had been drawn to the attention of the bishop by certain letters.[13]

Unlike in the York register, in this case the identity of the writer of these letters is not revealed. However, there is good reason for supposing that it may have been Biondo. In the summer of 1459, a few months before the issue of Bekynton's indulgence, the Pope had summoned a conference to Mantua to discuss arrangements for a crusade against the

---

[10] Vespasiano da Bisticci, *The Vespasiano Memoirs*, tr. W. George and E. Waters (London, 1926), 185; Weiss, *Humanism*, 89–90.

[11] Vespasiano, *Memoirs*, 415; Flavio Biondo, *Scritti inediti e rari*, ed. B. Nogara (Rome, 1927), xxx–xxxiii, 31–51; R. Fubini, 'Flavio Biondo', *Dizionario biografico degli Italiani* X (Rome, 1968), 551; Setton, 'Byzantine background', 73.

[12] *Official Correspondence of Thomas Bekynton (Memorials of the Reign of Henry VI)*, ed. G. Williams, Rolls Series 56, vol. 1 (London, 1872), 169–71, 241–2; M. R. James, *A Descriptive Catalogue of the Manuscripts in the Library of Corpus Christi College Cambridge*, vol. 1 (Cambridge, 1912), 494–5; Weiss, *Humanism*, 71–5.

[13] Somerset Record Office, Taunton, D/D/6, fol. 246; *The Register of Thomas Bekynton*, eds H. C. Maxwell-Lyte and M. C. B. Dawes, Somerset Record Society 49–50, vol. 1 (Frome and London, 1934), 330.

Turks. Not only Biondo, but also a number of refugees from Constanti-nople were among those present.[14] It does not seem unreasonable to suggest that Biondo might have recommended Stauracios to Bekynton and that this accounts for the presence of a Greek refugee in the West of England.

A third example is that of George Neville, Archbishop of York, who issued an indulgence for two refugees from Corinth and Negroponte in March 1475.[15] Here too there is evidence of links with Bessarion's house-hold. Neville, according to Pietro Aliprando, the Milanese ambassador in France in 1472, was not only known to the Greek cardinal but the two were good friends. Some doubt has been cast on this statement on the grounds that Neville, so far as is known, never went further from his native land than Calais, while Bessarion never visited England. It is not impossible, however, that they had exchanged letters, in the same way as Biondo and Bekynton had, even if the correspondence has not survived.[16]

Finally, there is John Shirwood, Archdeacon of Richmond and later Bishop of Durham. His archidiaconal register contains a similar indul-gence dated 1471.[17] While there is no direct evidence for any links be-tween Shirwood and Bessarion's circle, as a close friend and protégé of George Neville, he must at least have known something about the Greek cardinal. It is, perhaps, not without relevance that Shirwood later pos-sessed a copy of Gaza's Grammar copied by John Rhossos of Crete, one of the scribes who worked for Bessarion in Rome.[18]

The significance of these indulgences therefore seems clear. We know from the York register that refugees were arriving in England bearing letters from Cardinal Bessarion. We know that four English clergymen were acquainted with Bessarion or members of his circle, and that these same men all issued indulgences on behalf of refugees. It therefore seems likely that the refugees were specifically directed to these particular individuals in England by Bessarion or others in Italy.

This argument can be taken further. Those same links may well have acted to bring Emmanuel of Constantinople, George Hermonymos and other Greek scribes to England. The English clergymen who issued in-

---

[14] Biondo, *Scritti*, clvi–clvii; K. M. Setton, *The Papacy and the Levant (1204–1571)*, vol. 2 (Philadelphia, 1978), 196–230.

[15] Borthwick Institute of Historical Research, York, Reg. 21, fols 7A–7Av.

[16] *Calendar of State Papers (Milan)*, ed. A. B. Hinds, vol. 1 (London, 1912), 169; M. Lowry, 'John Rous and the survival of the Neville circle', *Viator* 19 (1988), 333–4.

[17] John Rylands Library, Manchester MS Latin 333, fols 63v–64; A. Hamilton-Thompson, 'The Register of the Archdeacons of Richmond, 1442–1477, pt.2 – 1465–1477', *Yorkshire Archaeological Journal* 32 (1936), 127.

[18] Cambridge, University Library, Ii.IV.16; *Catalogue of the Manuscripts Preserved in the Library of the University of Cambridge*, vol. 3 (Cambridge, 1858), 453–4.

dulgences for refugees obviously shared Bessarion's concern for those
displaced by the victories of the Turks. It would seem, moreover, that
some of them also shared his preoccupation with Hellenic literature.
While there is nothing to suggest that Thomas Bekynton was ever interested, the other three certainly were. William Grey of Ely possessed a
Graeco-Latin lexicon among his collection of books, and George Neville
of York was apparently able to write some Greek letters, although neither seems ever to have learned the language properly.[19] John Shirwood,
on the other hand, was not only interested but later went on to learn
Greek to a high standard.[20]

Not only, therefore, did Grey, Neville and Shirwood have contacts with
Bessarion's circle in Rome; they also shared its primary interest. It can
hardly come as a surprise, therefore, turning back to the colophons of the
manuscripts copied in England, to find two of these same men associated
with the Greek scribes. Both Emmanuel of Constantinople and George
Hermonymos dedicated examples of their work to Neville, while a Latin
translation of Aristotle's *De Virtutibus*, copied by Hermonymos, carries a
dedication to John Shirwood.[21]

It would appear, then, that the chain of recommendation which worked
in the case of destitute refugees could also work for scribes. Emmanuel
of Constantinople or Demetrius Cantacuzenus may well have come to
England armed with testimonials from Bessarion or, after his death in
1472, from one of his Italian associates. These may have been directed to
Grey, Bekynton, Neville or Shirwood or to some of the other English
clergymen who were interested in the Greek language, such as William
Selling, the Prior of Christchurch, Canterbury, or possibly the Bishop of
Winchester, William Waynflete.[22]

The evidence of the episcopal registers, therefore, offers a solution to
the problem of the Greek scribes in England. It suggests that they did not
leave Italy merely on speculation and happen to end up in England
where they were lucky enough to stumble on an employer: they were
specifically directed both to the country and to a patron.

---

[19] R. A. B. Mynors, *Catalogue of the Manuscripts of Balliol College, Oxford* (Oxford, 1963),
140; Weiss, *Humanism*, 142.

[20] *British Library Harleian Manuscript 433*, eds R. Horrox and P. W. Hammond, vol. 3
(London, 1982), 57–9; Weiss, *Humanism*, 150–52.

[21] London, B.L., Harley 3346, fol. 4v; Oxford, Bodleian Library, Rawl. G.93 (14821);
James, 'Scribe of the Leicester Codex', 445–7.

[22] Weiss, *Humanism*, 154; Gray, 'Greek visitors', 107, 110.

9. Fair exchange? Old manuscripts for new printed books

Colin Davey

As a by-product of my research on inter-church relations in the early seventeenth century, and particularly those between the Orthodox Church and the Anglican and other Reformed Churches, I came across in the correspondence of successive English ambassadors in Constantinople two intriguing stories about dealings in manuscripts and in marbles. But I shall confine myself now to the story of an attempt to obtain old manuscripts in exchange for new printed books – rather like 'new lamps for old' in the pantomime *Aladdin*.

In 1621 Sir Thomas Roe succeeded Sir John Eyre 'in his Embassy to the Ottoman Porte', as the title of his published correspondence puts it.[1] Thomas Smith describes Roe 'as a Gentleman of excellent parts, and of great honour and integrity, and one who served the interests of his Prince and country in Turkey with great courage and fidelity, and with an agreeable success; before whose times', he adds,

> the affaires of our Merchants were in great disorder ... he having to his immortal reputation recovered the respect due to Ambassadours, which had been utterly lost for several years before, by a succession of insolent Viziers; and that he deserved most highly not onely of the Greek Church, by his generous protection of it against those who endeavoured, as much as in them lay, to destroy its very being; but of Christendom in general ...[2]

The Patriarch of Constantinople, Kyrillos Loukaris, had already benefited from his acquaintance with Roe's predecessors. Through one of them, Sir Paul Pindar, he had corresponded with the Archbishop of Canterbury, George Abbot, who then, with the approval of King James I,

---

[1] *The Negotiations of Sir Thomas Roe in his Embassy to the Ottoman Porte* (London, 1740).

[2] Thomas Smith, *An Account of the Greek Church* (London, 1680), 252.

From *Through the Looking Glass: Byzantium Through British Eyes*, eds Robin Cormack and Elizabeth Jeffreys. Copyright © 2000 by the Society for the Promotion of Byzantine Studies. Published by Ashgate Publishing Ltd, Gower House, Croft Road, Aldershot, Hampshire, GU11 3HR, Great Britain.

invited him to send Greek priests to study at Oxford – the first, and only one of whom, Metrophanes Kritopoulos, arrived in England in 1617.[3]

Roe wrote to Archbishop Abbot in September 1622:

> The Patriark hath visited, and feasted mee. Hee wilbee the best of my conversation and friendship. He appears a grave and wise man, and one that hath great intelligence. By the next post I shall receave letters from him to your Grace, being now at his vintage absent.[4]

The following spring, as Roe reported to Archbishop Abbot, 'the patriarch came to mee for counsell and assistence, which I could not denye him', following the discovery of a plot to depose him. Roe then added: 'I beseech your grace, vouchsafe me some of your counsell in all these: I walk in blyndness, without any rule but myne owne discretion, which by too much zeale may err *errore amoris*'.[5]

Kyrillos Loukaris is described by Roe as 'in profession of his religion opposite' to 'those of the Romish faction' in the Orthodox Church and their supporters, the French ambassador and the Jesuits,[6] whose plot was 'to remove him from his sea, and to advance that other their proselite to his dignity, who should by little and little sowe the Romish doctrine, and privately subscribe the pope's universality, and in tyme subject the Easterne church wholly to his holyness'.[7]

A second attempt to depose Loukaris succeeded, as Roe reported in early May 1623, adding: 'Your grace may now see the universal practice of these engines; no church shalbe safe that is not theirs: Germany, France, Bohemia hath lately felt it; Greece is now in project, and God defend thy little flock in England'.[8]

In August Archbishop Abbot replied:

> I have acquaynted his majesty with the oppression and violence which is offered to that patriarke ... His majesty willed mee to write unto you, that you should give him such assistance as is in your power; and I will hope, that if his life bee preserved, there may come another turne ... If you see the patriarke, commend my love unto him, and let him know how affectionate and compassionate I am in his sufferings; wishing, with all my heart, that I were able any way to releeve him and comfort him.[9]

---

[3] Colin Davey, *Pioneer for Unity: Metrophanes Kritopoulos (1589–1639) and relations between the Orthodox, Roman Catholic and Reformed Churches* (British Council of Churches, 1987), 67–8, 72–3.

[4] Public Records Office: State Papers, Turkey 97:8:256, letter of 20/30 September 1622.

[5] *Negotiations*, 133: letter of 8/18 March 1622(3).

[6] *Negotiations*, 133, 146.

[7] *Negotiations*, 133.

[8] *Negotiations*, 146.

[9] *Negotiations*, 171: lettter of 12 August 1623.

Given this encouragement, Roe worked hard for Loukaris's restoration to the patriarchal throne, which took place in October 1623, and continued to support, counsel and assist him thereafter.

In the following year, 1624, we find the first reference to manuscripts in Roe's correspondence with Archbishop Abbot: 'I hear your grace hath written by one Mr Petty, that is arrived at Smirna, ymployed by my Lord of Arundell to buy books and antiquities. Hee will find', he adds, 'that barbarisme hath worne out all the footsteps of civility and learning: yet manuscripts are plenty, old Greeke books, that are little worth; they have been cerned over by many of good judgement, and I think the gleanings are very poore.'[10] This sounds suspiciously like the first step in any Middle Eastern bargaining or bartering process: declare the object of your search to be almost worthless.

However, a month later, in January 1625, Roe writes, rather gleefully, to the Earl of Arundel himself:

> I have lately fallen into a way that may leade me to some things ancient, and of estimation … By meanes of the patriarch, … I may procure some bookes; but they are indeed Greeke to mee: one only hath he given mee, for his majestie, with the express promise to deliver it; being an autographall bible intire, written by Tekla the protomartyr of the Greekes, that lived in the tyme of St Paul; and he doth averr yt to be true and authenticall, of his owne writing, and the greatest antiquitye of the Greeke church.[11]

In about June 1625, after the death in March of King James I which made Archbishop Abbot 'forbeare to write further, or to sende to the patriarke',[12] Sir Thomas Roe, in reply, 'finding in the conclusion of your grace's letter, a purpose to write to him', declared: 'I will presume to become a suitor, that you will be pleased to doe it …', for

> your grace shall doe me some advantage and enable mee thereby to doe more in my purpose of collecting Greeke authors, that are lost to us, and not in print; of which the patriarch is able richly to store England, and hath thereunto a good inclynation. I have an old manuscript of the seaven first councells in my possession, but not yet myne owne, lent mee by him to compare with the edition of Bynius, who pretends to have taken his from that very copy, in the Arabicque tongue, the booke having antiently belonged to the patriarchs of Alexandria, and from thence brought, as a great jewell, by Cyrillus.[13]

---

[10] *Negotiations*, 320: letter of 9/19 December 1624.

[11] *Negotiations*, 334: letter of 20/30 January 1624(5).

[12] *Negotiations*, 371, letter of 30 March 1625.

[13] *Negotiations*, 414: letter undated but, as a reply to one of March 1625, probably about June 1625.

Now comes the proposed 'fair exchange' of 'new books for old manuscripts':

> I have begunne to deal playnly with the patriarch, who hath made a great collection, that his old books rott and rust by him, among ignorant Greeks, that never will understand, nor make use of them: that in right they belong to the church of God, that will publish them; that they are weapons fit for champions, and not for colloyres. I find he scarce knowes the names of many, I am sure, not their contents, nor the reputation of their authors; many histories, ecclesiasticall and civill, that may be great lights unto us of the darker tymes; and have motioned to make him an exchange, and to furnish him with a compleate library of all classical authors, and bodyes of learning, which the Greeke church have not, which wilbee of use to him, and his successors, to leave to his sea, from whence those learnings may bee drawne, of which they are now wholly ignorant, in exchange of such of his which doe no good, being buried in obscurity. Hee hath promised to hearken unto mee, and to bestowe some upon the libraryes of England; and others hee purposeth to other places of Christendome: but my ambition is to keepe them together.
>
> Therefore [he concludes] if your grace will give mee encouragement, and by his majestie, or some other able meanes, make mee provision to trade for this rich merchandise, I make no question but to give you a good retorne; and to direct me herein, your grace's chapleynes will take paynes to send mee a catalogue of such authors as are mentioned in any bibliotheque, and are not extant: it is very likely, from hence may be supplied; for here are great numbers that none of us knowe, and [he admits honestly] my judgement is belowe this worke. I knowe doctor Goade [the archbishop's chaplain] is able to enstruct me in two howers, for my search for many months.[14]

In November Archbishop Abbot replied enthusiastically, enclosing a letter for the patriarch, and telling Roe:

> I do marvellous well like of your traffiking with him for his Greek copyes, which there do no good, and may serve for singular use here ... There shall not bee wanting a good librarye of bookes to returne him, if those which hee desireth may be had in these partes, and they bee to be compassed with any convenient summe of money. I pray you advertise mee what it may be guessed will give satisfaction for those copies ...; certainely those bookes are a great treasure, which now lyeth not only neglected, but a man may say almost buryed where they now are.[15]

Meanwhile in October Roe had written to Loukaris:

> Many things lie hidden in your libraries, most holy Father, which could be of use to the Church of God, and throw light on obscure controversies. The

---

[14] Ibid.

[15] *Negotiations*, 459: letter of 11 November 1625.

lamp should not be placed under a basket but on a lampstand, so that it can shine on all who are in the house. And Your Grace is in a position to emulate or excel not only our king but also … all your holy predecessors. Concealment does a disservice to the truth. Open your treasure for the good of all, and provide bread for the hungry. Thus you will receive the gratitude of all, renown richly deserved in the church militant, and the reward of an eternal crown in the church triumphant.[16]

The postal service between London and Constantinople being slow, and often unreliable,[17] it was only in April 1626 that Roe wrote to ac-knowledge receipt of Abbot's letters of November 1625 to the patriarch and himself, which, he adds, 'being arrived in the holy weeke, when our devotion and their ceremonies are at highest, I must defer the delivery until after Easter; and therefore can give your grace no full satisfaction, either what I shall gett of him, nor upon what conditions'. He then refers again to the 'old and great manuscript in Arabicque' which 'conteynes all the first councils' and encloses a transcript of what he calls 'the 37th Canon … in Arabicke and our Latine, never before, as I suppose, extant', and comments: 'The words give great praeeminence to the pope, but in my opinion, make the other patriarchs, in matters of their church, inde-pendent, and his equalls'[18] – a vitally important piece of evidence to use in arguments frequently then taking place between the Roman Catholic and the Anglican and other Reformed Churches. The same day, Easter Eve, he wrote to Dr Goade, but not very optimistically:

What I have done, I have related to his grace, who, I doubt not, will acquaint you; what I shall doe, as yet I cannot judge. The patriarch [he admits] is fast handed, and his promises are misteriall: I doe believe he hath treasures he doth not know: for he gathers bookes from monasteries, and by vacancies of bishops; some I shall gett, if I were able to choose.[19]

Nine months later the shrewd and well-educated Patriarch Kyrillos Loukaris said 'no' to the proposed exchange of 'new books for old'.

In a letter to Archbishop Abbot offering condolences on the death of King James I and good wishes for King Charles I, he wrote: 'This is my

---

[16] *Negotiations*, 442: letter, in Latin, of 14/24 October 1625.

[17] *Negotiations*, 213: 'by my letters of 14th October and 15th November which I hope have arrived', letter of 24 January 1623(4); ibid., 487: 'I have longe expected from your grace, some answer of his letter, which would advantage mee, in getting books', letter of mid-February, 1626; ibid., 663: 'it being now 15 moneths since I wrote you the enclosed … and not hearing from you … I doe conclude that both originalls and duplicates have miscarried by some envious hand in Venice; where my letters have often found takers up in the Bola', letter of 7/17 July 1627.

[18] *Negotiations*, 499: letter of 8/18 April 1626.

[19] *Negotiations*, 500: letter of 8/18 April 1626.

prayer for his royal majesty; and I most especially beg your blessedness to mention it to him in my name, and humbly to kiss the hands of his royal majesty, and earnestly to entreat him to continue to us his royal favour.' Then he went on:

> Meanwhile, with respect to the books of which your blessedness wrote to me, I do not think that I can satisfy you. If I can do anything, I will communicate with my most kind friend, protector and patron, Thomas Rowe, your most prudent Ambassador at this Court, and by him you shall be acquainted with my success.[20]

'What answere the patriarck hath given your grace to your proposition of exchange', wrote Sir Thomas Roe to Archbishop Abbot on 27 February 1627,

> you will perceive by the enclosed letter, which was sent me a moneth since; but hoping to see somewhat, I deferred the conveyance till this occasion: for having invited him to lye and recreate himselfe at my home, I had tyme to discourse lardgly with him; and the substance of his promise is, that he will not by way of bargayne make any exchange; but that before I returne, I shall see what he hath, and take my choyce freely; which liberty he will use with mee in England, as his studyes and use shall require. So as I make no doubt but to bring your grace somewhat that shall be worthy, and recompense my fruictless search.[21]

This last statement by the disappointed Ambassador is in many ways the most astonishing understatement. For his letter had already announced:

1. his 'being possessed of no more raretyes ... than of Isach Syrus, and a piece of Origen';
2. 'the patriarck also, this new yeares tyde, sent mee the old Bible, formerly presented to his late majestie, which he now dedicated to the Kyng' – that is, Charles I – 'and will send with yt an epistle, as I thincke he hath signifyed to your grace ... What estimation it may be of, is above my sckill; but he valewes yt, as the greatest antiquitye of the Greeke church ... I doubt not his majestie will esteeme yt for the hand by whom it is presented'; this was in fact the priceless early fifth-century Greek manuscript of the Bible, the Codex Alexandrinus, now in the British Museum;
3. and here Sir Thomas Roe was aware of its value, 'The councells are yet in my hand, and I hope to keepe them, which are alone worth a librarye';

---

[20] J. M. Neale, *A History of the Holy Eastern Church,* vol. 2 (London, 1847), 421–3, letter of 16 January, 1627.
[21] *Negotiations,* 618: letter of 27 February 1627.

4. as he wrote hopefully, 'some other bookes I shall procure, though', and he added petulantly, 'Mr Petty by his learning and industrye preventeth mee, and hath gotten many'.[22]

Roe's disappointment comes out again in a letter to Dr Goade of July 1627. 'The patriarch', he writes, 'seeming to thincke it unworthy to bargayne, hath promised, at my departure, that hee will let me choose in his store.' Then he goes on:

> He hath many vertues to commend him; but a Cretan by birth, and long bred among these degenerate Greekes and tirannous infidells, that it were more than humane force to resist the infection and corruption of dayly conversation and example. Therefore how I shall come off, I know not: sure I am, I have meritted much, and many wayes, of him, and not liked all his courses; and that perhaps will hinder mee. *Obsequium amicos, veritas odium parit*. But wee remayne good friends, and he professeth that I shall see the reall fruicts.[23]

The following February he wrote again to Dr Goad, not only referring to the arrival of Nikodemos Metaxas and the Greek printing press, and to his having 'saved Metaxas life and defended the Patriarch from calumny and danger'; but telling him 'that I have gotten some more bookes: and two dayes since the Patriarch sent me ten', including 'a part of Chrysostome upon the Psalmes, very wormeaten and ancient'.[24]

He then adds, giving us another glimpse of envy among rival manuscript hunters:

> The booke of councells formerly mentioned I have procured to be studied by an ingenious Duch man professor of the Arabique, in Leyden, mayntayned in the Eastern parts by the States: he tells me it is not such a treasure as I hoped, and that it is a coppy, written in the thicknes of ignorance, about 350 years since, full of confusion and corruption.

So he adds, shrewdly: 'Perhaps he would discredit it, to keepe it, for he seekes Arab bookes: therefore I will bring it home, for it hath much more than any other coppy; and learned men will distinguish the Corne, from Chaffe.'[25]

After nearly seven years in Constantinople, Sir Thomas Roe concludes his letter to Dr Goade with a heartfelt prayer:

> This is all that I have to write, unless I should trouble you with the Infirmities of this Empire *Nullis Medicabilis Herbis*: from whence God soone

---

[22] Ibid.

[23] *Negotiations*, 663: letter of 7/17 July 1627.

[24] PRO S.P. Turkey 97:14:53.

[25] Ibid.

deliver me, to whose mercy I desire to be commended in your Devotions, and so I faythfully rest.[26]

His prayer for deliverance was duly answered, and Roe left Turkey in the summer of 1628.

In September 1630 Sir Thomas Roe wrote from London to his former colleague, Cornelius Van Haga, the Dutch ambassador in Constantinople:

> I beeseech you to kiss the hands of the most reverend Patriarch Cyrillus on my part: his bible I presented to his Majestie, who did most graciously accept it, both for the dignity, antiquity and rarety of the book, and for the hands, which had preserved and sent it. The rest of his, and all the other manuscripts, which I gott, I have given to the most famous librarye of Oxford; which were so highly esteemed, that they were received with great solemnitye, and to his honour commemorated in their publique act, and for which I know they determine to make some due acknowledgement to his sanctity.[27]

Ever seeking more, Roe continued:

> We all hope, he will not end with this one bounty, but extend his liberality further, to the glorye of the Greeke, and benefitt of God's universal Church: for it is infinite pittye and sinne, that so many excellent lights should be kept in darkenes, and so rare jewells perish by dust, and wormes.[28]

The search for manuscripts continued, as Roe's successor, Sir Peter Wych, reported a few years later:

> Heere are arrived by waie of Ligourne two schollers of Oxford, the one of name Pococke ... the other of name Greves ... They pretende they are imployed by the universitie to study the Arab tongue, and to gett some manuscripts wherein they have some insight in that language.[29]

---

[26] Ibid.

[27] PRO S.P. Turkey 97:15:45–7, letter of 7/17 September 1630.

[28] Ibid.

[29] PRO S.P. Turkey 97:16:133, letter of 4 November 1637 to the Secretary of State.

10. The Gospels of Jakov of Serres (London, B.L., Add. MS 39626), the family Branković and the Monastery of St Paul, Mount Athos

Zaga Gavrilović

The Serres Gospel book, written in Serbian-Church Slavonic, was brought to England in 1837 from the Athonite monastery of St Paul, by Robert Curzon, later 14th Baron Zouche. It was deposited at the British Museum by his son in 1876 and is kept in the British Library as Additional Manuscript 39626.

The prosperous Byzantine city of Serres in eastern Macedonia, situated in the proximity of Via Egnatia, in the lush valley of Strumica, came under Serbian rule in 1345, during the reign of King, later Tsar, Dušan. Following Dušan's death in 1355, it was governed by his widow Jelena (the nun Jelisaveta). From 1365, Despot Jovan Uglješa Mrnjavčević, brother of king Vukašin, co-ruler with Dušan's successor Stefan Uroš V, appears as the sole governor of the city and of the adjoining region. After the death of both brothers Mrnjavčević in the battle against the Turks at Černomen in 1371, Serres was retaken by the Byzantines. It fell to the Ottomans in 1383.[1] The aim of this chapter is to review certain aspects of the cultural scene in Serres in this period of great political changes and to examine the relations of some of its prominent citizens with the monastic communities on Mount Athos, especially with the monastery of St Paul.

According to a colophon on fols 293–293v dated in 1354, the Serres Gospel book was copied for the metropolitan of Serres, Jakov, at the cathedral church of the Saints Theodore, during the reign of Tsar Dušan, his wife Jelena, their son king Uroš, and Patriarch Joanikije.[2] The scribe

---

[1] B. Ferjančić, *Vizantijski i srpski Ser u XIV stoleću* (Belgrade, 1994). On Despot Jovan Uglješa see J. S. Allen in *ODB*, vol. 2 (1991), 1070–71.

[2] Patriarch Joanikije died on his way back to Peć from Žiča on 3 September 1354. The colophon was written just before the news reached Serres. See A. Purković, *Srpski patrijarsi srednjega veka* (Düsseldorf, 1976), 62–3.

From *Through the Looking Glass: Byzantium Through British Eyes*, eds Robin Cormack and Elizabeth Jeffreys. Copyright © 2000 by the Society for the Promotion of Byzantine Studies. Published by Ashgate Publishing Ltd, Gower House, Croft Road, Aldershot, Hampshire, GU11 3HR, Great Britain.

was Kalist Rasoder, whose name is written in the shape of a cross on fol. 293v. With considerable literary talent, Kalist praises his patron thanks to whom the Tetraevangelion has been illuminated 'as a sky with shiny stars'.[3]

In fact, the manuscript does not contain many miniatures: there are four headpieces and a number of ornamented vignettes and initials, displaying a subtle use of colours and gold. The only full-page miniature, on fol. 292v, represents the Metropolitan Jakov in prayer before Christ to whom he is offering the book (Figure 10.1).[4] On the left of Jakov, an inscription in red letters on the gold background reads:

смѣреныї | митрополꙗн, сѣра грⷣ | и сⷬ҇ранамь к҃ | кїр іакѡⷡ [5]

On the right, between Jakov and Christ, another inscription reads:

сйи чеⷮвⷡ|робⷧаго|вѣстн҃|кь, прї|ношⷹ ти | вь дарь | влко | мои х҃е [6]

A clypeus, rather awkwardly placed within an ornamented border above the Metropolitan's figure, contains an epigram:

с8дїи сѣдецⷹ8, | и аг҃глоⷨ прѣстоєцⷨи. | р8вѣ гласецїй, и пламе|нї горецⷹ8. что сьтворⷨиши | дш҃е моа ведома на сочдⷦь, | тогⷣа ꙋбо ꙁлаа твоа прѣста|нꙋⷮтⷮи. и таинїⷩ грѣси ⷮбⷩои о|вличетсе. нь прѣжⷦе конⷰ | вьꙁⷷпїⷩи х҃8 бⷪⷢꙋ · [вⷤⷶе] ѡ|цⷦѣсти ме и сп҃[си] | ме ꙿ   7

---

[3] Kalist's colophon is reproduced (in two parts) in Lj. Stojanović, *Stari srpski zapisi i natpisi* I (2nd edn, Belgrade, 1982), No. 103 and III (2nd edn, Belgrade, 1984), No. 5544. On the style of Kalist's writing see Dj. Trifunović, *Pisac i prevodilac inok Isaija* (Kruševac, 1980), 16–17. The scribe's nickname 'rasoder' is unusual. It refers to his monastic habit 'rasa' (from the Greek *rason*), which is in tatters or which he himself has torn, as a sign of utmost humility. Kalist also calls himself 'vile' and 'slow-spirited'. A Greek term corresponding to 'rasoder' would be *rakendytes* ('wearer of rags'), as in Ptochoprodromos, Poem III, line 20 (ed. Pernot). Cf. M. Alexiou, 'The poverty of écriture and the craft of writing: towards a reappraisal of the Prodromic poems', *BMGS* 10 (1986), 38.

[4] J. Maksimović, *Srpske srednjovekovne minijature* (Belgrade, 1983), 102–3, colour plates 14–18. M. Harisijadis, 'Les miniatures du Tetraévangile de Jacob de Serrès', *Actes du XII Congrès international des études byzantines, Ochride 1961* (Belgrade, 1964), 121–30, contains references to the earliest bibliography. C. Walter, 'The Portrait of Jakov of Serres in London, Additional 39626', *Zograf* 7 (1977), 65–72, concentrates on the iconography and on the type of the head-dress worn by Bishop Jakov. See also I. Spatharakis, *The Portrait in Byzantine Illuminated Manuscripts* (Leiden, 1976), 89–90, figs 57, 58.

[5] 'The humble metropolitan of Serres and its region, kir Jakov.'

[6] 'This tetraevangelion I am offering to Thee, Christ, my Lord.'

[7] 'While the Judge is sitting and angels standing before [Him], while the trumpet is sounding and the flame is burning, what will you do, o my soul brought to judgment!? Then thy evil deeds will be brought before [Him] and thy secret sins will be revealed. But before the end, beseech Christ the Lord: God make me pure and save me.' I wish to thank Professor Dj. Trifunović of the University of Belgrade for helping me with the translation of this prayer.

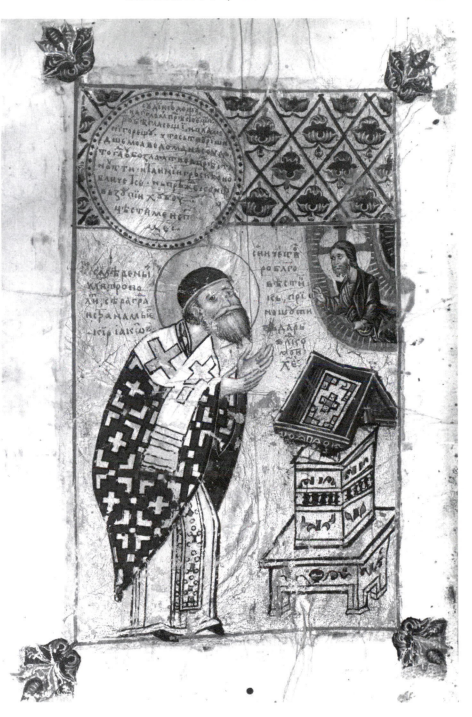

Fig. 10.1. Serres Gospel book (London, B.L., Add.MS 39626), fol. 292v: Metropolitan Jakov before Christ, 1354 (photograph: British Library)

Describing the manuscript, Anne Pennington has commented on its fine quality and on the unusual style of the portrait of its patron.[8] The impression of Robert Curzon, when he saw the book among some two hundred and fifty Slavonic manuscripts still kept in the library of St Paul's in 1837, was similar: 'It was a noble manuscript'. He mentions also that the igoumenos of St Paul was happy to present him with that volume, as well as with the Gospel of the Bulgarian Tsar Ivan Aleksandar, dating from 1356 (London, B.L., Add. MS 39627).[9]

Jakov occupied the metropolitan's throne of Serres from 1345 until his death, between 1360 and 1365. Earlier, he was the first igoumenos of Dušan's newly built monastery of the Holy Archangels near Prizren. A respected and influential prelate, his role and activity are well documented. He is known to have sent books to the monastery of the Virgin on Mount Sinai and was himself an author.[10]

It was during Jakov's term of office that the monastery of St John the Prodromos on Mount Menikeion near Serres received some of its finest fourteenth-century paintings.[11]

Frescoes in the chapel of St Nicholas on the floor above the outer narthex date from around 1358–64. A fresco of the Virgin Eleousa (Figure 10.2) is placed in the southwestern corner of the chapel, above a tomb (now empty). Next to it, an inscription in Greek states that this is the burial place of three women: 'kira Jelena, sister of the most noble Despot Uglješa and wife of the most noble kir Nikola Radonja and of their two daughters'.[12] It seems that it was an epidemic of plague which struck the family of Nikola Radonja Branković. After the deaths of his wife and his

---

[8] *The Anne Pennington Catalogue. A Union Catalogue of Cyrillic Manuscripts in British and Irish Collections*, compiled by R. Cleminson; general eds V. Du Feu and W. F. Ryan (London, 1988), 119–21.

[9] R. Curzon, *Visits to Monasteries in the Levant* (London, 1849), 424. See also the next chapter.

[10] G. Ostrogorsky, 'O serskom mitropolitu Jakovu', *Zbornik Filozofskog Fakulteta u Beogradu* 10 (1) (1968), 219–26; G.C. Soulis, *The Serbs and Byzantium during the Reign of Tsar Stephen Dušan (1331–1355) and his Successors* (Washington, 1984), 151–2; Ferjančić, *Vizantijski i srpski Ser*, 95–100; Dj. Trifunović, *Pisac i Prevodilac*, 16–19.

[11] A. Xyngopoulos, *Ai toichografiai tou Katholikou tes Mones Prodromou para tes Serras* (Thessaloniki, 1973). For a discussion of the chronology of the wall-paintings, after they were cleaned in 1979, see I. Djordjević and E. Kyriakoudis, 'The frescoes in the Chapel of St Nicholas at the monastery of St John Prodromos near Serres', *Cyrillomethodianum* 7 (Thessaloniki, 1983), 167–209.

[12] Djordjević and Kyriakoudis, 'The frescoes'. G. Subotić and S. Kissas, 'Nadgrobni natpis sestre Despota Jovana Uglješe na Menikejskoj Gori', *ZRVI* 16 (1975), 161–81. Subotić and Kissas were able to correct the former readings of the name RADOHNA (Slavonic, 'Radonja') in the inscription and thus to identify the husband of Jelena, Uglješa's sister. He was Nikola Radonja Branković, the eldest son of Dušan's nobleman Sebastokrator Branko Mladenović.

Fig. 10.2. Virgin Eleousa, *St John the Prodromos on Mount Menikeion near Serres, Chapel of St Nicholas, 1358–64 (from Ch. I. Pennas,* Oi toichographies tou katholikou tes mones Prodromou stes Serres, *Athens, 1978)*

Fig. 10.3. Mara Branković (far right) Group portrait of the family of Djuradj Branković on his chrysobull to the Monastery of Esphigmenou, 1429 (detail). (photograph: G. Subotić)

Fig. 10.4. The Monastery of St Paul, Mount Athos in 1883 (from A. Riley,
Athos or the Mountain of Monks, *London, 1887)*

Fig. 10.5. Monastery of St Paul, Mount Athos, Chapel of St George on the walls
(photograph: G. Subotić)

daughters, he and his wife's brother, Despot Uglješa Mrnjavčević, sponsored the fresco decoration of this chapel. Nikola then became monk at the monastery of Hilandar, on Mount Athos. Sometime before 1385, in association with Antonije Bagaš, another nobleman who had retired into monastic life, he rebuilt the Athonite Monastery of St Paul from its foundations (Figure 10.4). Nikola Radonja's monastic names were Roman/ Gerasim. Antonije's name in *megaloschema* was Arsenije. At first a monk at the monastery of Vatopedi, Arsenije was renowned for his translations of Greek theological works into Serbian.[13]

The monastic settlement of St Paul had been a dependant of the monastery of Xeropotamou and was probably named after the hegoumenos Paul, the tenth-century founder of that monastery. Even before its renovation by Gerasim Branković and Arsenije Bagaš, the caves around the ruins were inhabited by some Serbian monks who practised hesychia in them. The best known was the learned Isaija, translator of the complete works of Pseudo-Dionysius the Areopagite into Serbian-Church Slavonic. He too had been at the court of Despot Uglješa at Serres in the 1360s.[14]

Thanks to its enterprising new *ktitori*, the new monastery of St Paul prospered, as gifts were lavished upon it by various members of the founders' families.[15] With the silver and gold mines still active in Serbia, and still free of Ottoman control, the most generous donations came from Gerasim's younger brother Vuk Branković, and their relations, Prince Lazar, Princess Milica and later their son Despot Stefan Lazarević. This was continued during the time of Gerasim's nephew Despot Djuradj Branković, who in 1446/7 built a new church (alongside the old catholikon), dedicating it to his patron saint, St George. Both churches were demolished in the nineteenth century when the new catholicon was erected.[16]

---

[13] G. Subotić, 'Obnova manastira svetog Pavla u XIV veku', *ZRVI* 22 (1983), 207–58; idem, 'Manastir Svetog Pavla', in *Kazivanja o Svetoj Gori* (Belgrade, 1995), 111–34. D. Sindik, 'Srpske povelje u svetogorskom manastiru Svetog Pavla', *Miscellanea de l'Institut de l'histoire* 6 (Belgrade, 1978), 183–205.

[14] Dj. Trifunović, *Pisac i prevodilac*.

[15] One of the earliest recorded gifts dates from 1385 when Arsenije's brother, Nikola Baldovin Bagaš, transferred the ownership of his monastery of the Virgin Mesonisiotissa and its lands and properties to St Paul's. G. Subotić has determined that Mesonisiotissa was situated in the marshy lands near Vodena (Edhessa); it should not be confused with the Mavriotissa of Kastoria: 'Obnova manastira' and idem, 'Manastir Bogorodice Mesonisiotise', *ZRVI* 26–7 (1987), 125–71. The much-venerated icon of the Virgin Nisiotissa, originally from Mesonisiotissa and probably brought to Athos during Ottoman times, is still kept by the altar of St Paul's monastery.

[16] S. Binon, *Les origines légendaires et l'histoire de Xéropotamou et de Saint-Paul de l'Athos. Etude diplomatique et critique* (Louvain, 1942), 193, 202–3; G. Subotić, 'Manastir Svetog Pavla', 124–34.

One of the most interesting benefactors of St Paul's monastery was Carica Mara Branković, Djuradj's daughter and great-niece of Gerasim Branković (Figure 10.3). In 1435, as a vassal of Murat II, her father was obliged to give her in marriage to the Sultan. After Murat's death she came back to Serbia, but following the death of her parents in 1456–7 she returned to Turkey. Her step-son Mehmed II, who greatly respected her, gave her property at Ježevo, near Serres. With her own court there and active until her death in 1487, she played an important diplomatic role between Dubrovnik, Venice and Serbia on the one hand and the Ottoman court on the other.[17]

As Mara had remained a Christian, she took care of several Athonite monasteries, especially of Hilandar and of St Paul: the first was a foundation of Stefan Nemanja and St Sava of Serbia; the other was linked to her own family Branković.

Research into Ottoman sources is likely to reveal further details on this remarkable woman and her part in the history of Mount Athos. According to a document dated 1469, Mara bequeathed three parts of all her possessions, land as well as gold, silver and precious textiles to Hilandar and two parts to St Paul.[18]

An Athonite legend speaks of Mara's attempt to visit the monastery of St Paul: as soon as she set foot on the shore, a voice from heaven reminded her that she should not go further on the land of the Holy Mountain. In the meantime, St Paul's monks had come towards her to greet her and receive gifts. A cross still marks that spot, with a well-kept small kiosk sheltering an illustration of the event; an earlier chapel was destroyed in the nineteenth century.[19]

Later generations of the Branković family, including those who married into the nobility of Romania, continued supporting the monastery of St Paul through the sixteenth and seventeenth centuries when the community counted predominantly Serbian, Bulgarian and Romanian monks (Figures 10.5 and 10.6). It ceased to be a Slavonic monastery in the first half of the eighteenth century.

In view of this historical development, it is quite easy to understand how the Gospel book of the Metropolitan Jakov of Serres found its way

---

[17] Mara Branković is styled 'Carica' (Tsaritsa) in Serbian sources, 'Imperatrix' in Ragusan and 'Despina Hatun' in Ottoman documents. Modern research has thrown much light on her life and personality. See especially R. Ćuk, 'Carica Mara', *Istorijski Časopis* 25–6 (1978–79), 53–97; V. Boškov, 'Mara Branković u turskim dokumentima iz Svete Gore', *Hilandarski Zbornik* 5 (1983), 189–214; M. Živojinović, 'Svetogorci i Stonski Dohodak', *ZRVI* 22 (1983), 165–206. D. Nicol, *The Byzantine Lady: Ten Portraits 1250–1500* (Cambridge, 1994), 110–19, devotes a chapter to Mara Branković, without including the results of that research.

[18] V. Boškov, 'Mara Branković', 193.

[19] R. Ćuk, 'Carica Mara', 93; V. Boškov, 'Mara Branković', 198.

Fig. 10.6. Monastery of St Paul, Chapel of St George, Virgin with child in the naos, 1551 (photograph: G. Subotić)

into the library of St Paul's monastery, although one cannot be sure of the precise date of that transfer. It is known also that the Gospel book of the painter Radoslav, copied around 1429 in Serbia, and containing a colophon by the monk (*inok*) from Dalša, was found at St Paul's library by the Russian bishop Porfirij Uspensky in the nineteenth century. Twelve leaves with miniatures (and the colophon) are now in St Petersburg's Public Library.[20]

Among unpublished works of art from the treasury still at St Paul's is an early fifteenth-century epitaphios, gift of the metropolitan of Belgrade, Isidor.[21]

A section of an embroidered fourteenth-century belt or border, bearing the name BRANKO written in Cyrillic, as well as some heraldic motifs and other ornaments, has been kept in the Hermitage Museum at St Petersburg since 1902. It is believed that it was part of the attire of Sebastokrator Branko Mladenović, father of Gerasim Branković and great-grandfather of Carica Mara Branković. Branko Mladenović was a nobleman at the court of King, and later, Tsar Dušan. From around 1334 he was governor of Ohrid (d. before 1365). A longer section of the same embroidery was acquired by the British Museum in 1990.[22] Although it is impossible to tell which medieval treasury gave shelter to that particular work of art before it reached other collections, and appeared finally on the market at the beginning and at the end of this century, the monastery of St Paul is among the first that come to mind. Just as likely, however, is that it was found among the deposits of the Serbian aristocracy in Dubrovnik, valuables sent for safekeeping in the decades of the Ottoman invasion and mentioned in numerous Ragusan archives of the period.

---

[20] J. Maksimović, *Srpske srednjovekovne minijature*, 123–4, colour plates 56, 57, 58.

[21] I owe this information to my friend and colleague G. Subotić who is preparing a detailed study of St Paul's monastery.

[22] H. Granger-Taylor and Z. Gavrilović, 'Embroidered belt or border', in D. Buckton, ed., *Byzantium: Treasures of Byzantine Art and Culture from British Collections* (London [British Museum], 1994), 208–11, with colour plate.

Section III

Interpreters

11. 'A Gentleman's Book': attitudes of Robert Curzon

Robin Cormack

The travel account and the biography are well known as the surest routes to a bestselling book. In the case of the Honourable Robert Curzon's *Visits to Monasteries in the Levant*, the book was an instant bestseller as an autobiographical travel book. Apart from its accounts of the hazards of foreign travel, the book gave its Western readership an influential perception of the character of the Orthodox monastery and Byzantine art. It retrospectively described Curzon's travels and experiences in Egypt and Palestine, Meteora and Athos, and was published in the summer of 1849. He had first gone to Egypt, Syria, Turkey and Greece in 1833–34; returned to Egypt and Constantinople in 1837–38, and made the trip to Mount Athos. He was in Constantinople and Turkey during the years 1841 to 1843, but returned home after a severe illness struck him at Erzerum. It seems he never went back after this to the East.[1]

The publishers John Murray originally planned to print a thousand copies and to give Curzon half the profits, but they ultimately produced four editions in his lifetime and one posthumously before the text went on to other publishing houses. John Murray printed 7,250 copies in all, and the book was commended in its first reviews for 'its total absence of all conceits and affectations', and it was conspicuously 'on every table'. For Ruskin in the *Stones of Venice*, it was 'the most delightful book of travels that he ever opened'.[2] Nevertheless as a literary achievement, it was always regarded as subordinate to Kinglake's *Eothen* of 1844 (a book which was still obligatory reading at my school over a hundred years

---

[1] Ian H. C. Fraser, *The Heir of Parham. Robert Curzon 14th Baron Zouche* (Alburgh, Norfolk, 1986).

[2] *Stones of Venice*, I (London, 1886), 15.

From *Through the Looking Glass: Byzantium Through British Eyes*, eds Robin Cormack and Elizabeth Jeffreys. Copyright © 2000 by the Society for the Promotion of Byzantine Studies. Published by Ashgate Publishing Ltd, Gower House, Croft Road, Aldershot, Hampshire, GU11 3HR, Great Britain.

later). It was almost certainly *Eothen* and its immediate popularity that
acted as the stimulus to Curzon to write about his own experiences, for
he talks about writing a book in January 1845 and had finished three
hundred pages by April that year. Its particular selling point to other
Victorians was, one can be fairly sure, its bibliomania; as a record of one
avid collector's tips and experiences, both good and bad, it would have
had a ready public among the gentlemen of the period – hence the
description of it as a 'gentleman's book'.[3]

The lively combination of anecdotes about book collecting and observations about local life and colour (however much another generation
might characterize his observations as 'Orientalist' in character) endeared
it to a reading (and potentially travelling) public, for whom the new
development of the steamboat was opening up unprecedented possibili-
ties of visiting exotic places. Yet it was this potential mass tourism which
was to change the character of the East, as Curzon himself saw and
deplored in his new preface to the 1865 edition:

> These pages describe a state of affairs so entirely passed away that the
> account of them seems to belong to a much more remote period than the
> year 1833. Those countries were, however, much better worth seeing at
> that time than they are now; they were in their original state, each nation
> retained its own particular character, unadulterated by the levelling dis-
> course with Europeans, which always, and in a very short time, exerts so
> strong an influence that picturesque dresses and romantic adventures dis-
> appear, while practical utility and a commonplace appearance are so gen-
> erally disseminated, that in a few years more every country will be alike,
> and travellers will discover that there is nothing more to be found in the
> way of manners and customs that they may not see with greater ease in
> their own houses in London.

Since the book had begun with the claim that 'the monasteries of the East
are particularly interesting to the lovers of the picturesque', Curzon may
have felt that by the time of the later edition a defensive statement was
necessary in case the picturesque aspects of the tour had worn thin.

The expressed attitudes of Robert Curzon, not so much as a travel
writer but as a witness of a particular early Victorian response to Byzantine art and architecture, are evidence for the nature of the British experience of the Orthodox world at his time, and as a constantly re-read

---

[3] The edition published by Arthur Baker Ltd of London in 1955 (based on the edition of
1865), *Visits to Monasteries in the Levant* by the Honourable Robert Curzon, Jun. with an
introduction by Seton Dearden, a preface by Basil Blackwell, and a series of photographs
by Ralph Richmond Brown, attributes the description 'A gentleman's book' to Robert
Bridges in conversation with Basil Blackwell (p. 5). The publication figures quoted here
come also from the prefatory note of B.B.

document for many years after. It would of course be possible to explore at some length his writing as a way of defining the nature of Englishness through setting out how Curzon recognizes the 'Other' – how for example he contrasts the open expression of joy by the emotional Easterners and the silence of repressed Westerners, like himself, on first seeing the city of Jerusalem in 1834 (yet at the same time makes a clever historical point by pointing out that the modern Easterner reacted exactly like the medieval Crusader from the West). But this chapter will focus on Curzon as an individual witness of Byzantium in the middle of the nineteenth century.

The portraits of Robert Curzon and his family (an engraved portrait of Robert was given to all the members in 1858 on his entry to the Grillion's Club, as required by the conventions of the founder) may prompt the question whether the Honourable Robert Curzon, subsequently the 14th Baron Zouche and heir to the Sussex Downs country seat at Parham, was anything much more than a privileged British aristocrat with more money than knowledge who, like so many contemporaries in the nineteenth century, collected books as a respectable sideline and hobby. However, in comparison with his younger brother Edward, the seriousness of Robert Curzon's ambitions are more evident – Edward married secretly without permission in the summer of 1834 and refused to take the easy option of Holy Orders. Instead he decided to buy a house in Regent's Park with a view to obtaining something not too taxing, 'like a job in the British Museum'.[4]

Robert Curzon was born in London on 16 March 1810 at 58 Welbeck Street and made his name as a writer and collector of manuscripts (127 of his manuscripts passed in 1917 into the British Library as the bequest of his unmarried daughter Darea Curzon, Baroness Zouche, including the fourteenth-century Gospels of Tsar Ivan Alexander from the monastery of St Paul on Athos). His life has been usefully charted by Ian H. C. Fraser[5] in a biography which sets out the details of his life and, most important for the purposes of this chapter, records information from the letters to his friend Walter Sneyd (which are now in the archives of the University of Keele). These letters contain anecdotal information about his travels that he did not publish, and reveal that either his memory was at fault as he put the narrative together, or that the narrative was more subtly contrived than may appear. For example, the story, connected with the monastery of St Mary Deipara at the Wadi Natrun in March 1838, that some of the manuscript folios were 'doing duty as coverings to

---

[4] Fraser, *Heir of Parham*, 73.

[5] Fraser, *Heir of Parham*. On Curzon and his manuscript, see also the previous chapter.

a couple of large open pots or jars which had contained preserves, long since evaporated' seems something of a flexible *topos* rather than an accurate memory of his visit. It suited his narrative to portray the monks of the Levant as ignorant and incapable of valuing their heritage. It excused his own actions in removing this heritage.

Robert Curzon was abnormally short, reaching five foot three inches at the age of sixteen. His physical undersize and his highly strung and intensely shy personality were a problem to his family, although they thought it was 'nothing that a good school with well-ventilated dormitories could not put right'. After a number of schools he ended up at Charterhouse, which he left at the age of fifteen in 1825, and then after three years of private tutoring went up to Christ Church, Oxford. He failed Responsions, and left without a degree in 1830 after four terms, because his Greek did not match his knowledge of Latin grammar, and because his tutor told him he was wasting his time. We know most about Curzon's personal thinking from the letters written over the years to the Revd Walter Sneyd (born 1809); all but two of his 509 letters survive. They were at Oxford together and Sneyd also was short (five foot five-and-a-half inches) and both come over in their letters as hypochondriacs. They were also both highly enthusiastic bibliophiles, and were equally under the spell of Walter Scott's romantic novels.

When Curzon came down from Oxford, his father offered him a seat in the House of Commons, but he initially declined, instead making a tour of Ireland and then visiting Weimar (and other centres in Europe) between August 1830 and January 1831. Curzon had an annuity of £500 a year. Later this was increased by a dowry of £300 when he got married in 1850 at the age of forty to Emily Julia Wilmot-Horton (aged twenty-eight). Soon after the marriage they went to Rome, where she suffered from morning sickness. Curzon had an audience with Pope Pius IX and gave him a copy of the *Catalogue* of his manuscripts for the Vatican Library. Emily had two children, Robin (b. 1852) and Darea (b. 1860), before dying in 1866. Robert Curzon became the Baron Zouche in 1870 on the death of his mother, and died in 1873 at the age of sixty-three, the member of several London clubs (such as the Philobiblon Society to which he was elected in 1854). He spent much energy in later life developing the house at Parham.

Curzon was not yet twenty-one when he decided to enter the Commons, but he was soon unseated by the Reform Bill, and he compensated with travelling, culminating with his first visit to the Levant. In 1832 he went through Europe, travelling with Sneyd, who was involved in collecting manuscripts, preferably of the Classics. Inscriptions in two of Curzon's manuscripts in the British Library show that he was already collecting when a student at Christ Church (London, B.L., Add. MSS 39338 and 39643). One of his earliest acquisitions was a thirteenth-century Bible, and this interest in the Middle Ages marks his distinctive expertise as a collector. His thinking was deeply coloured by his passion, as clearly documented in a private letter written to Sneyd in London on 10 July 1835:

> I met Mrs Beaumont at a Ball, who looked so pretty that I have thought of nothing else since. I never saw an illuminated manuscript half so beautiful as she is, and as for pages of the first of Caxton's, the blackness of their letters are no more to be compared to the darkness of her eyes than the fine white margin is to the fairness of her skin.

Robert Curzon was soon to be parted from Sneyd as a travelling companion; in 1832 Sneyd had to return to England for financial reasons and get a job – the easiest option was the Church. Consequently, instead of going to Egypt with Sneyd as first planned, Curzon travelled with George Palmer, a fox-hunting squire. They went by boat from Malta to Egypt, arriving at the end of July 1833, a singularly bad choice of time of year. They nevertherless hired a Nile boat for four months, returning to Cairo in the New Year.

Curzon's writings on Egypt are perhaps the most rounded historically and socially of his travel accounts. He was there in 1833–34 and again in 1837–38; he was in Jerusalem and Mar Saba in 1834. It was in November 1834 that he visited the monasteries of Meteora, and the important visit to Mount Athos was undertaken from Constantinople in the spring of 1837. In 1841 he was a private secretary in the British Embassy on the Bosphorus, and his final departure from Turkey took place in 1843, after he was taken seriously ill while attending a pistol-shooting competition at Erzerum.[6]

The question that this chapter pursues is whether the writings of Curzon offer anything more than elegant but detailed documentation on the pillaging of the treasures of Orthodox monasteries in the nineteenth century, undertaken on the pretext of saving their treasures for a more enlightened audience. Inevitably people have called Curzon the 'Elgin of the Athonite Monasteries' and suggested that he took his books illegally. His own defence that he always offered a fair price and was prepared to take no for an answer (in the preface of 1865, no doubt in the face of criticism) has been perhaps surprisingly persuasive. It may be that the issue for us is not whether his appropriations were legal, but how much truth there was in his portrayal of the guardianship of their possessions

---

[6] His second travel book, *Armenia: a Year at Erzeroom, and on the Frontiers of Russia, Turkey and Persia*, appeared in 1854, published by John Murray. His other books also appeared in this period: *Book of the Prophet Moses* (1855–56) and the *Short Account of the most celebrated libraries of Italy* (1854).

by the Athonite and other Eastern monasteries. His allegations seem to be at variance with the evidence of the 1997–98 exhibition of the treasures of Mount Athos which were transported to Thessaloniki. This exhibition suggested a contrary scenario of alert monks and attention to their treasures and heritage over the centuries, so that each monastery has collected within its precincts a considerable *mélange* of Athonite history and possessions.[7] Curzon created an adverse picture of the Orthodox monastery to cover his own actions. It has been a remarkably durable distortion.

This chapter looks at his attitudes rather than his deeds, and suggests that his medievalism marks an important stage in nineteenth-century intellectual history. It is true that at first glance his catalogue of his books, published in 1849 and produced in fifty copies, may suggest an amateur's work. This would be a superficial impression, and in any case the emotive word 'amateur', which often crops up in discussions of Curzon, is a word of dubious value in the history of Byzantine studies. He was certainly more than an ignorant collector, for he had a strategy of travelling in the East for a particular kind of book, and his concept of Byzantium and Byzantine art emerged out of first-hand experience. He justified his acquisition of books and other materials on the grounds that his mission was to write a history of writing. The full title of his catalogue is *A Catalogue of Materials for Writing; early writings on tablets and stones, rolled and other manuscripts and oriental manuscript books, in the library of the Hon. Robert Curzon at Parham in county of Sussex*, and in the preface he writes: 'It is to be hoped that the possessor of these manuscripts may escape in some measure the imputation of folly which is given to those Bibliomaniacs, who heap up accumulations of old books which they can neither use or understand'.

Nevertheless the *Catalogue*, although relatively learned (and he presumably had some assistance in its compilation), is not as promising a book as the *Visits*. When he comes to describe his key illuminated possession, given to him, so he says, by the Abbot of St Paul and St George on Athos, the Gospels of Ivan Alexander, which we attribute to Tirnovo in the middle of the fourteenth century, and which is clearly based on a fully illuminated Byzantine manuscript or manuscripts of the eleventh century, Curzon writes:

> It would be difficult for any book, whatever its ostensible subject might be, to give a more perfect view of the costume, manners and customs of the country to which it owes its origin, for almost every common-place occupation is listed; dinners, boats, and houses are represented in the drawings. As

---

[7] *The Treasures of Mount Athos* (Thessaloniki, 1997).

well as battles, processions, churches and other things more usually seen in ancient illuminations. Almost every page is laboriously illuminated with pictures of battles, feasts, ships and scenes of everyday life of the Bulgarians and other nations subject to the Byzantine empire, giving an insight into their manners and customs, such as is not found in any other manuscripts, illustrating many things which Gibbon attempted to describe in the 'Decline and Fall of the Roman Empire' and of which little is known to the antiquarians of the present day. The book is altogether one of the most curious monuments of bygone days to be found in any library in Europe.[8]

He also compares the illuminations with the Bayeaux Tapestry: both lack a painted background.

Curzon's interpretation at face value of the miniatures as accurate representations of everyday life obviously contrasts with modern notions of the copied and derivative character of Gospel imagery, usually now seen as owing more to pictorial models than the observation of the real world. Yet the idea that these miniatures might offer the best illustrations for the world verbally described by Gibbon is perhaps no more contentious than the descriptive use of medieval art in many history books today. However, when it comes to the *Visits*, Curzon's art history comes out as more considered and sophisticated. His travelling in the Levant had a stated purpose, influenced by the writings of a number of famous predecessors. This is clear from the preface of 1865, but equally transparent throughout the text of the book:[9]

The origin of my researches in libraries of ancient monasteries ... was that I wished among other hobbies to make such a collection of early manuscripts and printed books as would enable me to illustrate a history of the art of writing from specimens in my own collection ... I was the pioneer who first in modern times undertook this sort of literary campaign.

Of his and others' efforts in the monasteries he adds:

So thoroughly were these ancient libraries explored in the fifteenth century, that no unknown classic author has been discovered, nor has any manuscript been found of greater antiquity than some already known to the British Museum and other libraries.[10]

---

[8] *Catalogue*, 42. Curzon was himself interested in daily life, and the *Travels* were illustrated with 'costume drawings made by a Maltese artist; they represent costumes worn at the present day in different parts of the Turkish empire'. Some drawings and sketches are by Curzon, but one of the best is by Lord Eastnor.

[9] One might say that Curzon's references to earlier scholarly literature are predictable. But the fact is that they represent an efficient coverage of the mainstream literature on the historical materials of the region: Gibbon, Didron, Montfaucon, Tischendorf, Clarke, Carlyle, Tattam, Dallaway.

[10] Curzon, *Visits*, 22.

In other words, Curzon, like others before him, entertained the perpetual, if fading, hope that they would find some famous lost book of antiquity. This is the aspect of exploration that we find in previous endeavours, and it was a great spur to fame and fortune. A particular stimulus was the book by the Revd James Dallaway, *Constantinople. Ancient and Modern* (1797). Dallaway, while reporting that it was 'morally impossible' for a Christian to enter the library of the Seraglio, yet said that there were 120 manuscripts there, and that perhaps they included unknown works of classical authors. Lord Elgin, as ambassador, worked to get access to the Seraglio for the Revd Joseph Dacre Carlyle and even achieved this in 1800. Carlyle, Professor of Arabic at Cambridge, declared that there were no classical authors represented there. He equally found nothing in the library of St Sophia, but acquired manuscripts from other places, and thus pointed to the fruitful monasteries for the future: he visited Mar Saba and Mount Athos. He came home with twenty-seven Greek manuscripts, saying 'I have not stolen even one'. Of the questions which were asked of Carlyle after his death in 1818, one was why all his manuscripts went to the library of Lambeth Palace, and the other was whether he was right about the Seraglio Library.

Another influential predecessor of Curzon was Edward Daniel Clarke, Professor of Mineralogy at Cambridge in 1808 and University Librarian in 1817 (one of Curzon's manuscripts was purchased from Clarke's collection). Clarke quarrelled with Carlyle, but he too got into the Seraglio library. His great *coup* was to extract five manuscripts from the monastery of St John on Patmos, including the Arethas *Plato*, which the Bodleian Library purchased with alacrity in 1809. Carlyle and Clarke publicized the existence of large numbers of manuscripts in the Bazaar at Constantinople – they estimated perhaps 50,000 books as on sale, and between them they mapped out the targets in the East for the avid book collector. Curzon wrote of his visit to Patmos in a letter to Sneyd. He saw the famous Job (of the tenth century), and dated it because of the script to the fifth or sixth centuries, comparing it with the Vienna Dioscurides, 'the most ancient manuscript that I have ever seen in the Levant'. He offered 'all my money, and my other coat and my old hat and my little finger – but to no purpose'.[11]

Other important characters in this period came on to the scene later than Curzon, and were actually more effective operators. One was Tischendorf, who saw the Codex Sinaiticus in 1844. Another was Coxe, in the Levant in 1857. Another was the Coptic scholar Henry Tattam, who sought manuscripts in order to edit and print the contents. He went

---

[11] Fraser, *Heir of Parham*, 34.

to Sinai in 1839, but operated most successfully in the Natron valley. He was there in 1838 and purchased forty-nine manuscripts; by 1842 his good relations with the patriarch gained him another two hundred manuscripts. It was something of a *coup* to have beaten the French to these manuscripts, and they were packed up and sent to the British Museum where they arrived in poor shape.[12] In this company, one can see how Curzon might be described as the last amateur collector, and in the preface of 1865 he comments on the fact that the 'British Museum had acquired the ancient Syriac library of the Natron Lakes at a far less cost than what I had paid to those same monks and others for the ancient books which were no use to them'. He also compliments Tischendorf on rescuing fifty uncial manuscripts.

In this context one sees how the targets had already been defined for Curzon, and his visits to the picturesque sites of the Levant were planned according to a practical programme of treasure hunting. In Constantinople, for example, Curzon, in the course of his stay as private secretary to the ambassador in 1841–42, went into St Sophia and admired it without much enthusiasm, probably because he failed to gain entrance into its library or that of St Eirene. He lingered in the bazaars. He was perpetually in hope that the monasteries and bazaars were full of lost Classics. Although Curzon was obviously conventionally optimistic in these respects, his attitudes and knowledge were not limited to the Classics. His acquisition of a thirteenth-century manuscript at the beginning of his career and his sympathies for Christian medieval art opened his eyes to a broad spectrum of aesthetic appreciation. Perhaps his disastrous Oxford career in the Classics had its bonus.

One major visit of Curzon was so unsuccessful that he omitted it from the published travels, although some of the details are probably transposed into the text. This was his visit to the monastery of St Catherine's on Sinai in March 1834, described in a letter to his parents which was probably written in Cairo.[13] The letter gives a clear account of the operation and confesses its failure. This was one of the early indications to Curzon that removing manuscripts from famous sites was not going to be easy. He describes the episode with bitterness. Even the journey through the desert was unpleasant, as his companion Palmer was weary of desert travel, and Curzon had to travel by himself, just with his servants and three Greek pilgrims. The monastery looked 'like an old Gothic castle, where a mon-

---

[12] The British Museum's fourteenth-century icon with Four Church Feasts arrived with a package of Syriac manuscripts from the monastery of St Mary Deipara in the region of the Natron Lakes in 1851: see D. Buckton, ed., *Byzantium: Treasures of Byzantine Art and Culture from British Collections* (London [British Museum], 1994), cat. 221.

[13] Fraser, *Heir of Parham*, 36.

strous giant or terrible enchanter might reside, much more than the abode of a few quiet old monks'. On arrival, a shot from his gun got a reaction – a rope was sent down. He spoke to the abbot in a few words of Arabic and modern Greek, but 'It is a horrid place, nothing looks cheerful and the mountains are not high enough to give the sublime appearance of the Alps or other mountains I have seen'. Curzon saw that the monastery was a 'treasure-house': the church and chapels were lit with silver chandeliers and glittered with precious icons and relics mounted in gold. It had white marble walls, tiles of oriental porcelain and rich Persian carpets on the floors. But all was covered with dust. He reckoned that the library had over three thousand manuscripts and he rummaged through a tenth-century Gospels, an illustrated Psalter, a Lives of Saints, and a quarto manuscript of the Gospels written in 'Gold Uncial Greek', given by Honorius. Curzon asked the abbot if he would sell some of the books and was told that he could have had any number of them had not a certain Englishman taken some away fifteen years earlier in exchange for a telescope. This was probably Bankes, who in London in 1832 had suggested the visit to Sinai to Curzon. As a result of the deal, the abbot at the time had been downgraded to the status of a common monk. The present abbot had no intention to risk a fate that might be worse.

Curzon gives the dialogue which he claims followed:

> 'But I will give you half a dozen bottles of liqueur.'
> 'Where is it ?', asked the abbot.
> I gave it to him on the spot.
> 'This is excellent', says the abbot.
> 'Yes and nobody will know anything about it', says Curzon.
> 'But there is a catalogue and you can't have any books at all.'[14]

The outcome is graphically portrayed. The abbot consumes all the good 'Rosolio', while Curzon leaves Sinai with a useless gift: not the Codex Sinaiticus, but the skin of a gazelle, stuffed with dates and almonds. The expedition took three weeks and Curzon said he never wanted to ride a camel again. Curzon did not publish his story at the time, but no doubt it represents what he soon learned about the strategies that both sides could employ. In comparison, the published account of his acquisition of the Ivan Alexander Gospels from St Paul's on Athos seems almost suspiciously low-key. He admits that this Bulgarian monastery was prosperous and kept its books well. Consequently Curzon saw little hope here, until the abbot asked him to choose a memento. He 'impertinently' chose the Alexander Gospels. He offered to buy another manuscript and was given that too.

---

[14] Fraser, *Heir of Parham*, 36ff.

As a result of his travels, Curzon was in as good a position as any mid-nineteenth-century antiquarian to gain a working knowledge of Byzantine art. At St Paul's on Athos he is given an engraving of the monastery, and he compares it with Byzantine paintings which

> always have a line or two of description explanatory of the subject, as in this curious Greek engraving. It is copied from one of the prints given to pilgrims who visit the monasteries of Athos and gives a good idea of the appearance of a Byzantine building and the character of Greek art in modern times.[15]

What he writes about Byzantine art emerges from the usual Victorian pastiche of sources and observation. This is seen in the 'Introductory chapter' of the *Visits*, in which he sets out a way of viewing Byzantine art and architecture. Significant for seeing the context of his thought is what he wishes to emphasize. Curzon is struck by the fact that these are the very monasteries in which one can trace a continuity from the Fathers who lived in them in the Middle Ages to the present day, so that 'after the remains of the private houses of the Romans at Pompei, they are the most ancient specimens extant of domestic architecture'. But unfortunately the architecture is 'hardly ever fine', and monasteries are usually small, being calculated for the needs of the monks alone. Accordingly, St Sophia is the only Byzantine church of any magnitude. For Curzon, Byzantine church architecture is in every respect inferior to that of the West; poverty and subjection to Islam have been a feature of the East. The churches are all of the same character.

For Curzon the term 'Byzantine architecture' is meant to describe a style. He must therefore define its essence. He tells us that it is not Romanesque, not Lombardic, not Saracenic, though it resembles and is inferior to those styles. His whole tone is deeply critical: because of the decay of science at the time of its origins, the architects could not produce better imitations of Roman architecture. They were blundering architects, equally unable to produce sculpture and so always reusing classical pieces, as in the ancient metropolitan church of Athens which, when Curzon was last there, was used to contain the few volumes dignified by the name of public library. This curious church was built in the sixth century. It seems as if the model for Byzantine churches was public baths, not the basilica, as in the West.

The three qualities of classical architecture – proportion, symmetry and grace – are found to be as absent from Byzantine architecture as they were from the work of British architects of Curzon's time. The Byzantine architect made up for good taste by the richness of colour, inlaying the

---

[15] Curzon, *Visits*, 30.

walls with marble or fresco or, in the richest churches, with mosaic with a gold background and a few words explaining the subject.

Curzon's viewing of Byzantine architecture (and the architecture of his own time) was deeply pessimistic, and depended on a taste for the Classical. After such a conservative and critical viewing of Byzantine church architecture and its structural logic, we might expect an equally negative approach to Byzantine painting. Unexpectedly, in his appreciation of the pictorial arts of Byzantium and the Orthodox world Curzon is interestingly positive. His characterization of painting is that it falls into one of two categories: art either addresses itself to the intellect or to the passions. Byzantine art belongs to the first category, as does early Italian art. Although Byzantine is inferior and less noble than the Italian primitives, because it is stiff and conventional, yet he concedes that

> no one who studies these ancient works of art can fail to appreciate and reverence that high and noble spirit which animated the pencils of these saintly painters, and irradiates the composition of their sublime conceptions with a dignity and grandeur altogether lacking in Rubens, Titian, Guido Reni, Domenichino and even later Raphael.[16]

Curzon's artistic knowledge of the cinquecento paradoxically helps him to appreciate Byzantine art, which he calls devotional art and which, he regrets, began to decay in the fifteenth century, just when Italian art was flowering. Yet Byzantine art succeeds in his view in conveying feelings of devotion and religious awe and a kind of grandeur which was absent from works of the artists of his time. He has learned from Didron's publication of the *Painters' Guide of Mount Athos* of 1845 about the limitations of Byzantine subject-matter and concludes that it was controlled by the church and stereotyped. The question is whether it is this control that explains the continuity and similarity of Byzantine art.

Curzon's feeling about Byzantine art suggests some kindred ideas with the Pre-Raphaelite aesthetic frame and a romantic view of the medieval artist seen to be constrained by the control of the Church. This was the frame of reference for much of the second half of the nineteenth century and beyond. The importance of Curzon as a contributor to this tradition is that he knew the material in the Byzantine world at first hand. Although he spent time in Italy, particularly after 1850, he did not, like Ruskin and others, view Byzantine art through an Italian haze. His knowledge of Byzantine monumental decoration and architecture is striking for a man who is wrongly seen as a myopic manuscript collector. The popularity of his book must therefore have been one of the main reasons for the increase in sensitivity to Byzantine art in the next hundred years,

---

[16] Curzon, *Visits*, 34.

and its influence is no doubt to be traced in such books as Robert Byron's *The Station*.

Yet Curzon the traveller and observer did remain the British gentleman abroad, though sensitive to the customs of the Levant, as he himself recorded in a sketch made during his visit to 'the Abyssinian Library, in the Monastery of Souriani on the Natron Lakes' in Egypt (Figure 11.3). Robert Curzon is seated and dressed in the long robes of a merchant of the East. The room is dark, with bright sunlight seen through the door and a small window. It is whitewashed and plain. There is a shelf with dishes and other utensils, and manuscripts hang on wooden pegs around the room. There is a low round table with frugal food, and an animal skin acts as a carpet. Curzon's armed Egyptian servants stand on the right, and a Black Ethiopian monk dressed in leather (gazelle skins) is on the left. On the floor in front of Curzon is a case from which a manuscript has been taken and is held in the hands of the monk seated beside him. Standing over Curzon is the blind Coptic abbot of the monastery. The setting and the details are described by Curzon, but the pictorial image of the young Westerner sitting and reaching out towards the precious manuscript book eloquently describes the scholar facing the elusive East.

Fig. 11.1. From the original 1849 edition of Robert Curzon, Visits to Monasteries in the Levant: 'View of the Great Monastery of Meteora, from the Monastery of Barlaam, with the River Peneus in the distance (from a Drawing made on the spot by Viscount Eastnor)'

VISITS TO MONASTERIES
IN
THE LEVANT

BY THE
HONOURABLE ROBERT CURZON JUN.

From a Sketch by R. Curzon.

Interior of the Court of a Greek Monastery. A monk is calling the congregation to prayer by beating a board called the simandro (σιμανδρο) which is generally used instead of bells.

WITH NUMEROUS WOODCUTS

LONDON:
JOHN MURRAY, ALBEMARLE STREET.
1849.

Fig. 11.2. Facsimile of original 1849 title page: Robert Curzon, Visits to Monasteries in the Levant

| Abyssinian monk clothed in leather. | The dining table. | The blind abbot leaning over the Author. | Abyssinian monk. | The books hanging from wooden pegs let into the wall. | The Author's Egyptian servants. |

Fig. 11.3. From Chapter VIII (Natron Lakes, Egypt), Robert Curzon, Visits to Monasteries in the Levant; 'Interior of the Abyssinian Library, in the Monastery of Sourianin on the Natron Lakes'

12. Bury, Baynes and Toynbee

Averil Cameron

If you go into a classical and Byzantine bookshop today, one of the books you will almost certainly find there is J. B. Bury's *History of the Later Roman Empire* (1923). Like his *History of Greece* (1900), later revised by Russell Meiggs and commonly used as a textbook until very recently, Bury's *Later Roman Empire* has served generations as a guide and an introduction to the period from the death of Theodosius I to that of Justinian; it is even now in many ways the most detailed narrative of the period. It is less easy to find his first version, the *History of the Eastern Roman Empire from AD 395 to 800* (1889), or his *History of the Eastern Roman Empire from the Fall of Irene to the Accession of Basil I (AD 802–867)* (1912), but if you can, they are worth having. Bury's annotated edition of Edward Gibbon's *History of the Decline and Fall of the Roman Empire* in seven volumes (1898–1900) is still the edition of choice for any Byzantinist reading Gibbon. His introduction to the original Byzantine volume of the *Cambridge Medieval History* (vol. 4, 1923), of which he was the editor, was reprinted out of *pietas* in the new version of 1967, which kept to the same effective starting date of 717. Where are they now, the polymaths like Bury?

It was Norman Baynes, who followed so much in Bury's footsteps, who produced the standard memoir of his predecessor.[1] Bury was only some sixteen years older than Baynes himself – they were born in 1861 and 1877 respectively – but he died in 1927 at the relatively early age of sixty-five, whereas Baynes lived on until 1961; there are still people who knew and remember him.[2] Joan Hussey has written of the difference

---

[1] Norman H. Baynes, *A Bibliography of the Works of J.B. Bury, compiled with a memoir* (Cambridge, 1929).

[2] I am indebted to the appreciation by J. M. Hussey written for the British Academy, 'Norman Hepburn Baynes, 1877–1961', *PBA* 49 (1965), 365–73; see also her contribution in

From *Through the Looking Glass: Byzantium Through British Eyes*, eds Robin Cormack and Elizabeth Jeffreys. Copyright © 2000 by the Society for the Promotion of Byzantine Studies. Published by Ashgate Publishing Ltd, Gower House, Croft Road, Aldershot, Hampshire, GU11 3HR, Great Britain.

between them that, while Baynes had a deep appreciation of his predecessor, he felt that in Bury critical analysis at times impeded creative
vision, whereas, she writes, Baynes himself 'was never afraid to combine
critical and exact scholarship with imaginative reconstruction'... 'it was
Baynes, his follower and successor, who was able to bring to life the
civilization of Byzantium for an immeasurably wider audience than that
commanded by Bury'.[3] I shall return later to this question of audience.
They had met by 1903, and corresponded thereafter; Bury asked Baynes
to contribute to the *Cambridge Medieval History* (though not to vol. 4 itself,
which indeed Baynes later criticized in a review in the *Times Literary
Supplement*).[4] At that time Bury was already Regius Professor of Modern
History at Cambridge, while Baynes only went down from Oxford in
1903 and then went to the Bar; he was not appointed Assistant Lecturer
at University College London until 1913 or Reader till after the First
World War. Baynes's life and career were less varied than was the case
with Bury. He never married, and spent all his academic career at University College London.[5] His mother continued to be an important force
in his life for many years, and he was supported by a deep religious
sense derived from his Baptist family background. Baynes gave much of
himself to evening teaching of history to the wider public, and is remembered for his thrilling voice, and for his talent for companionship among
colleagues and pupils. He was known more widely to ancient historians
in the University College London Ancient History Circle and through
the annual Baynes Weekend at Wellingborough, a place chosen because
it was said to be equidistant from Oxford, Cambridge and London. Hugh
Last, Frank Adcock (Professors of Ancient History at Oxford and Cambridge) and Norman Baynes were the triumvirate who began it and
dominated it for years (I am glad to have been one of the first women to
be invited to attend, though sadly that was after Baynes's death). With
Last and Adcock he also shared his attachment to the Roman Society, of
which he served as President and which commemorated him in the
Journal of Roman Studies for 1947.

Baynes's interests and the circumstances of his life led him to publish,
in addition to what he wrote on Byzantium and the later Roman empire,
bibliographies on the Classics for the wider public, on Old Testament

---

the *Bulletin of Dr Williams's Library*, 72 (1967), on the occasion of the opening of the
Norman Baynes Byzantine Collection at the Library (hereafter, Hussey, *Bulletin*).

[3] Hussey, 'Baynes', 372.

[4] Hussey, *Bulletin*, 4–5.

[5] As Professor of Byzantine History from 1931 until his retirement in 1942. In 1937 he
was relieved of all duties in teaching ancient history and made Honorary Professor of
Byzantine History and Institutions.

Israel and, during the Second World War, on Hitler and National Social-
ism.[6] But Bury's range and output were much wider, as well as differently focused.[7] Throughout his life his publications alternated between
the Byzantine and the classical, and between the historical and the literary. At Trinity College Dublin he held a Chair of Greek simultaneously
with his Chair of Modern History. He was an expert on Browning, and
had published editions of the poems of Pindar. While holding his Regius
Chair of Modern History at Cambridge from 1902 onwards, he published on the ancient Greek historians and St Patrick, and supplemented
his large scholarly output with a stream of literary pieces, Latin and
Greek verses and translations. He wrote on the education of women,
praising Christianity for the many 'fine women' it had produced, who
might act as models and prototypes for the modern emancipated woman,
and eliciting an appreciative response from Mrs Fawcett.[8] Though a
classicist by training, and one who won a Fellowship of Trinity College
Dublin by examination, he also studied Sanskrit, Syriac and Hebrew at
Göttingen for six months during his undergraduate career, and later
learned Russian. Sir Steven Runciman remembers that Bury was only
prepared to take him seriously as a prospective Byzantinist when he
learned that he too knew some Russian. This Bury took as a good sign
and promptly sent the young Runciman away, telling him to review two
articles in Bulgarian.[9]

The third and youngest of the scholars considered here is Arnold
Toynbee. Born in 1889, Toynbee was also a classicist by training, who
had won scholarships to Winchester and Balliol, and was elected a Fellow of Balliol as soon as he graduated; he then married into what was in
effect the British classical aristocracy, choosing as his wife the daughter
of Gilbert Murray.[10] Neither Baynes nor Toynbee were directly pupils of
Bury. Although, as I have said, Baynes met Bury in 1903 and had written
his Lothian prize essay on Heraclius by then, he left academic life in
favour of law for some years after taking Greats, while Toynbee's period
as Fellow of Balliol was cut short by the start of the First World War. Yet
in his preface to his late book, *Constantine Porphyrogenitus and His World*
(1973), Toynbee states that he owed his inspiration and his enthusiasm

---

[6] See the bibliography included in *JRS* 37 (1947), 1–9, also with prefatory note by J. M.
Hussey.

[7] Very useful also is the article by George Huxley, 'The historical scholarship of John
Bagnell Bury', *GRBS* 17 (1976), 81–104.

[8] See Baynes, *Memoir*, 71.

[9] Steven Runciman, *A Traveller's Alphabet. Partial Memoirs* (London, 1991), 15.

[10] For Toynbee's life, see W. H. McNeill, *Arnold J. Toynbee: A Life* (New York, 1989):
critical review by G. Martel, 'Toynbee, McNeill and the myth of history', *The International
History Review* 12 (2) (1990), 330–48.

for Constantine Porphyrogenitus to Bury: 'my mother had been giving me the volumes of Bury's edition of Gibbon in instalments, and it was Bury's appendix to volume vi, published in 1902, that had set me off'.[11] He dedicated this book, in effect, to Bury: 'I publish this as a small tribute to Bury, who, besides being a very great historian, was also a masterly editor of Greek texts.'[12]

The three men were very different. In his memoir of Bury, Baynes has left a sympathetic and scrupulous discussion of one whose views did not, in some important matters, coincide with his own. After an extended treatment of Bury's rationalism, for instance, he writes that 'perhaps' one thing is clear: 'the discreet student will not go to Bury's books for his church history'.[13] Toynbee in turn was very unlike Baynes; yet he was among the many signatories to the admiring address presented to Baynes in 1942, the year of Baynes's retirement from University College London, and that in which he gave the Romanes Lecture at Oxford and received an honorary D.Litt. there. In the preface to this address, incidentally, Bury is described as Baynes's 'friend and master', and Baynes himself as being 'universally recognised as Bury's successor'.[14] The list of names reads like a litany of the great and the good. Professor Hussey has already commented on the remarkable warmth of affection which was expressed towards Baynes – *amicus carissimus* – by his friends and academic colleagues, here in Britain and elsewhere.[15] Toynbee continued to be a friend of Baynes, and to urge him to write the larger studies of Byzantium which sadly never came.[16]

These personal connections are important, and are still very relevant to the Byzantinists of today. The world of Byzantine scholarship is not very large, even now; moreover, Toynbee's career subsequent to his leaving the Koraes Chair at King's in 1924 continued to lie in London. I know that there were people present at the Symposium in 1995 who knew Toynbee, and one person – Sir Steven Runciman – who must have known all three.

They differed markedly, however, in their teaching and influence. Steven Runciman writes of Bury that he was a 'frail, shy man', who may have had a few pupils at Dublin, but who, after he moved into Byzantine

---

[11] A. J. Toynbee, *Constantine Porphyrogenitus and His World* (Oxford, 1971), vi.

[12] Toynbee, *Constantine Porphyrogenitus*, viii.

[13] Baynes, *Memoir*, 88.

[14] *An Address Presented to Norman Hepburn Baynes with a Bibliography of his Writings* (Oxford, 1942), 20.

[15] Cf. the concluding reference (p. 21) to the 'kindnesses which Baynes has shown to a variety of causes and to all sorts and conditions of men'; cf. especially Hussey, *Bulletin*, 9–11.

[16] Hussey, *Bulletin*, 6.

studies, 'neither had nor wished to have any more'.[17] Toynbee spent little time or effort on regular teaching at King's during his tenure of the Chair there, giving on average only seventeen lectures a year, to few students, and with few or no other duties. His appointment had been conditional on his brushing up his modern Greek so as to be able to teach it, and his failure to teach played a major part in the complaints that were eventually made against him.[18] After leaving King's he held what effectively became, *faute de mieux*, a research chair, with no teaching duties.[19] The trajectory of Baynes was quite different. He took his responsibilities very seriously. Arnaldo Momigliano wrote in his Inaugural Lecture in the Chair of Ancient History at University College London in 1952 that 'to teach Ancient History in the College of George Grote and Norman Baynes must have seemed a severe responsibility for my predecessors Professor Cary and Professor Jones'.[20] Baynes was as interested in introducing teachers to ancient history as in writing books on Byzantium, and taught for many years in both day and evening schools for the purpose; he also made regular broadcasts, including broadcasting to schoolchildren, and produced bibliographies for those without Latin or Greek. He is still (just) remembered for his thrilling voice and powers of explanation, and again, Professor Hussey cites examples from surviving letters of appreciation, which were evidently many. He was proud to see himself as first and foremost a teacher, and a teacher who valued pupils of every kind of background. This surely had much to do with the sense of mission inculcated in his early years at home, but, like his Ancient History Circle, it also showed his talents for friendship and the lively part he took in meetings and theatricals.[21] He was evidently a performer even in his teaching: he gave a memorable rendering of the chorus of frogs in Aristophanes' *Frogs* – the precursor of a similar performance which I well remember at Oxford by Eduard Fraenkel.[22] This personal involvement is one of the things most often mentioned about him, and difficult for those of us of a younger generation to recapture; he was, for instance, 'best friends' with Hugh Last, the Camden Professor of Ancient History

---

[17] Hussey, *Bulletin*, 6.

[18] See R. Clogg, *Politics and the Academy. Arnold Toynbee and the Koraes Chair* (London, 1986), 62–6; also R. Beaton, 'Koraes, Toynbee and the Modern Greek heritage', *BMGS* 15 (1991), 1–18.

[19] Martel is particularly scathing on his failure to teach ('Toynbee', 348).

[20] A. Momigliano, 'George Grote and the study of Greek history', Inaugural lecture at University College London, 19 February 1952, repr. in *Studies in Historiography* (London, 1966), ch. 3.

[21] For instance as Burglar Bill and (very differently!) the Voice of God: Hussey, *Bulletin*, 8, 10.

[22] See Hussey, 'Baynes', 370.

at Oxford, who was by all accounts an unusually austere and reserved person. They wrote to each other as often as we would telephone our friends nowadays. But for a long period at the end of his life, from 1953 onwards, Baynes's activity was severely curtailed by ill health, and he was unable to write the books his friends so much wanted him to complete, or to reply to his many correspondents from all walks of life.

A very obvious difference between the three lay in their personal ideas and beliefs. Bury's late nineteenth-century rationalism, as I have already said, is discussed by Baynes in his *Memoir* ('the disciple of Gibbon was, like his master, a Rationalist').[23] It was a high-minded late Victorian rationalism which, at that date, still required its upholder to debate seriously and form a view on the role of religion in history. Bury's conclusion was that Christianity was in no way miraculous, and that any argument from its success must be discarded; however, 'viewed modestly as a great social phenomenon, Christianity has had a distinguished and instructive history'. But its days were over: 'it began to decline when it ceased to be fully adequate to the needs of the time and to correspond to all the tendencies of progress. The decomposition, like the growth, can be traced step by step.' He took this belief to the logical limit, and excluded also any kind of dilute theism: 'There is nothing for it but to trust the light of our reason. Its candle power may be low, but it is the only light we have.'[24] Bury, the historian of the idea of progress and advocate of freedom of thought,[25] believed in contingency rather than in laws of history. Yet his inaugural lecture at Cambridge set out his belief that history was a science – no more and no less.[26] Articles he produced during the First World War, setting out his rationalist principles and his views on causation and contingency in history are, as Baynes rightly said, a necessary background for understanding Bury's work, not simply explaining why he came to write on freedom of thought, but also why he wrote his history as he did. Indeed, Bury's views and his approach to history led him, in Baynes's view, to omit a whole dimension from his understanding of the early Byzantine state. When, later, Peter Brown was to praise the use made of the vast Christian literature of the early Byzantine empire by A. H. M. Jones, he cited Baynes as an example of the kind of empathy which these sources would make possible.[27] But for

---

[23] Baynes, *Memoir*, 76 ff.

[24] See Baynes, *Memoir*, 81.

[25] *A History of Freedom of Thought* (London, 1914); *The Idea of Progress* (London, 1920).

[26] Inaugural Lecture, 26 January 1903 (Cambridge, 1903).

[27] Peter Brown, 'The Later Roman Empire', in *Religion and Society in the Age of St. Augustine* (London, 1972), 50. 'Brilliant' is used more than once by Brown when writing of Baynes (e.g., *Religion and Society*, 50, n.3; 334).

Bury, belief in human progress, a belief which he retained despite the experience of the war, was to be the nearest he came to an act of faith, and indeed he himself described it as such.[28]

That particular kind of rationalism, combined with a liberal belief in progress, now seems very much in period. Others, for instance Anthony Bryer, have shown how crucial were the years from 1908, the date of the foundation of the Bywater and Sotheby Chair at Oxford, to the early 1920s, for the development of the academic study of Byzantine and modern Greek in this country,[29] and we must go on to comment on the importance of the First World War and its aftermath for each of my subjects.

During the war, the young Toynbee was writing official propaganda, while Baynes worked on intelligence while lecturing in ancient history to the University College Evening School, though he was still a law tutor until 1916. But Baynes's background and inclinations were quite unlike those of Bury. Baynes was not simply a Protestant, but had been brought up as a Baptist. Both his parents were closely connected with the Baptist Missionary Society, and Baynes himself was deeply religious; when he wrote to his father as an undergraduate about his plans for a subject for the Lothian Prize Essay, he used revealing language: 'the wars of Heraclius are really a crusade before the time and the victory of the Holy Mother was that of truth over error'.[30] His essay on icons, 'The supernatural defenders of Constantinople', and his article 'The thought-world of East Rome' show the kind of empathy which is now the hallmark of the writings of Peter Brown. It is no surprise that Brown has frequently referred to these works, and made much use in his earlier writings of the saints' lives translated in Dawes and Baynes, *Three Byzantine Saints* – a modest publication which, like Baynes's collaborative volume of essays on Byzantium, has been a basic tool for English students.[31] A review of Ernst Stein's history of the later empire published by Baynes in the *Journal of Roman Studies* in 1928 made his own approach very clear. He took Stein gently to task for his limited, and largely political focus; 'there is no attempt to initiate the reader into the thought-world of the fourth and fifth centuries – the conflict of the adherents to the classical tradition with those who were for pouring new wine into the old bottles'. In the pages on monasticism, 'Dr. Stein has but little interest for a great religious move-

---

[28] See Baynes, *Memoir*, 87–8.

[29] A. A. M. Bryer, 'Byzantine and Modern Greek studies: a partial view', *BMGS* 12 (1988), 1–26.

[30] Cited by Hussey, *Bulletin*, 4.

[31] E. Dawes and N. Baynes, *Three Byzantine Saints* (Oxford, 1948); N. H. Baynes and H. St L. B. Moss, *Byzantium. An Introduction to East Roman Civilization* (Oxford, 1948).

ment … we are not helped to look upon the world as a Byzantine saw it'.[32] Two other subjects dear to Baynes – Augustine and Constantine – demonstrate his emotional involvement with Christianity; the first links him again with Peter Brown, and of the second, Peter Brown himself wrote that Baynes's Raleigh lecture on Constantine[33] 'saved' us in England from the extreme scepticism with which Constantine's Christianity has been viewed by continental scholars.[34] With all due allowance for the passage of time and the large recent bibliography on Constantine, that essay still stands as the best refutation of the sceptics, and is a basis, for example, of T. D. Barnes's presentation of Constantine as a committed Christian.

Though Peter Brown was, like myself, a pupil of Momigliano, the creative and empathetic dimension of Baynes's work, together with his feel for Eastern Christianity, were clearly strong influences upon him. Brown learned from Momigliano to develop further both the emphasis on creativity and imagination and the deep interest in the working of religion, and from others the benefits of approaching religious history from the context of social anthropology.[35] But the distinctive approach of Baynes was one of the clear influences in the conception of late antiquity so characteristic of Brown and his followers.

Toynbee's religious stance changed more than once during his writing career. During and after the First World War he took the view that religion was an illusion, but in 1930, through what he claimed as a mystical experience, he again became convinced of the existence of God, and eventually he became a Roman Catholic, claiming now that Christianity was the highest of the religions and made Western civilization worth saving; by the 1960s, however, he had fallen back on a kind of universal pantheism with no one supreme religion.[36] The *Study of History*, then, which comprises twelve volumes in all, including the last, a *Reconsideration*, and was published over the period from 1934 to 1961, embraced many twists and turns of the author's mind, just as it includes a bewildering juxtaposition of examples to illustrate its sprawling argument.[37]

---

[32] *JRS* 18 (1928), 217–28, at 217.

[33] 'Constantine the Great and the Christian Church', *PBA* 15 (1929), 341–442, repr. with preface by H. Chadwick (Oxford, 1972).

[34] Brown, *Religion and Society*, 256.

[35] See, e.g., L. Cracco Ruggini, 'All'ombra di Momigliano: Peter Brown e la mutazione del tardoantico', *Rivista Storica Italiana* 100 (1988), 739–67, at 741; A. Rousselle, 'Jeunesse de l'antiquité tardive. Les leçons de lecture de Peter Brown', *Annales E.S.C.* 1985 (3,) 521–8.

[36] See Martel, 'Toynbee' (as in note 10 above), 342–3.

[37] I–III (1934); IV–VI (1939); VII–X (1954); XI (maps and gazetteer, 1959); XII (1961). Dimitri Obolensky's interesting article, 'Toynbee and Byzantium', in I. Hutter and I. Sevcenko, eds, ΑΕΤΟΣ (Berlin, 1998), 243–56, appeared three years after the present paper was written.

But a shifting position as to the force of religion in history did not stand in Toynbee's way or undermine other certainties as to the 'essence' or 'character' of alleged civilizations, any more than it restrained him from repetition, lack of organization or the replacing of argument by categorical statement. The same mixture of undigested elements can be seen in two late works, *Hannibal's Legacy* (1965), which deals with the Roman Republic, especially after the Punic Wars, and *Constantine Porphyrogenitus and His World* (1973). The successive volumes of the *Study of History* sold enormous numbers in their day. Yet reading even a part of this vast work today is an uncomfortable experience, so unwilling are we nowadays to accept such grand generalities, and so repelled, if that is not putting it too strongly, by the crudity of Toynbee's assumptions about race and ethnicity. The constant resort, in a work on what we would now best call 'societies' or 'cultures', rather than 'civilizations', to metaphors of sickness and health,[38] youth and age, family relationships and moral weakness and vigour, is so completely out of date in a postmodern age in which all former certainties are open to question that one can hardly read Toynbee without feeling an almost physical discomfort. This is compounded by his extreme clumsiness of style, coining words like 'unavoidableness', and filling his books with prolix annexes and digressions; finally, his emotive language – terms like 'fatal', clutches', 'dead civilizations' – is not such as we would like to see from our students or use ourselves. Unlike Bury or Baynes, Toynbee has attracted violent criticism from historians such as Hugh Trevor-Roper and others, partly in reaction to the adulation which he had attracted during his lifetime,[39] and the biography of him by W. H. McNeill is in large part a rehabilitation against these attacks. Like *Constantine Porphyrogenitus and His World*, *Hannibal's Legacy* presents an extraordinarily broad sweep, 'amply documented by references to ancient sources and modern scholarship', as one reviewer put it, 'and written apparently without regard for the cramping restrictions which publishers are apt to impose on scholars of lesser stature'.[40] Both books are sprawling and undisciplined, but both, it is true, contain sections that are memorable as pieces of historical writing. Nevertheless, the questions they provoke are twofold: is it worth ploughing through even part of the rest, and even more important, do the categorical assertions and position-taking not diminish what value the works might otherwise have?

---

[38] Metaphors of decay in O. Spengler's *Decline of the West* (trans. 1962, orig. 1918); J. A. Tainter, *The Collapse of Complex Societies* (Cambridge, 1988), 77–9; on Toynbee, 79–80.

[39] See Martel, 'Toynbee'; C. T. McIntire and M. Perry, eds, *Toynbee: Reappraisals* (Toronto, 1989).

[40] E. S. Staveley, *JRS* 57 (1967), 244.

In that this generation is still trying to free itself from the old idea of Byzantium as a static and totalitarian state, it must be said that reading Toynbee does not represent a helpful enterprise.[41] He insists on the contrast between Hellenic civilization on the one hand, characterized by secularization, hatred of autocracy and love of freedom, and 'Byzantine' civilization. He sees the latter's essence as encapsulated in the act of *proskynesis*, in which a subject expressed his servitude to the emperor and the state.[42] In this he emphasizes a break with the past, even 'an eager receptiveness', not continuity.[43] As elsewhere, he proceeds by assertion, not by argument.

Toynbee himself wrote to Baynes to encourage him to give a complete expression to the dualism in Byzantine culture between Hellenism and the Judaeo-Christian tradition which Baynes had set out in his essays on 'The Hellenistic civilization' and 'The thought-world of East Rome'.[44] It is a dualism recently restated, with reference to Toynbee, by Speros Vryonis in his contribution to the Dumbarton Oaks publication *Byzantium. A World Civilization*.[45]

As we all know, the history of academic posts in Byzantine and Modern Greek in British universities has not been an easy one. Questions of range and ideological stance have too often been left unresolved, with difficult consequences. For Bury this did not seem to pose any difficulty. Bury believed in cultural continuity between the ancient Greek world and that of Byzantium,[46] even asserting that 'the civilization of the later Roman Empire was the continuation of that of Ancient Greece';[47] there was no incompatibility for him between this and his expressed view that 'No "Byzantine Empire" ever began to exist; the Roman Empire did not come to an end until 1453'.[48] He showed an early interest in the later Greek language and became a serious traveller in Greece; he picked up languages with ease. As George Huxley has noticed, he expressed the view in 1919 that Greece had the best claim to Constantinople.[49] Bury held Chairs of Greek and of Modern History simultaneously and Baynes

---

[41] See A. Kazhdan and G. Constable, *People and Power in Byzantium* (Washington, D.C., 1982), 117–20.

[42] *Constantine Porphyrogenitus*, 526 ff., 541 ff.; see Kazhdan and Constable, *People and Power*, 119.

[43] *Constantine Porphyrogenitus*, 5.

[44] See Hussey, *Bulletin*, 6.

[45] A. E. Laiou and H. Maguire, eds, *Byzantium. A World Civilization* (Washington, D.C., 1994), at 19–20.

[46] See Huxley, 'Bury' (as in note 7), 101 f.

[47] *Cambridge Medieval History*, vol. 4, viii, cited by Baynes, *Memoir*, 17.

[48] *History of the Later Roman Empire*, vol. 1 (1889), v; cited by Baynes, *Memoir*, 64.

[49] Huxley, 'Bury', 103; cf. Baynes, *Memoir*, 166.

taught ancient history while occupying a Chair of Byzantine History; no one apparently thought this odd. Baynes retained his fascination with Augustine while writing on Byzantine topics, though he was never to write about him at full length – a topic for retirement, he thought. Toynbee had been a student at the British School at Athens in 1911, and learned fluent modern Greek, although he confessed to Principal Burrows that by 1919 it had become rusty, and promised on appointment to go and polish it up; nor did he show any interest in modern Greek literature, a fact which the electors also had to take into account. But as a young Fellow and Tutor in Ancient History at Balliol, and while working on intelligence during the war, he was already interested in later Greek history and published on Greece since 1882 and on the Armenians in the Ottoman Empire.[50] The main rival candidate for the Koraes Chair, A. W. Gomme, himself an excellent classicist, was also competent and interested in Modern Greek language and literature.[51]

Bury, by a long way the oldest of the three historians, spent the First World War in Cambridge, where he wrote a series of articles in the *R.P.A. Annual* in which he set out some of his ideas about history. He also defended the views as to the supremacy of free expression of thought upheld at the beginning of the war in his *History of Freedom of Thought*, and his book *The Idea of Progress* appeared in 1920. He believed that progress, like history, was contingent and not guaranteed, and clung to the idea even through the experience of the war.[52] For Baynes the war years represented the time of his move from the law to scholarship; he had already published a set of articles on Theophylakt Simokatta, and on Heraclius and on the Persian campaigns, which remained basic for a very long time. But like Toynbee, he also worked in intelligence (and during the Second World War was to edit Hitler's speeches and write on fascism). As for Toynbee, the foundations were laid during these years for his later involvement with current affairs and international history. Greece, Toynbee said in his inaugural lecture in 1919, was about to take the place of the Ottoman Empire as the bridge between Europe and the East.[53] If Greece could not have Constantinople, Bury had written to *The Times* in February of the same year, then it should be placed under the League of Nations.

There is not the space here to consider the relationship of this range of works by British – or it would be better to say, English and Irish – scholars with broader trends in European scholarship. They were cer-

---

[50] See Clogg, 'Toynbee' (as in note 18), 35–6.

[51] Clogg, 'Toynbee', 36.

[52] Baynes, *Memoir*, 81–8; cf. 88, 'the *Idea of Progress* was his working faith'. See also 78.

[53] Clogg, 'Toynbee', 43–4.

tainly far from being influenced by class-based, Marxist or economic explanations, and seem equally far from either M. I. Rostovtzeff or Max Weber. The emphasis on continuity on the part of both Bury and Baynes also set them apart from such historians as Ernst Stein or Ferdinand Lot, with their conceptions of decline, and from the preoccupation of so many others with finding an explanation for the fall of the Roman Empire and the end of classical antiquity.[54] Their connection with European scholarship was rather a connection with Byzantinists like Ostrogorsky, Grégoire and Dölger, with *Byzantinische Zeitschrift* and with the East European academies.

Of the three historians, if we consider the point of view of students and university curricula, Bury must be the one who has been the most read. Toynbee was for a time immensely popular, but not, surely, in academic teaching. It was, however, an important achievement that he should have placed Byzantium within the wider context of world history, something that most Byzantinists have failed to do. Toynbee has inspired great hostility from historians as well as enjoying periods of immense influence with the general public. His flaws are obvious, and indeed the sprawling breadth of his interests, combined with his outmoded or objectionable ideas about the growth and fall of civilizations and their inherent characteristics, make even his more specialized works like the book on Constantine Porphyrogenitus appear eccentric. Nevertheless, Byzantium does need – even more so today – to be considered against the broad context and the *longue durée* of European history. *Constantine Porphyrogenitus and His World* appeared in the same year as Dimitri Obolensky's *The Byzantine Commonwealth*, and I believe that Obolensky acknowledged a debt to Toynbee. Few other scholars have even attempted so broad a view. Perhaps there is now the need to return – not, certainly, to Toynbee's notions of affiliations and parentage – but to a real 'long view'. Though Toynbee's grand scheme of the decline and fall of cultures is unlikely to be revived, it has some resonances now in contemporary works on culture and imperialism, the supposed decline (or 'triumph') of the West, the 'end of history' and similar themes, as it does also in the archaeologists' attention to complex societies and the causes of their collapse. Especially since 1989, Byzantium still has many aspects to be explored by a historian who is prepared to risk that long comparative view.

---

[54] For a discussion see E. Patlagean, 'Dans le miroir, à travers le miroir: un siècle de déclin du monde antique', in *Les études classiques aux XIXe et XXe siècles: leur place dans l'histoire des idées*, Entretiens Hardt 26 (Vandoeuvres-Genève, 1980), 209–40; A. Momigliano, 'After Gibbon's *Decline and Fall*', repr. in *Sesto Contributo alla Storia degli Studi Classici e del Mondo Antico* I (Rome, 1980), 265–84.

As for Bury's histories, while they have been much read, they have perhaps, as Baynes implies, been less appreciated for themselves than they would have been if they had brought the subject more to life. Yet it was surely Bury, as well as Rostovtzeff, whose example lay behind A. H. M. Jones and the solid school of late Roman history which he inspired.[55] His attention to detail, his pragmatism and his interest in constitutional and administrative history (as also in his work on the *Kletorologion* of Philotheos) have left very recognizable traces in others. But it was Baynes who provided a model and example for those who, like Peter Brown, have been more inclined to the emotive and spiritual. Baynes's article, brilliantly titled 'The supernatural defenders of Constantinople',[56] lies behind much recent writing on images, relics and holy men. In 'The icons before iconoclasm',[57] he outlines the very arguments in the Christian anti-Jewish dialogues that have received so much attention in recent publications. His work on Constantine now represents the new orthodoxy. And his attention to 'the man in the East Roman street' foreshadowed by more than a generation the approach of Alexander Kazhdan and the *Oxford Dictionary of Byzantium*. I can see merits in Toynbee despite his defects; I owe a great debt and pay due respect to Bury; but if I had to choose one of the three, I would choose Baynes.

---

[55] On Jones see J. H. W. G. Liebeschuetz, 'A. H. M. Jones and the *Later Roman Empire*', in D. F. Clark, M. M. Roxan and J. J. Wilkes, eds, *The Later Roman Empire Today, Papers given in honour of Professor John Mann* (London, 1993), 1–8 (*University of London Institute of Archaeology Bulletin* 29 [1992], 1–8).

[56] Originally published in *Analecta Bollandiana* 67 (1949), 165–77.

[57] *HThR* 44 (1951), 93–106.

13. O. M. Dalton: 'ploughing the Byzantine furrow'

Christopher Entwistle

In 1860 the Director of the British Museum, Anthony Panizzi, was summoned before a Select Committee at Westminster and asked by its chairman: 'You have also, I imagine, Byzantine, Oriental, Mexican and Peruvian antiquities stowed away in the basement?' Panizzi replied: 'Yes, a few of them; and, I may well add, that I do not think it any great loss that they are not better placed than they are.'[1] A perusal of the Synopses of the British Museum, published annually from 1808 to 1856, and of subsequent guides to the Museum reveals that until the mid-1870s the only early Christian antiquities on public display were a number of gilded glasses from Rome; Byzantium was represented by a bronze lamp. An attitude of persistent neglect towards the Museum's early Christian and Byzantine collections prevailed until the turn of the century, when a remarkable curator, O. M. Dalton, with the connivance of a sympathetic keeper, Sir Hercules Read, effected a remarkable transformation in the Museum's attitude to both the display and publication of its Byzantine antiquities.

Ormonde Maddock Dalton (Figure 13.1) was born in Cardiff on 30 January 1866, the second son of Thomas Masters Dalton, a wealthy solicitor.[2] He was educated at Harrow and won an exhibition to New College, Oxford, in 1884, where he read Classical Moderations and Literae Humaniores, taking a First in each. After briefly considering a diplomatic career, Dalton decided to travel and spent most of the period

---

[1] *Report from the Select Committee on the British Museum* (Parliamentary Papers, House of Commons), 1860, xvi, p. 183, para. 18.
[2] For the bare bones of Dalton's life see *DNB*, vol. 2 (Oxford, 1975), 2591. A fuller appreciation of Dalton, written by his life-long friend Sir George Hill, appears in *PBA* 31 (1945), 357–73.

ORMONDE MADDOCK DALTON
Keeper: 1921 – 1928

Fig. 13.1. Ormonde Maddock Dalton (photograph: British Museum)

between 1888 and 1893 abroad, both in Europe and Asia. In the summer of 1893 he decided to return to England and, after a brief period teaching in Derbyshire, he learnt of a vacant position in the Department of British and Medieval Antiquities at the British Museum, applied, and was appointed an Assistant of the Second Class on 7 June 1895.

Dalton was initially employed on the research and development of the department's ethnographic material. He was elected a Fellow of the Royal Anthropological Institute in 1895 and was honorary secretary and editor of its *Journal* from 1896 to 1897. In 1899 Dalton published in tandem with the Keeper of the Department, Sir Hercules Read, a volume on the antiquities of Benin.[3] Although Dalton was to maintain a life-long interest in ethnography, he was next assigned to prepare a catalogue of the early Christian and Byzantine antiquities in the Museum's collection.

This volte-face was in part, as Dalton later acknowledged, a reflection of the burgeoning growth of Byzantine studies on the Continent in the 1890s, exemplified by the appearance of such periodicals as *Byzantinische Zeitschrift* and *Vizantijskij Vremennik*, as well as the works of, *inter alia*, Schlumberger, Strzygowski, Kondakov, Graeven and Smirnoff. The acquisition of the Franks Bequest in 1897 must also have acted as an additional stimulus to the publication of the collection. Sir Augustus Wollaston Franks, who had been Keeper of the Department from 1866 to 1895, was a polymathic collector whose interests ranged from subjects as diverse as neolithic flints to Chinese porcelain.[4] His bequest of 3,330 objects included many early Christian and Byzantine pieces of great importance: in all, about a third of the catalogue subsequently compiled by Dalton comprised objects either acquired by Franks during his keepership or from his bequest. Dalton took a little over two years to complete a catalogue of the just over a thousand objects which constituted the Museum's collection and it represents, given Dalton's purely classical background, a rapid and formidable accumulation of expertise in the field of Byzantine archaeology.[5]

Dalton's research in the pre-war period remained primarily concerned with the early Christian and Byzantine collections. His publications, many of which appeared in the *Proceedings* of the Society of Antiquaries, to which he had been elected a Fellow in 1899, are too numerous to list here. Altogether unconnected with the Byzantine collections, Dalton also

---

[3] C. H. Read and O. M. Dalton, *Antiquities from the City of Benin and from other parts of West Africa in the British Museum* (London, 1899).

[4] See David M. Wilson, *The Forgotten Collector: Augustus Wollaston Franks of the British Museum* (London, 1984).

[5] O. M. Dalton, *Catalogue of Early Christian Antiquities and Objects from the Christian East in the ... British Museum* (London, 1901).

published a book on the Oxus Treasure in 1905,[6] a gallery guide to the Museum's medieval antiquities in 1907 and, in 1908, the first of three novels under the pseudonym W. Compton Leith.[7] Three further publications on the British Museum's collections of ivories[8] and finger-rings[9] and the McClean bequest of medieval antiquities to the Fitzwilliam Museum[10] further extended Dalton's area of expertise.

It was the appearance, however, in 1911 of Dalton's *magnum opus*, *Byzantine Art and Archaeology*, that established him as the pre-eminent expert in the field in Britain.[11] Over 700 pages long, the volume covers virtually every aspect of Byzantine art, with the exception of architecture. Although the bulk of the volume is descriptive, Dalton does address the leading theoretical controversy of the time, the 'Orient oder Rom' debate. In essence this concerned the respective roles played by the East and Italy in the development of early Christian art. Dalton, who saw no formal break in continuity between pagan and Christian art, favoured the East, though with some circumspection:

> If the question 'Orient or Rome' only implies that the elements of Roman Christian art were not indigenous to Italian soil, if it only assumes that for their due development a continued foreign influence was necessary, the answer must be given in favour of the East ... The researches of recent years in Anatolia, in Syria, and Egypt have enabled us to adjust more nicely the balance between the East and Rome. The Eastern scale sinks lower with the growth of knowledge; when Mesopotamia has been explored it must sink lower yet.[12]

Dalton's attitude to Byzantine art, while broadly sympathetic, was not without its ambiguities. His classical education made him ill disposed to certain of its features: sculpture and the glyptic arts too often betray themselves as 'a pensioner of antiquity, living upon traditional types';[13] in the art of the goldsmith he saw the disappearance of 'the old Greek insistence on beauty of form ... it was no longer necessary to model well, or to apply to the creations of the goldsmith's craft that fine restraint

---

[6] O. M. Dalton, *The Treasure of the Oxus* (London, 1905).

[7] *Apologia Diffidentis* (Cambridge, 1908).

[8] O. M. Dalton, *Catalogue of the Ivory Carvings of the Christian Era in the ... British Museum* (London, 1909).

[9] O. M. Dalton, *Franks Bequest. Catalogue of the Finger Rings in the ... British Museum* (London, 1912).

[10] O. M. Dalton, *Fitzwilliam Museum, McClean Bequest: Catalogue of the Medieval Ivories, Enamels, Jewellery, Gems and Miscellaneous Objects Bequeathed to the Museum by Frank McClean, M.A., F.R.S.* (Cambridge, 1912).

[11] O. M. Dalton, *Byzantine Art and Archaeology* (Oxford, 1911).

[12] Dalton, *Byzantine Art*, 8–9.

[13] Dalton, *Byzantine Art*, 118.

which preserved the Greeks from the love of empty splendour', and the abandonment of 'the honest solidity of early Roman work'.[14] On the other hand he saw in the art of the Macedonian and Comnenian periods a flowering of the arts 'as brilliant and prolific' as in any preceding era and that

> every branch of art was now illustrated by important works, and that the repute of Byzantium was raised to a height never previously excelled. In mosaics, in architecture, in painting, in almost all the minor arts, the period was one of prolonged and distinguished achievement.[15]

He concluded his introductory chapter with the following paean:

> The absolute greatness of Byzantine art will be affirmed or denied in proportion as the relationship of art to ethics is regarded as near or remote ... In its theory Byzantine art is at one with our great mediaeval art; in its practice, though upon different paths, it attains an equal level of achievement.[16]

Dalton was also concerned with the promotion of Byzantine studies outside the immediate orbit of the Museum. This manifested itself primarily through his involvement in the Byzantine Research and Publication Fund. As early as 1907 Sir Hercules Read, under Dalton's prompting, had written to John Coote Adams, the administrator of the Estate Offices of Viscount Astor, a generous patron of archaeological excavations both in Britain and abroad, about the Fund. He described its intentions as such:

> a number of well-equipped young scholars are desirous of working at Byzantine archaeology in the Mediterranean area ... The subject of the investigation would be principally the Byzantine churches many of which are falling into ruins, and so far the matter is urgent: and it is proposed to publish the results in a uniform manner.

The Fund was formally established in 1908 under the presidency of Edwin Freshfield. The Committee appointed to administer the Fund had Read as the president and Dalton as joint secretary with the architect Robert Weir Schultz.

Dalton was particularly concerned that the Fund and the Museum should involve themselves in promoting excavations abroad, particularly in Egypt. In a 1910 review of Oscar Wulff's catalogue of the Byzantine antiquities in the Königliches Museum in Berlin, Dalton remarked on the astonishing rapidity with which that museum was accumulating

---

[14] Dalton, *Byzantine Art*, 540.
[15] Dalton, *Byzantine Art*, 16.
[16] Dalton, *Byzantine Art*, 37.

early Christian sculpture from Egypt, and lamented, 'It is especially to be regretted that the illustration of the Christian art of Egypt should not be systematically pursued by the country which has for years occupied the position of the most favoured nation in the Nile valley'. To this end negotiations were entered into with Sir Guy Maspero in Cairo whereby both the British Museum and the Fund might be involved, with appropriate concessions, in future excavations at either Saqqara or Bawit. This came to nothing, but the Museum and Fund did secure the early Byzantine cemetery site of Wadi Sarga, approximately fifteen miles south of Assiut. This was excavated by the American archaeologist R. Campbell Thompson during the winter of 1913–14, but was discontinued with the outbreak of the First World War. Thereafter Dalton's involvement on the Committee became tenuous due to what one of his colleagues alluded to as 'squabbles'; he further remarked that Dalton was 'clearly immensely disappointed with the failure of a cherished project'.

Dalton's research was severely circumscribed by the outbreak of war, although his catalogue of gems in the British Museum, a project on which he had been working for a number of years, appeared in 1915,[17] as did a translation, with introduction, of the letters of Sidonius Apollinaris. The war years saw Dalton involved first in voluntary work with the Red Cross, then seconded by the Admiralty to work in their Intelligence Department: here he produced maps and guides to the more obscure parts of the empire which were involved in hostilities. This work was curtailed in 1916 when he was knocked down by a bus outside the Royal Geographical Society and suffered a severe leg injury. To his experiences in hospital we owe the last of his three novels, *Domus Doloris*, a meditation on the nature of pain.

In 1921 Dalton succeeded Sir Hercules Read as Keeper of the Department. Both the administrative demands of the Keepership and the reorganization of the department's galleries led, not surprisingly, to a diminution in the rate of Dalton's publications. Much of his attention in the early 1920s was given over to substantially revised editions of the gallery guides to both the Byzantine and medieval collections. Dalton's last major contribution to Byzantine studies, *East Christian Art*, appeared in 1925.[18] This covered much the same ground as his earlier *Byzantine Art and Archaeology*, but also included a long chapter on architecture. In this he provides an able summary of the latest ideas on such problems as the origins of the vault and dome, and the evolution of the cruciform church plan. Dalton was largely content with presenting the conflicting argu-

---

[17] O. M. Dalton, *Catalogue of the Engraved Gems of the Post-Classical Periods in the ... British Museum* (London, 1915).

[18] O. M. Dalton, *East Christian Art: A Survey of the Monuments* (Oxford, 1925).

ments and, in summation, allowing that their 'relative truth or falsehood has yet to be finally determined'. If anything, he favoured an intermediate approach which attached more importance to Hellenistic rather than Italian or Oriental influences.

The last two years of Dalton's keepership saw him issue a substantially revised edition of the Oxus Treasure and a translation of the *History of the Franks* by Gregory of Tours. By now, however, Dalton was tiring of both the Museum and Byzantium. In 1927 he wrote: 'I want to reaffirm the opinion that the B.M. suffers no essential loss by my disappearance. I may have exaggerated when I once told you that the long Byzantine furrow had broken my back; but it has permanently bowed it!' After his retirement in 1928 Dalton's interest in Byzantine matters faded completely. The following year he wrote: 'it is true that my soul is still deadly weary of Byz. archaeology. I may recover in time, but at present I feel as though I would rather subscribe to *anything* else'. Projects to translate Fortunatus and the Dialogues and Letters of Sulpicius Severus failed to come to fruition, and although as late as 1939 he agreed to serve on the British Byzantine Archaeological Committee it was only on the condition that he was 'not to be bothered with active attendance'. Dalton spent his retirement years, first in Bath, and then from 1940 in the White Cottage at Holford in the Quantocks, where he died on 2 February 1945.

14. R. M. Dawkins and Byzantium

Peter Mackridge

If one were to give a paper on Dawkins as a Byzantinist, there would be rather little material to talk about. I would call Dawkins a medievalist rather than a Byzantinist. He was not particularly interested in what is known as Late Antiquity; what he found attractive was Greek culture from about the end of the iconoclast period onwards.

As my title makes clear, I shall be dealing with Dawkins's work on Byzantine culture. I shall not be touching upon his work on Frankish-occupied Greek lands, such as his edition of the fifteenth-century Cypriot chronicle of Makhairas.[1]

R. M. Dawkins (1871–1955) was the first holder of the Bywater and Sotheby Professorship of Byzantine and Modern Greek Language and Literature at Oxford from 1920 to 1939. In his first job as an archaeologist he excavated a number of sites in Greece, notably the sanctuary of Artemis Orthia at Sparta and the Minoan city at Palaikastro in eastern Crete. His long stay at the British School at Athens, of which he served as Director from 1906 to 1914, brought him into contact with post-classical Greece, and he soon became a historical linguist and dialectologist of the Greek language in its medieval and modern phases. His most notable contribution to this field was his timely study of the Cappadocian dialects of modern Greek[2] – timely because within a decade of its publication the speakers of these dialects had been ejected from their homeland and resettled in various parts of Greece. Through the collection of folk-tales as material for linguistic study he gradually became interested in mod-

---

[1] *Leontios Makhairas, Recital concerning the Sweet Land of Cyprus, entitled 'Chronicle'*, edited with a translation and notes by R. M. Dawkins (Oxford, 1931).

[2] R. M. Dawkins, *Modern Greek in Asia Minor* (Cambridge, 1916).

From *Through the Looking Glass: Byzantium Through British Eyes*, eds Robin Cormack and Elizabeth Jeffreys. Copyright © 2000 by the Society for the Promotion of Byzantine Studies. Published by Ashgate Publishing Ltd, Gower House, Croft Road, Aldershot, Hampshire, GU11 3HR, Great Britain.

ern Greek folklore, and he published three substantial volumes of Greek folk-tales after his retirement from his Oxford Chair. From his early years until the outbreak of the Second World War Dawkins was a keen and adventurous traveller, and he was both fortunate and pleased that in those days the terms of the Bywater and Sotheby Professorship not only permitted him to absent himself from Oxford for one term each year, but positively encouraged him to travel. He was particularly fond of exploring the northern and southern shores of the Mediterranean, and more especially the eastern parts of the Greek world (Asia Minor and the eastern islands), which held a special fascination for him – those areas that had not become part of the modern Greek state, or which had only recently been incorporated into it.

In his capacity as an archaeologist during the years 1902–12 Dawkins published a number of short papers on Byzantine finds that had come to his notice during his excavations: these include notes on Byzantine pottery from Sparta, on churches and cruciform fonts, and on an inscription on the land walls of Constantinople.[3]

Later, as a folklorist, he published a substantial and fascinating article entitled 'Ancient Statues in Mediaeval Constantinople' in the journal *Folk-Lore* in 1924. Here Dawkins displays the attitude that was beginning to characterize his work at the time, namely his interest in the way that oral traditions and popular beliefs associated with objects from an earlier age express the living and constantly evolving dialogue between past and present. In writing this article his interest was to emphasize that while comparatively few inhabitants of and visitors to Constantinople read books, all of them, learned and unlettered alike, encountered in their daily lives the remains of the ancient pagan world in the form of statues, columns, reliefs and inscriptions. Dawkins showed how these remains were regarded and explained, paying particular attention to the beliefs that were attached to them. His chief sources were the eleventh-century work *De Signis*, attributed to George Kodinos, and the appendix, entitled *De Aedeficiis*, to Niketas Choniates' account of the Fourth Crusade, whose adherents were responsible for destroying the majority of these ancient remains. Dawkins was particularly attracted by what he called 'mediaeval fancy',[4] and he considered that the Byzantines' attitude to these ancient remains summed up very concisely their view of the ancient pagan world in general. He concentrates on the idea that these remains were regarded as having been made by

---

[3] 'Byzantine pottery from Sparta', *ABSA* 17 (1910–11), 23–8 (with J. P. Droop); 'Cruciform fonts in the Aegean area', *ABSA* 19 (1912–13), 123–32; 'An inscription on the land-walls of Constantinople', *Byzantion* 7 (1932), 239–40.

[4] 'Ancient statues in mediaeval Constantinople', *Folk-Lore* 35 (1924), 217.

the powerful magicians of the days of heathendom; days of which the legend had remained that men were then more learned and had more power over nature than Christians had, or perhaps ought to have ... The men of old were regarded as wonder-workers, magicians, doctors, and sages, and the works they left had been endowed by their arts with all sorts of magical powers and gifts, or could give lessons in wisdom to such as were able to read their meaning ... There seems to have been no feeling that the relics left by the ancients were impure or ungodly, but simply that they were at once beautiful, of greater power and efficacy in the sphere of magic than anything which could be produced by men of their own day.[5]

Some monuments were believed to prophesy disaster, others to protect the city from its enemies. Dawkins also lists the enchanted statues, many of which were reputed to be the work of Apollonius of Tyana: for example a gnat, a fly, and other insects made of bronze that protected the city from real insects, or a statue of an eagle that kept away snakes. He also points out that the medieval Greek word for an enchanted statue, τέλεσμαν, is the origin of the French and English word *talisman*, which comes directly from the Greek (with the medieval final -*n*) and not, as the etymological dictionaries tell us, by way of Arabic. Dawkins concludes that his study has thrown light on what he calls the 'mental outlook' or 'mental attitude' of the Greeks of Constantinople – what historians of a school later to be developed in France would call their *mentalité*.

Dawkins's activities as a teacher of Byzantine and modern Greek language and literature at Oxford have left few traces, although he did give lectures on Byzantine historiography, some typescripts of which are still to be found in his archives. Hardly any undergraduates read modern Greek during his tenure, but he did supervise the research of one graduate student, namely Georgina Buckler's D.Phil. thesis on 'The Intellectual and Moral Standards of Anna Comnena', which was published in 1929.[6] It is amusing to think that the only doctoral thesis supervised by this notorious misogynist was the work of one woman historian about another.

Dawkins's fascination with the medieval probably went back to his boyhood, when the work of William Morris exercised an especial charm on him, although he was far from sympathetic to the socialist aspects of Morris's ideas. Later, when Dawkins was a Fellow of Exeter College, he no doubt felt that Morris, who had been an undergraduate there, was still a haunting presence. For Dawkins, as for Morris, the medieval past was an exotic country to which he was fond of escaping from the modern world. It may have been Morris's Romantic fascination for the Ice-

---

[5] 'Ancient statues', 217–18.
[6] Georgina Buckler, *Anna Comnena: a study* (Oxford, 1929).

landic sagas that first awoke Dawkins's interest in Norse literature and lore. At all events, during his undergraduate studies in electrical engineering at King's College, London, and while he was working for an electrical engineering firm at Chelmsford immediately afterwards – a profession imposed on him, much against his will, by his father – Dawkins spent much of his spare time learning Icelandic. He had already taught himself Sanskrit, and he went on to learn enough Finnish to read the Kalevala; he also studied Middle Irish as well as Egyptian and Hebrew grammar – all this before he went to Emmanuel College, Cambridge, as a mature undergraduate around 1899 to read Classics.

Many years later, around 1930, Dawkins put together the first draft of what he intended to be a book entitled 'The Varangian Guard at Constantinople', which was initially based on two lectures that he had given at Pembroke College, Cambridge, in 1929. He considered himself almost uniquely qualified to write on this topic, since he was in a position to read both the Byzantine and the Norse sources; and we should bear in mind that the Icelandic sagas which relate the legendary adventures of the Varangians in rhapsodic terms were familiar to him well before he was able to read the Byzantine Greek writers who provide a more sober, laconic and sometimes contemptuous view of the blond barbarians who formed the imperial bodyguard. Of this projected book the Dawkins archive, housed in the Taylor Institution Library at Oxford, contains not only the 1930 draft but a revised and expanded version he made in 1944, consisting of 155 typed pages.[7] Although he omits it in the second version, the first draft begins with a reference to Walter Scott's novel *Count Robert of Paris* (1832). This mention is an indication that Scott's novel, no doubt read when he was a boy, may have been one of Dawkins's initial sources of inspiration for his study of the Varangians, and indeed for his interest in Byzantium in general, which always retained an element of Romantic medievalism. As I have said in an earlier paper,[8] Dawkins was interested in the Greece of Herodotus rather than the Greece of Thucydides: Asia Minor and the eastern islands interested him more than the mainland of Greece, and particularly the southern Greek mainland. As a historian, too, Dawkins was a follower of Herodotus rather than Thucydides; he was more interested in gathering together stories

---

[7] Since Dawkins's death a monograph on the Varangians, written by an Icelandic contemporary of his, has appeared in English: Sigfús Blöndal, *The Varangians of Byzantium: an aspect of Byzantine military history*, translated, revised and rewritten by Benedikt S. Benedikz (Cambridge, 1978). Neither the author of the book (who lived from 1874 to 1950) nor the reviser appears to have been aware of Dawkins's project.

[8] See Peter Mackridge, '"Some pamphlets on dead Greek dialects": R. M. Dawkins and Modern Greek dialectology', *ABSA* 85 (1990), 201–12, where further biographical details on Dawkins may be found.

based on oral tradition than in establishing the positive truth concerning events of the recent or distant past.

His book on the Varangians is divided into seven chapters, with the following titles: (I) The Sources and the Scandinavians in Russia, (II) The Routes to Mickelgard,[9] (III) Harald Hardrada, (IV) Sigurd the Crusader, Rognvald of Orkney and the later Varangians, (V) The Varangians in Service at Mickelgard, (VI) The Influence of Mickelgard on the North, (VII) Conclusions. His Norse sources are chiefly the thirteenth-century *Heimskringla* by Snorri Sturlason and other sagas such as the *Saga of the Earls of Orkney*. Although Scandinavian mercenaries had already been employed by the Byzantines for some time before this, Dawkins writes that the first Byzantine reference to the Rus fighting on the Byzantine side is in Kedrenos, who refers to an incident in 1034, while the two most notable relevant documents also date from the eleventh century, namely the appendix, entitled Νουθετητικὸς πρὸς τὸν βασιλέα, to Kekavmenos's Στρατηγικόν, which contains an account of Harald Hardrada, and Pseudo-Kodinos, who gives a detailed account of the part played by the Varangians in the ceremonial of the imperial court. It is characteristic of Dawkins's work as a historian that he confines himself to published sources.

After an account of his sources, Dawkins goes on to summarize the activities of the Northmen in Byzantine lands, first as raiders, then as traders, and then as pilgrims as well as guardsmen. After this, Dawkins traces the three chief routes taken by Northmen on their journey to Constantinople and Jerusalem: the eastern route (or 'Varangian way') via Novgorod and Kiev, the western route via the straits of Gibraltar, and the southern route by land via Rome. He then goes on to tell the story of Harald Hardrada, the only Varangian to be mentioned by name in a Byzantine text, who was no doubt of particular interest to Dawkins because of his death in England, at the Battle of Stamford Bridge in 1066. Dawkins compares the accounts of Harald's exploits in the saga devoted to him with the material provided by Kekavmenos and with other more reliable historical evidence, noting that the Norse accounts are not the work of eyewitnesses but are 'a reflexion of his fame in Norway rather than very precise historical evidence'.[10] The account of Harald's triumphal entry into Constantinople as it is related in the saga contrasts starkly with Kekavmenos's assurance that Harald was quite content with the lowly title bestowed on him by the emperor. But Dawkins is interested just as much in legends attached to Harald which cannot have originated

---

[9] Mickelgard was the Norse name for Constantinople.

[10] 'The Varangian Guard at Constantinople' (unpublished typescript in the Dawkins Archive, Taylor Institution Library, Oxford), 1944 version, dossier III, p. 2C.

from his actual exploits as in those activities for which we have historical evidence. Nevertheless, on the subject of Harald, Dawkins refers to the runic inscription on the lion which used to stand at the Piraeus but was removed to Venice by Francesco Morosini in 1688, pointing out that although Bugge's reading of the runes in 1875 discredits the original reading by Rafn in 1856, later writers have persisted in repeating the erroneous view that the inscription mentions Harald by name; according to Dawkins, there is nothing to suggest that the runes mention Harald Hardrada; they are so badly effaced that probably no reading at all is possible. Blöndal concurs with Dawkins that the connection with Harald is a modern myth.[11]

Chapter IV indicates Dawkins's recurrent difficulties in structuring a book. King Sigurd the Pilgrim and Earl Rognvald of Orkney, to whose stories the chapter is chiefly devoted, were not members of the Varangian guard, but pilgrims to Jerusalem who visited Constantinople during the course of their journey; yet the Herodotean Dawkins cannot resist the temptation of including them in his book. As for the later history of the Varangians, Dawkins was possibly attracted to them once again by their English connections. Pointing out that in their latter years, before the Crusade of 1204, the Varangians were made up primarily of Englishmen, Dawkins writes that the English serving Alexios Comnenos at the siege of Durazzo in 1081 had the satisfaction of fighting against the kinsmen of their Norman conquerors who, led by Robert Guiscard, were attacking the Greek empire. Dawkins goes on to summarize the duties and position of the Varangians in Byzantine ceremonial, as these are given by Pseudo-Kodinos, and ends by referring to what the Northmen brought back home with them from Byzantium: tales of the wonder of the East; gold and jewellery; weapons; church ornaments and the relics of saints; and – a typically Dawkinsian touch – even the word *fengari* (moon) which appears in poetic Icelandic.

Dawkins concludes by stressing the successful way in which the Byzantines kept the Varangians under control, and he contrasts this favourably with the failure of the Sultans of Egypt and Turkey to deal with their own foreign imperial guards, namely the Mamelukes and the janissaries respectively. Finally, despite their reputation for heavy drinking, Dawkins comes down very much in favour of the Varangians, whose Norse ferocity, harnessed by the Byzantines, was directed to a constructive goal. He concludes his book with the following words:

> In the service of the emperors the Northmen helped to give stability to the one city which preserved through the savagery of the middle ages the lamp

---

[11] Blöndal, *Varangians*, 230–33.

of learning for the future: a better occupation for the 'ira Normannorum' than was to be found in their own seas, where for the same motives they were apt to throw themselves into the opposite scale, burning and destroying such frail arks of learning as Iona and Lindisfarne, where Celtic monks kept some remains of the learning and culture of a better age.[12]

In an unpublished autobiographical note, Dawkins writes that he abandoned his Varangian project for two reasons. First, he realized that his lack of Russian prevented him from reading essential sources, and in particular Vasilievski's book on the Varangians. I cannot take this reason entirely seriously, since, given his background in languages, one would have thought he could have learned enough Russian to read what he needed to; though it would obviously have been more difficult for him to do so by this advanced age. His second reason is more convincing, since it accords with the impressions that we gain from reading his work: he found 'writing historical narrative was quite beyond my powers'.[13] Elsewhere in his autobiographical reminiscences he writes: 'My love of accumulation and spadework and a certain reluctance I have to formulate wider ideas have always made the production of short papers ... more congenial to me than anything else.'[14] Indeed, he published five brief articles, based on parts of his Varangian book, four of them between 1935 and 1937, and the fifth in 1947.[15] It is characteristic that all four were published as a result of requests to him to provide a contribution to homage studies dedicated to other scholars.

The last work by Dawkins devoted to Byzantine culture that I want to talk about is his book *The Monks of Athos*, published in 1936. Like the titles of some of its chapters, the title of this book is rather misleading. According to the Preface, his original intention was

to bring together a collection of legends of Athos. As I proceeded, I found it necessary to include some account of the life of the monks and the constitution of the monasteries, as a background to the legends and traditions. Then, as I intended from the beginning to trace out as far as I could the historical foundation of these legends, I could not dispense with ac-

---

[12] 'The Varangian Guard', first version, dossier VII, p. 8.

[13] Dossier 6(5), Dawkins Archive, p. 89.

[14] Dossier 6(5), Dawkins Archive, p. 93.

[15] 'The visit of King Sigurd the Pilgrim to Constantinople', in *Eis mnemen Spyridonos Lamprou* (Athens, 1935), 55–62; 'Greeks and Northmen', in *Custom is King: essays presented to R.R. Marett* ... (London, 1936), 35–47; 'The Catalan Company in the traditions of Mount Athos', in *Homenatge a Antoni Rubió i Lluch: Miscellània d'estudis literaris històrics i lingüístics*, vol. 1 (Barcelona, 1936), 267–70; 'An echo in the Norse sagas of the Patzinak war of John II Komninos', *Annuaire de l'Institut de Philologie et d'Histoire Orientales et Slaves* 5 (1937) [Mélanges Emile Boisacq, vol. 1], 243–9; 'The later history of the Varangian Guard: some notes', *JRS* 37 (1947) [Papers presented to N. H. Baynes], 39–46.

counts of the foundation of monasteries and of the development of monastic life on Athos.[16]

Thus the book is not so much about the monks themselves as about the
legends which they and their predecessors have told with reference to
their monasteries and to the icons they contain. Dawkins travelled to
Mount Athos on four occasions, in 1905, 1931, 1933 and 1935, during
which he spent a total of more than ten weeks in the monasteries. It is
clear from these dates that most of the preparation for his 'Athos book'
was carried out in the first half of the 1930s. In the book Dawkins tells
us nothing about the personalities and opinions of the monks he encountered there, nor about the daily routine and annual round of their
chapel services and the purpose and content of these observances; he
also says little about Orthodox theology except in so far as it concerns
the cult of icons. *The Monks of Athos* is partly a description of the
topography and flora of the Athos peninsula, and of the buildings and
paintings of the monasteries, but most of all it is concerned with the
legends attached to the monasteries and their icons, particularly the
foundation legends of the monasteries – how, for instance, their founders were miraculously guided to build the monastery in a specific spot
– and the stories that tell how certain icons came to be painted or how
they found their way to their present home – often by miraculous
means to escape destruction or desecration – and the miracles associated with these icons.

For Dawkins, legends were images of the past still living in the present,
and, as I have said, he was more interested in these than in what we
might think of as more 'objective' history. He says himself that in *The
Monks of Athos* he collected together legends he heard orally and those he
found in books, but made no use of unpublished material. He hardly
ever refers to manuscript documents such as *typika* and chrysobulls,
whose contents do not seem to have interested him. He prefers what he
terms 'pious fancy' to the 'slender thread of fact'.[17] By this time Dawkins
was a fully fledged folklorist, and he was interested in living legend as
the organic and constantly developing mediation between past and
present, a reflection of what people think and believe in the present
about the past, and as such a kind of knowledge about the past, different
from the knowledge contained in historical documents, but equally valid
and valuable. We might compare the way in which historical linguistics,
in which Dawkins had been trained, reconstructs earlier stages of a language on the basis of later evidence, except that we do not know of any

---

[16] *The Monks of Mount Athos* (London, 1936), 9.
[17] *The Monks*, 86.

strict laws governing the development of legends in the way that linguistic laws govern the historical development of languages.

Dawkins writes that the 'Athonite mentality' has led to

> a corpus of traditional stories which can hardly be paralleled anywhere
> else in the world of the present day, and it is all the more worthy of our
> attention, because the relation of tradition to the actual facts of history
> throws a practical and not merely a theoretical light on the value of leg-
> end: we are testing the value of what is usually called folk-memory.[18]

On Athos Dawkins found what he believed to be the survival of the
medieval Byzantine world-view, preserved more or less intact by virtue
of Ottoman domination, which had protected Athos from the inroads of
Western modernity. The Athonite 'way of thinking, or rather ... way of
feeling', he believed, could teach us much more about the Byzantine
mentality than could the study of Byzantine history as it is recorded in
texts. We notice here an interest in collective mentalities which, together
with his distaste for history as a narrative of political events, brings him
close to the *Annales* school that was being developed in France at the
same time. It is a significant coincidence that two chapters of Marc Bloch's
La société féodale, published three years after Dawkins's Athos book, are
entitled 'Les façons de sentir et de penser' and 'La mémoire collective'
respectively; we may compare Dawkins's references to 'way of thinking,
or rather way of feeling', and 'folk-memory', which I have just quoted.

Once again Dawkins's difficulties in organizing his material are clearly
visible in *The Monks of Athos*. In the opening pages he claims that his
book is not laid out like a travel book, but that he uses a rough chronological scheme, connecting sets of legends to the relevant historical events
out of which they have grown, but allowing himself 'such digressions as
would be natural to men talking freely and discursively on any subject';[19] we may note the emphasis on the 'orality' of his own discourse.
Yet in practice he is constantly caught between chronological, spatial and
thematic principles of structuration: the chronological principle entails
the telling of the history and legends of the monasteries in chronological
order; the spatial principle shows in his inclusion of the various legends
and lore attached to a particular place and its environs; while the thematic principle involves grouping together similar legends from different times and places. In fact there are many divagations from the topic in
hand, generally motivated by geographical propinquity.

Dawkins was no doubt attracted to the Athonite monasteries, particularly the cenobitic ones with their central courts and their chapels, by the

---

[18] *The Monks*, 43.
[19] *The Monks*, 26.

similarities with the collegiate life of Oxford and Cambridge with which he was familiar. The Holy Mountain of Athos, as a confederation of exclusively male monastic communities devoted to prayer and meditation, appealed to Dawkins's taste for male company and his desire for a refuge from modernity. He expresses his admiration and sympathy for the simplicity of the monks' hard work and devotion; and it is characteristic that he writes, after describing a scene of monks working in a little cottage workshop, that the sight would have pleased William Morris.[20]

Yet Dawkins tried to avoid imposing his own preconceptions on the monastic life of Mount Athos. As he states in the 'Conclusion' to his book, he was concerned to provide the picture that an Orthodox pilgrim would get of the Holy Mountain, not the view obtained by the scholar, art historian, or other traveller from the West. He is especially sensitive to the significance of icons in Orthodox worship, and particularly the spiritual and emotional importance of icons to the ordinary Orthodox worshipper. Perhaps the finest part of his book is the central chapter, entitled 'On icons in general', which I would recommend to anyone wishing to understand why icons have played such an important role in the history of the Orthodox Church. In a later chapter, having related the legend of how the pious empress Theodora, wife of Theophilos the last of the vigorously iconoclast emperors, had preserved some icons of the Virgin for her own personal and secret adoration, Dawkins conveys the attitude of the ordinary Orthodox Christians who hear this legend:

> Greek pilgrims through all the centuries since the coming of the Turks would feel at once their kinship with the pious empress; the struggle against the evil iconoclasts would seem only an earlier chapter of their own resistance to Islam; and in a sense this was true, for both iconoclasm and Islam were enemies from the partly Semitic east, facing and opposing the more sensuous, more intimate, perhaps more material way in which the Greeks have always looked at religion and man's relation to eternity. Byzantine theologians had shown that the service of respect and love paid to icons was bound up with a true faith in the Incarnation and the redemption of God's created, material world: the common man has never had much need to think of these ancient subtleties; it has been enough for him to know that both Turks and iconoclasts rejected and scorned the holy icons, to him the cherished emblems of the orthodox faith.[21]

Dawkins frequently stresses the unique position of Mount Athos, which has preserved Byzantine Orthodoxy from both the Moslem East and the innovative West.

---

[20] *The Monks*, 143.
[21] *The Monks*, 242.

Dawkins's book, with its well-informed, sympathetic yet sober view of the 'Athonite mentality', succeeded in correcting many of the misconceptions that the English-speaking public might have gained from reading Robert Byron's mannered, opinionated and whimsically anti-Western book *The Station* (1928) and Ralph Brewster's scandal-mongering exposé of Athonite life in *The 6000 Beards of Athos* (1935).

For Dawkins Mount Athos allowed the visitor, through its legends, an insight into 'a way of looking at the world which has come down to us straight from the Byzantine age'.[22] His work on Athos and on the eastern regions of the Greek world had convinced him of the continuity of language, belief and culture between Byzantium and the simple Greeks of his own day, particularly those who were untainted by Western influence and a pseudo-classical veneer such as they tended to acquire in the educational establishments of the modern Greek state. Although he had been a classicist he shows little interest in the alleged continuity of Greek culture from antiquity to modern times; but in the unity of a culture that the Oxford undergraduate syllabus justly calls 'Medieval and Modern Greek' Dawkins had an unshakable belief.

---

[22] *The Monks*, 379. For the sake of completeness, I might add that the proposed 'second edition' of *The Monks*, of which a typescript dated 1940 is to be found in the Dawkins Archive, incorporates material from Ktenas and Barsky, and makes connections with legends from the rest of Greece. He made an article out of the material added to this 'second edition': 'The arrangement of wall-paintings in the monastery churches of Mount Athos', *Byzantina-Metabyzantina* 1 (1946), 93–105. In addition Dawkins published some supplementary short notes to his book in the form of an article: 'Notes on life in the monasteries of Mount Athos', *HThR* 46 (1953), 217–31.

Section IV

Other perspectives

15. Du Cange and Byzantium

Jean-Michel Spieser

It is surprising that Charles Dufresne, sieur Du Cange, is so little known. In 1988, the three-hundredth anniversary of his death, which is also the three-hundreth anniversary of his *Mediae et infimae graecitatis glossarium*, was hardly celebrated. Du Cange was born in Amiens in Picardie, and the Société des Antiquaires de Picardie was alone in commemorating this anniversary. An issue of their *Bulletin* was devoted to him.[1] An unsigned note tells the reader that this Société received few encouraging responses when trying to arrange a commemoration, and was unable to organize a Du Cange exhibition. This same note recalls, in contrast, the erection earlier, at the initiative of the society, of a statue of Du Cange, and its inauguration with speeches by the representative of the minister, the mayor of Amiens, the president of the Académie des Inscriptions et Belles-Lettres and other representatives of the academic world – even a salvo of artillery was fired. That had all happened on 19 August 1849, a date which is not far away from one of the rare general publications on Du Cange.[2]

Du Cange was more celebrated by Latinists than by Byzantinists. In 1978, a colloquium was held on the lexicography of medieval Latin, on the occasion of the anniversary of the publication of the *Glossarium mediae et infimae latinatis*.[3] Some notes at the end of the volume are devoted

---

[1] Th. Girard, 'La formation intellectuelle de Du Cange et ses premiers travaux', *Bulletin de la Société des Antiquaires de Picardie*, 1988 (3rd quarter), 79–88; M. Evrard, 'Lettres de Du Cange à Nicolas Du Mont (1671–1676)', ibid., 89–128.

[2] L. Feugère, *Etude sur la vie et les ouvrages de Du Cange* (Paris, 1852). For a useful bibliography on Du Cange, see E. Bury and B. Meunier, eds, *Les Pères de l'Eglise au XVIIe siècle* (Paris, 1993), 529.

[3] Y. Lefèvre, ed., *La lexicographie du latin mediéval et ses rapports avec les recherches actuelles sur la civilisation du Moyen-Age, Paris 18–21 octobre 1978* (Paris, 1981), 11.

From *Through the Looking Glass: Byzantium Through British Eyes*, eds Robin Cormack and Elizabeth Jeffreys. Copyright © 2000 by the Society for the Promotion of Byzantine Studies. Published by Ashgate Publishing Ltd, Gower House, Croft Road, Aldershot, Hampshire, GU11 3HR, Great Britain.

to Du Cange and to the exhibition which was then held at the Bibliothèque Nationale.[4] This commemoration of the Latin *Glossarium* should remind us that Du Cange was not primarily a Byzantinist, even if we suppose that this word could have meant anything in the seventeenth century. His first interest was in fact in genealogy and in heraldry. He elaborated a very modern approach to heraldry, which could have brought it to the standard actually achieved only in the nineteenth century, but that part of his work remained unpublished.[5]

As far as we know, it is only in the 1650s, and perhaps not before 1655, that Du Cange, at the age of forty-five, began dealing with the Eastern world. It was French history which led him to Constantinople: his concern was to provide a new edition of Villehardouin and to translate it in 'modern' French. He expanded it in a *Histoire de l'empire de Constantinople sous les empereurs français* published in 1657.[6] In both the 'Epître au Roy' which opens the book and in the 'Preface', Du Cange underlines the links between the history of France and the history of Constantinople, because of the domination of the empire of Constantinople – these are the very words he uses – by French emperors. This was the justification for the book being published as part of the 'Byzantine du Louvre', whose official beginning was 1648. In the same place Du Cange exhorted Louis XIV to wage war on the Turkish empire, because he had a claim to occupy the imperial throne, earlier occupied by his ancestors. Du Cange explained also that the conquest of Constantinople in 1204 was not due to the ambition of the French kings: God used them to punish the Greeks for their cruelty and the purpose of the conquest was not to rule more countries, but to re-establish an emperor who had been blinded, and to unify the Church. Du Cange went so far in his glorification of the French past that he presented the conquest of Constantinople as a kind of successful remake of the storming of the Capitol by the Gauls, and he finished by saying that the subjects of the king were as courageous and generous as the Gauls and those who took Constantinople put together. He also alluded to the traditional refusal of the French kings to admit that the Habsburgs had a just claim to the imperial title and throne.

More than twenty years later, in 1680, Du Cange used the same themes when he dedicated his *Historia Byzantina* to Colbert. Again, Louis XIV is

---

[4] See *La lexicographie*, 497–500, a speech by Ch. Samaran, given in front of Du Cange's house; M. Pastoureau, 'Du Cange héraldiste', *La lexicographie*, 501–4; D. Bloch, 'Charles Du Cange (1610–1688), Exposition organisée à l'occasion du tricentenaire du *Glossarium mediae et infimae latinitatis* par la Bibliothèque Nationale. Catalogue', *La lexicographie*, 509–47 (511–12, with a chronology of his life).

[5] M. Pastoureau, 'Du Cange héraldiste'.

[6] At the turn of the sixteenth to seventeenth century Blaise de Vigenère had, in the same way, published an edition of Villehardouin and one of Chalcocondyles.

portrayed as the sovereign most able to defeat the Turks; France was the equal of the Eastern Empire. France, added Du Cange, has even a superiority over the Eastern Empire because of the stability of the succession, a remark which points to one of the reasons which made Byzantine history so difficult to understand in early modern Europe.

All these assertions recall the imperial ideology which, over the centuries, was to a greater or lesser extent stressed by the kings of France, and which played a by no means negligible part in Louis XIV's policy. But first we have to consider what value is to be given to the kind of declarations contained in dedicatory epistles, a very rhetorical genre indeed. For instance, A. Pertusi would dismiss such words as flattery.[7] He quotes the editor of the 'Correspondence administrative' at the time of Louis XIV, who stressed the omnipresence of this flattery.[8]

A. Pertusi tries to distinguish between the intellectual work done by scholars and the use made of it by the powerful. He seems to mean that scholars write their books as if they were far away from the concerns of the world that surrounds them. Such a dichotomy is no longer acceptable from an epistemological point of view. We can no longer see the evolution of the intellectual world as a history of ideas without trying to find out its connections with the surrounding world, which is not only a stage for the growing of ideas, but a component of intellectual evolution.

By chance, we have an insight into the connections between Du Cange and Colbert. Du Cange presented what we may call a draft for his dedication of the *Historia Byzantina* to Colbert through the abbé Gallois: the letter, dated 10 October 1679, in which Gallois reports to Du Cange Colbert's response to his demand, is preserved in the Bibliothèque Nationale.[9] Du Cange also asked for a new start for the 'Byzantine du Louvre': no volume had been published for almost ten years, since 1670, when the editions of Kinnamos and Paulos Silentarios (the description of Hagia Sophia), and of 'Niketas Akominatos', both volumes by Du Cange himself, were issued. Colbert, as Gallois reports, accepted the dedication. It is interesting to note that, despite his pleasure, Colbert asked Du Cange to cancel the end, 'ce que vous trouverez barré avec du crayon'. Alas, we do not know what displeased Colbert. Gallois tried also, he says, to persuade Colbert to manifest some interest in the continuation by Du Cange of the *Histoire Byzantine*, i.e. the 'Byzantine du Louvre'. In fact, over the following years some volumes, essentially by Du Cange

---

[7] A. Pertusi, *Storiografia umanistica e mondo bizantino* (Palermo, 1967), 89–90.

[8] G. B. Depping, *Correspondance administrative sous le règne de Louis XIV* (Paris, 1855), xxix (quoted by Pertusi, *Storiografia*, 89, n. 241).

[9] H. Omont, 'Du Cange et la collection byzantine du Louvre', *REG* 17 (1904), 33–4 (Paris, B.N., MS fr. 9503, ff. 147–8).

himself, were published by the Imprimerie Royale, first of all the volume whose dedication was the point of this letter.

It is obvious that Du Cange looked for the patronage of Colbert and the king to promote the edition of the collection of Byzantine history. It is also obvious that he thought he could base his request on the assumption that Byzantine history could support the greatness of France and the king's claim to the imperial crown. There is, however, little evidence to show that the beginning of the 'Byzantine du Louvre' has anything to do with this issue or this ideology: nothing has been found concerning this project in the published letters of Cardinal Mazarin;[10] nor does the famous *Protreptikon* by Father Philippe Labbé, which is considered as an 'ouverture' for the Parisian Corpus, touch on this topic.[11] Nevertheless, the suspicion that 'la grandeur de la France' has something to do with the decision to print this collection at the Imprimerie Royale, founded some years earlier in 1640,[12] is actually supported by a text, published by Omont and quoted by Pertusi, a 'mémoire' sent in March 1648 to Chancellor Séguier by Joseph-Marie Suarès, Bishop of Vaison.[13] Suarès recalls an older project he had, when he was the librarian of Cardinal Barberini, to publish from the Greek historians a history 'ab orbe condito ad captam usque a Turcis Constantinopolim' – from the creation of the world to the fall of Constantinople. Leo Allatius promised to help and mentioned his project in a book published in 1633.[14] At the end of this 'mémoire' Suarès recalls the rights of Louis to be the common emperor of East and West. He notes the recent conquest of Flanders, country of Baldwin and Henry, Emperors of Constantinople, and Catherine, from whom, says Séguier, Louis XIV inherited a claim to this throne: she was daughter of Philippe, Emperor of Constantinople (he means Philippe of Taranto), and granddaughter of Baldwin II. She was consecrated empress of Constantinople by Boniface VIII and then married to Charles of Valois, father of the Valois kings.[15]

It is well known that the kingdom of France laid claim to the imperial title as late as the seventeenth century, even if traditional historiography

---

[10] Pertusi, *Storiografia*, 89 and n. 242.

[11] For this text, see H. Omont, 'La collection byzantine de Labbé et le projet de J.-M. Suarès', *REG* 17 (1904), 18–32, esp. 18–19 and 19, n. 1.

[12] For a general view of the problem of books, printing and publishing in the seventeenth century, see the relevant chapters in R. Chartier and H.-J. Martin, *Histoire de l'édition française*, vols 1 and 2 (2nd edn) (Paris, 1990). A older still account provides valuable information on the Imprimerie Royale: A. Bernard, *Histoire de l'Imprimerie Royale du Louvre* (Paris, 1867).

[13] See Omont, 'La collection byzantine'.

[14] Pertusi, *Storiografia*, 82–5, uses this text to challenge the priority and the legitimacy of Labbé's claim to have been the first to have the idea of the Parisian Corpus.

[15] Omont, 'La collection byzantine', 31–2.

pays little attention to this aspect of royal propaganda, judging it a secondary topic.[16] But its importance should not be excessively downplayed. In 1658 the French king tried to be elected emperor; more generally, the obvious and lasting presence of the imperial theme cannot be without meaning in the very carefully organized propaganda of Louis XIV.[17] The Byzantine objects bought on behalf of Louis are part of this.[18] The relevance of this theme may be shown through the reactions of the Habsburg court every time some French initiative could be understood as a claim to the imperial dignity.[19] As late as the time of Leopold's death in 1705, the Habsburg crown was concerned to present itself as the legitimate successor of the Roman emperors. At his funeral, the statue of Leopold was surrounded by those of Constantine, Theodosius, Charlemagne and Otto I.[20]

Is it enough to establish a link between this imperial ideology and French interest in Byzantine history? Following A. Pertusi, it could be said that it has no significance. The seventeenth century was a time of great intellectual development and achievement. Despite the attacks from Cartesianism, a strong and optimistic erudition was able to develop in France.[21] Progress in historical knowledge has its place in general progress; and as Pertusi stressed, to deal with the history of the East or of Antiquity was less dangerous than to deal with national history, because of censorship and all kinds of other pressures from the State.[22] This conception reveals more what a scholar believes himself to be than what he really is. The opportunities that were given to the 'antiquarians' belong to what P. Bourdieu calls 'le champ des possibles', which is a part of the reality of the world in which they live and which can never be avoided. Du Cange's enormous breadth of interest may help to illustrate this point: many of his writings, as has already been said, were left unpublished, notably his work on heraldry.[23] What is more, in 1678, three years

---

[16] See, for this approach, G. Zeller, 'Les Rois de France candidats à l'Empire. Essai sur l'idéologie impériale en France', *Revue Historique* 53 (13) (1934), 257–311 and 497–534.

[17] See now P. Burke, *The Fabrication of Louis XIV* (Yale, 1992); for this particular topic, see pp. 192–4. See also, for more references, F. Waquet, *Le modèle français et l'Italie savante (1660– 1750)* (Collection de l'Ecole française de Rome 117; Rome, 1989), 328, n. 115.

[18] R. Cormack, 'The French construction of Byzantium: reflections on the Louvre exhibition of Byzantine art', *Dialogos* 1 (1994), 28–40, especially at 35.

[19] See the incident mentioned by Burke, *Fabrication*, 169, at the occasion of the birth of the second son of Leopold in 1682. See also F. B. Polleross, 'Sonnenkönig und österreichische Sonne', *Wiener Jahrbuch für Kunstgeschichte* 40 (1987), 239–56.

[20] F. B. Polleross, *Das sakrale Identifikationsporträt. Ein höfischer Bildtypus vom 13. bis zum 20. Jahrhundert* (Worms, 1988), 73.

[21] Waquet, *Le modèle français*, 297–332.

[22] Pertusi, *Storiografia*, 91.

[23] See note 5 above and also Girard, 'La formation intellectuelle'.

before trying to dedicate his *Historia byzantina* to Louis XIV, Du Cange
proposed to Louvois a project for the publication of the historians of
France, which was not accepted.[24] It should be obvious that the responses he received did influence his work and that an opposite answer
would have changed the perception we have of Du Cange. It would also
be absurd to say that Du Cange organized his researches in a way de-
signed to please a protector and gain advantages. But with the wide
range of his interests, too wide to let him believe that he could bring
everything to achievement, he took advantage of the opportunities given
by those who had power to pay and to print.

It could also be said that first Mazarin and then Colbert was moved by
a general desire to promote 'les arts et les lettres'. They chose to help the
very few who were interested in Byzantine history, because this field of
knowledge was not yet well explored. Far from promoting the ideology
of French power, interest in Byzantium would, in this case, have been
alive only among a narrow circle of priests and antiquarians helped by
the authorities. It is easy to show that this is not true. The use of Byzantine subjects in the *belles-lettres* is well attested and it is much larger than
is usually known; it deserves a study in itself. It points to a more substantial diffusion of Byzantine material in broader circles.[25] Even in the
field of narrative history, there is good evidence of a larger diffusion than
the names of Du Cange, Labbé and others lead us to expect.

One example is Louis Cousin, author of an *Histoire de Constantinople*
in French, which was in fact a translation, for those who did not know
Greek, of some Byzantine historians; in his work, however, there is no
evocation of the imperial theme.[26] Father Louis Maimbourg will be
more useful for our purpose.[27] This Jesuit, having spent the greater

---

[24] Published with notes by the abbé Gallois (who seems to have played a part on this
occasion too) in Father Lelong, *Bibliothèque historique de la France*, ed. Fevret de Fontette
(Paris, 1711), vol. 3, xviii–xxiii (quoted after Omont, *REG* 17 [1904], 33, n.1).

[25] See Pertusi, *Storiografia*, 93–103. Campistron, a writer of tragedies, wrote in 1685 an
'Andronic'; see N. Hepp, 'De la littérature à la rhétorique. Campistron, imitateur de
Racine', in Ch. Wentzlaff-Eggebert, ed., *Le langage littéraire au XVIIe siècle. De la rhétorique à
la littérature* (Tübingen, 1991), 295–306 (I thank Prof. Hepp for this reference).

[26] *Histoire de Constantinople depuis le règne de l'Ancien Justin jusqu'à la fin de l'Empire, traduite
sur les originaux grecs par M*^r*. Cousin, président en la cour des Monnoies, dédiée à Monseigneur de
Pompone, Secrétaire d'état*. The first edition was published in 4o, in eight volumes, between
1672–1674. The first volume of a new edition was published in Paris in 1685.

[27] For a general presentation of Maimbourg, even if the main part of the article deals
with a narrower topic, see G. Declercq, 'L'histoire du calvinisme de Louis Maimbourg et
sa réception par la critique protestante', in L. Godard de Dondville, ed., *De la mort de
Colbert à la révocation de l'Edit de Nantes: un monde nouveau?* (XIVe colloque du Centre
Méridional de rencontres sur le XVIIe siècle; Marseille, 1985), 199–32; and s.v. Maimbourg
in *Dictionnaire de Théologie Catholique* IX² (1927), col. 1656–61.

part of his life teaching rhetoric, preaching and indulging in polemics with the Jansenists and the Protestants, began writing history in 1673, at the age of sixty-three. He claims his wish was to write a history that would be as pleasant to read as a novel. Actually he was sometimes criticized for this, being accused of writing for the 'grand public', as we would say today. In just a few years (he died in 1686) he did write a good deal of history, mostly on two topics, the history of the Roman empire – we have to see in which sense he uses this word – and the history of heretics. He also managed to connect the two topics, because he tried to show that all stages of the decline of the Roman empire were due to some kind of heresy. As he himself suggested, we can link together four of his books that are of special interest to the question we are concerned with and almost the first he wrote as a historian. He began in 1673 with the *Histoire de l'arianisme*, followed in 1674 by *Histoire de l'hérésie des iconoclastes et de la translation de l'empire aux Français*. Then came *Histoire du schisme des Grecs* (1677), and, eventually, *Histoire de la décadence de l'empire après Charlemagne et des différends des empereurs avec les papes* (1679). These books were very successful and new editions were issued several times.

In this last book, in the address to the king, he speaks about the pitiful decline of the Roman empire.[28] The point is that this empire is not what we call the Roman Empire, not even our Byzantine Empire, but the German Roman Empire. In the first book of this work, he explains that the *Histoire de l'arianisme* was written to show how, after Constantine's death, the Western Empire fell into decline because of Arianism; the *Histoire de l'hérésie des iconoclastes* was devoted to 'the marvellous renovation of the western Empire when it was translated to Charlemagne'.[29] The *Histoire du schisme des Grecs* was supposed to explain the decline of the Eastern Empire as a consequence of this schism, beginning with Photius. Finally, the point of this present book, he continues, is to show how the Western Empire declined again. That happened in several stages: first the French emperors and the Roman Church, sustained by these emperors, reached the peak of their power; but mistakes and failures by the successors of Charlemagne and by the French nobles eventually allowed the Saxon kings to take over the empire. The final decline was due to those German emperors who tried to weaken the Roman Church.[30]

---

[28] *Histoire de la décadence*, f.5* v (edn 1681).

[29] *Histoire de la décadence*, 2. In the *Histoire de l'hérésie des iconoclastes* he had written that God provoked this translation of the Empire to the West (and to France) to punish the Greeks (Maimbourg uses the word 'Greek') for having rebelled several times against the Church (*Histoire de l'hérésie des iconoclastes* 4th edn [1683], 3).

[30] *Histoire de la décadence*, 3 (edn 1681).

We do not have to look for all the implications of Maimbourg's ideas, nor for the links between them and the relationship between the French Crown and the Roman Church. But we see again, and this time not in a small 'antiquarian' milieu, the French monarchy presented as the legitimate heir to the Roman Empire.

However, and this is the last objection we have to answer, French imperial ideology may have something to do with the Roman Empire, but not with the Byzantine one. And in fact, some features of Louis XIV's propaganda seem to give credibility to this argument: when in 1661 Louis XIV played the part of an emperor in an equestrian parade, he was called Imperator Romanorum. When he is portrayed like a new Apollo, he is again closer to Roman than to Byzantine models. We have pictures of Louis as Apollo, as Alexander, even as the Good Shepherd. We have no picture of him wearing the *loros*, even if Byzantine imperial pictures with the *loros* were known, at least by the learned.[31]

But in the world of the seventeenth century, what we call the Byzantine Empire is still, as it was in the Middle Ages, nothing other than the Roman Empire. We could say that Louis XIV had no reason to show himself as a Byzantine emperor: he did not claim to be the successor to the Byzantine emperors, but, like them, he saw himself as the successor of the Roman emperors. The place of antiquity in the intellectual world of the seventeenth century is not an easy problem and it would go beyond the scope of this chapter to discuss this issue. The contradiction between pagan or classical antiquity, and Christian antiquity, the contradictory use of this Christian antiquity by what can be called Gallican scholarship and Jesuit scholarship gives a picture in which the richness of details, the diversity of individualities, sometimes also the weight of traditional ideas, may hide the overall evolution.[32] Out of all this complexity one strong idea emerges, which is shared by many peoples for most of the seventeenth century, and that is the feeling of a continuity with the classical world, a continuity which was not interrupted by the changing fortunes of the Roman Empire.[33]

We have to insist on this point because the common historical sensibility of our day presents the Renaissance as a break with the past. True, it

---

[31] In one of his letters, Du Cange speaks of the 'loros, le manteau entortillé des empereurs grecs'.

[32] See, e.g., M. Fumaroli, 'Temps de croissance et temps de corruption. Les deux antiquités dans l'érudition jésuite française du XVIIe siècle', *XVIIe Siècle* 33 (1981), 149–68. The articles of B. Neveu are also valuable; some of the most important may now be found in B. Neveu, *Erudition et religion aux XVIIe et XVIIIe siècles* (Paris, 1994).

[33] On this problem, see the reflections of B. Neveu, 'Archéolâtrie et modernité dans le savoir ecclésiastique au XVIIe siècle', *XVIIe Siècle* 33 (1981), 169–84 (repr. in B. Neveu, *Erudition*, 365–83).

was; but the complexity of the evolution is sometimes hidden because we forget too readily how this picture of the Renaissance as a completely new world was only constructed slowly, and particularly in the nineteenth century by Michelet and Burckhardt.[34] On the contrary, many aspects of the intellectual life of the seventeenth century are to be understood only if we are aware that antiquity was felt as close, and its experience and its world of representation as still valuable.

We can now understand how the very notion of empire could still be important in terms of foreign relations for the European states and in the diplomatic language through which the states tried to assert their place and their role. The true empire, on which the legitimization of a contemporary empire was grounded, was of course the empire of Rome. Byzantium was not considered as a historical reality in itself, but what we call in French an 'avatar' of the Roman Empire.

Hence we may say that the interest in Byzantine history during the seventeenth century belonged to and was promoted by a cluster of facts, some of which – those related to the idea of empire and the glorification of France – I have tried to bring to light here.[35] Of course this cluster is more complex, and the situation of the Church and of religious thought should also be considered if one wants to be exhaustive. I have chosen to stress the idea of empire, which has seemed to me less prominent in existing literature. The validity of this connection finds some confirmation in the fact that what we may call a decline in Byzantine studies (even if, as I have tried to show, this vocabulary is in a sense anachronistic) coincided with a shift in the choice of models for the French king. Peter Burke speaks of 'a crisis of representation'.[36]

The background is again a very broad topic, ranging from the 'Querelle des Anciens et des Modernes' to the 'crise de la conscience européenne' to quote a famous book, which marks an epoch in the historiography. What concerns us here is that it is well known that Louis XIV and those who organized his propaganda reined back the use of models from Antiquity. Not only was the Roman imperial model used with more discretion, but Louis also gave up identification with Alexander the Great;

---

[34] W. K. Ferguson, *La Renaissance dans la pensée historique* (Paris, 1950), 163–6 (Michelet) and 167–80 (Burckhardt) (date and pagination from the French edition of *Renaissance in historical thought*).

[35] It is interesting to note that this motivation was still understood in the nineteenth century. See Father Ch. Daniel, *Les jésuites historiens au dix-septième siècle* (Lyon, 1879), a book where the author, a Jesuit himself, gives valuable information on Sirmond, Petau, Labbé, Baluze and generally on the Byzantine Corpus; also on Du Cange, as a pupil of the Jesuits and for having a brother who became a Jesuit. He stresses several times the fame gained for France by these men who dealt with Byzantine history.

[36] Burke, *Fabrication*, 125–33.

Saint Louis replaced both.[37] Scholars do not agree on the precise time when this happened. Such changes usually span a period of time, and anticipation, like archaism, brings confusion into the perception of such evolution. Burke reproduces an anonymous painting of Louis XIV identified with Saint Louis,[38] dated as early as 1660; on the other hand, the erection of a huge equestrian statue for Louis, as late as 1691, has still something to do with Roman imagery.[39] The edition in 1668 of a medieval biography of Saint Louis, dedicated to the king and comparing both sovereigns, may also be recalled.[40] But it can be assumed that the shift was in process in the 1670s and at the beginning of the 1680s.[41]

Now these are the very years when the Byzantine Corpus of the Louvre showed no progress. The contrast with the 1640s has to be stressed: great amounts of money were spent for the volumes then issued. We know that more than 300,000 pounds were spent in the Imprimerie Royale between 1640 and 1647.[42] Of course, this information does not help directly, because the Corpus had not yet begun. But if 1647 saw the lowest expense, in the following years, despite the financial crisis due to the war with Spain, many volumes which constituted the Byzantine Corpus were issued. If around 1680 Colbert allowed (which means paid for) new publications, starting with the *Historia byzantina*, only a few editions by Du Cange and Combefis were possible. And after Du Cange's death, the story of the 'Byzantine du Louvre' virtually comes to an end.[43]

It is amazing to see that progress in knowledge of Byzantine historians is contemporaneous with the last time that the French monarchy tried to assert its right to the imperial crown. What is more, the last volumes of this enterprise, as well as what is today considered as the crowning achievement of this time for our field, Du Cange's *Glossarium*, are the result of a request justified by arguments which were actually no longer supported.

Before leaving Du Cange and his century, we must also note that what is often seen as the most usual point of view on Byzantium, the stress of the idea of decline, seems not to have a central place in the historiography of this period. In 1685 L. Cousin published the first volume of what he

---

[37] Ch. Grell et Ch. Michel, *L'Ecole des Princes ou Alexandre disgrâcié* (Paris, 1988).

[38] Burke, *Fabrication*, 193, fig. 87; see also 113 and 115.

[39] Burke, *Fabrication*, 115 and fig. 50–51 (pp. 116–17).

[40] Burke, *Fabrication*, 113.

[41] See the discussion in Burke, *Fabrication*, n. 41.

[42] I found these figures in Bernard, *Histoire de l'imprimerie royale* (as in note 12 above), 73. He quotes Sauval, *Histoire et recherche des antiquités de la ville de Paris* (3 vols, Paris, 1724), vol. 2, 41.

[43] Only the Nikephoros Gregoras, edited by Boivin in 1702, and Banduri's *Imperium Orientale* (2 vols, 1711) were added.

called 'History of Constantinople', actually a translation of Byzantine historians.[44] In his foreword ('Avertissement'), he insists on the interest of this History and of the greatness of the Empire, even after Constantinople was its new capital.

The idea and the word of decadence were nevertheless already linked with Byzantium: Du Cange himself wrote a text called 'De la Grandeur et de la Décadence de l'Empire de Constantinople', which was presented to Colbert, but which, as far as I know, was never published.[45] But obviously the very title given by Blaise de Vigenère to his French translation of Chalcocondyles, 'Histoire de la Décadence de l'empire d'Orient', had a much more lasting influence. It is surely not by chance that Chalcocondyles is mentioned several times by Voltaire in his *Essai sur les moeurs*.[46] As everybody knows, the topic of decline and decadence dominated all other points of view in the eighteenth century. And, of course, in a renewed conception of history, where it was men who played the major part, not God, the end of an important empire gave much to think about.

But the titles just mentioned, the one chosen by Vigenère and that of the unpublished text of Du Cange, invite us to give some attention to something that appears quite puzzling when we take heed of the vocabulary used in the eighteenth century. Following our own usage, I have spoken about Byzantium. But you may have noted that in the titles of seventeenth-century historians other expressions are more frequently used. The history of the words 'Byzantium' and 'Byzantine' from the fifteenth century on has not yet been written, and it is also beyond the scope of this chapter to deal with this question. Nevertheless, it is obvious that Du Cange uses it principally when he writes in Latin: see his *Historia Byzantina* and the first part of this book *Familiae Byzantinae*. But in French and even in Latin, alongside 'histoire byzantine' – I wonder if anywhere he writes 'empire byzantin' – he makes equal use of 'empire de Constantinople', 'bas-empire', 'empire oriental', 'empire grec'. I would say that this is not only due to a desire for stylistic variation, but that it has something to do with a concept that is still undefined. His hesitations appear distinctly when he invites Colbert, in the 'Epître' mentioned above, to look at the Roman world: he adds 'vel graecanici potius (quando de illo hic praesertim sermonem instituimus)'.[47] The same expressions

---

[44] See above, note 26.

[45] See Bloch, 'Du Cange' (as in note 4 above), 518. This autograph manuscript (Paris, B.N., MSS, n.a.fr. 10245) was shown in the 1978 exhibition.

[46] Voltaire, *Essai sur les moeurs et l'esprit des nations*, ed. R. Pomeau (Paris, 1963), vol. 2, 981, s.v. Chalcocondyle.

[47] 'or better the Greek one, because it is about that we shall here speak principally'.

are used by Maimbourg. I confess I have not read all the histories he wrote, but again I wonder if ever he used the word 'byzantine': he speaks of the Western and Eastern Empire, of the Roman Empire of course, and of the Greek Empire (which seems quite definitely to mean the Eastern Empire, after the 'translation', and is also a way to stress that this empire no longer holds a legitimate position). In the same way Nikephoros Phocas is called 'a perfidious Greek'.[48] This vocabulary asserts that Byzantium was not yet an independent or very definite concept, and may be used to confirm that, as we said before, the seventeenth century was a time when older representations and the conception of a lasting Roman Empire were still valid.

---

[48] Maimbourg, *Histoire de la décadence*, 65.

16. Pyotr Ivanovich Sevastianov and his activity in collecting Byzantine objects in Russia

Olga Etinhof

Pyotr Ivanovich Sevastianov was one of Russia's most distinguished travellers and collectors of Christian antiquities in the nineteenth century.[1] Born in 1811 in the town of Krasnoslobodsk in Penza province, he was a son of Ivan M. Sevastianov, a merchant of the first guild and an honorary citizen. Pyotr was first educated at home, with the participation of M. M. Speransky. In 1822 he was sent to Staff Captain I. I. Galushka's Moscow boarding school for sons of the gentry. From 1826 to 1830 he studied at a law faculty of Moscow University, obtaining a candidate's degree in moral–political sciences. For the next twenty years, from 1831 to 1851, Pyotr Sevastianov worked as a lawyer, in the Caucasus (1833–36), in Moscow (1836–38) and in St Petersburg (1838–51), rising to the rank of actual state councillor. During this time he travelled extensively in Russia, mostly in the south, and in the Caucasus, Georgia in particular. In 1840 he made his first long-awaited journey abroad.

As the documents in his archives show, Pyotr Sevastianov first began collecting as a pastime during his travels.[2] Not possessing a historical

---

[1] G. Vzdornov, *Istoria otkrytia i izuchenia russkoi srednevekovoi zivopisi XIX veka* (Moscow, 1986), 83–9; G. Dovgallo, 'Sobranie P. I. Sevastianova (f. 270)', in J. Rykov, ed., *Rukopisnye sobrania Gosudarstvennoi biblioteki imeni V. I. Lenina. Ukazatel 1/1 (1862–1917)* (Moscow, 1983), 139–51; G. Dovgallo, 'P. I. Sevastianov – archaeolog, puteshestvennik, sobiratel', *Moskovsky zurnal* 1 (1993), 11–17; G. Dovgallo, 'Sobiratelskaia deiatelnost P. I. Sevastianova (po materialam ego lichnogo archiva)', in A. Komech and O. Etinhof, eds, *Drevnerusskoie iskusstvo. Balkany. Rus* (St Petersburg, 1995), 242–56; I. Kyzlasova, 'Novoie o collecii P. I. Sevastianova', *Voprosy slaviano-russkoi paleographii, kodikologii i epigraphiki, Trudy Gosudarstvennogo istoricheskogo museia* (Moscow, 1987), 71–6; J. Pyatnitsky, 'Proishozdenie icon s Aphona iz sobrania P. I. Sevstianova', *Soobschenia Gosudarstvennogo Ermitaga* 53 (1988), 42–4; J. Pyatnitsky, 'O proishozdenii nekotoryh icon iz sobrania Ermitaga' in A. Bank and V. Lukonin, eds, *Vostochnoie Sredizemnomorie i Cavcas IV–XVI vv. Zbornik statei* (Leningrad, 1988), 126–40.

[2] Dovgallo, 'Sobranie Sevastianova', 142.

From *Through the Looking Glass: Byzantium Through British Eyes*, eds Robin Cormack and Elizabeth Jeffreys. Copyright © 2000 by the Society for the Promotion of Byzantine Studies. Published by Ashgate Publishing Ltd, Gower House, Croft Road, Aldershot, Hampshire, GU11 3HR, Great Britain.

education, he collected as a self-taught amateur. Yet his interests were so broad and his enthusiasm so great, that he soon acquired extensive knowledge of palaeography, archaeology and history and devoted himself entirely to collecting objects of Christian archaeology. In 1851 he retired. From 1851 to 1866 Pyotr Sevastianov travelled abroad to Western and Southern Europe and to East Christendom. He collected all sorts of items: medieval manuscripts, early printed books, icons, fragments of frescoes, mosaics and architectural decoration and sculpture, church plate, enamels, textiles, coins, seals and so on.

He did not collect works of art only. The making of a collection for him had no distinct educational character. His collecting was aimed broadly at the 'furtherance' of sciences, so he included everything that could be of interest to Christian archaeology and to the study of monuments, such as maps, topographical plans, moulds, casts, copies, sketches, drawings, written descriptions and photographs. He was interested not only in Orthodox objects (Byzantine, Slavonic and Russian), but also in those relating to East Christian and West European culture.

Pyotr Sevastianov concentrated above all on works from Palestine, Rome and, in particular, Mount Athos, where his main collections were formed. In Palestine he made a study of the topography of the Holy Land. He then commissioned a plan in relief of Jerusalem which was exhibited in Russia in the 1850s. Among his travels to Italy the last visits to Rome, particularly that of 1863, were the most fruitful for his collection. He made five visits to Mount Athos: in 1851, 1852, 1856–57, 1858, 1859–60.

In 1856–57 Sevastianov began systematic work at Mount Athos at his own expense. This work went well beyond an amateur pastime and attracted attention of scholars. In 1858 an exhibition was organized in Paris of his collections from Mount Athos comprising medieval objects, drawings and photographs that produced a great impression. Sevastianov's travels to Mount Athos and his collecting activity coincided with the beginning of the spread of photography in Europe and Russia. He mastered photography in France and Russia and was one of the first enthusiasts to make extensive use of photography in the study of antiquities. On 5 February 1856 at a meeting of the Paris Academy of Inscriptions and Letters, he presented a paper 'On photography with respect to archaeology', which was greeted with great interest.[3] He proposed preparing photographic copies of medieval manuscripts in the major European collections, thereby making them accessible to scholars everywhere. In

---

[3] 'O svetopisi v otnoshenii k archeologii. Zapiska P. I. Sevastianova, chitannaia 5 fevralia 1858 g. v sobranii Parizskoi Akademii nadpisei i slovesnosti', *Izvestia Imperatorskogo Russkogo archaeologicheskogo obschestva* 1 (5) (1859), cols 257–61.

1859 Sevastianov's collections of photographs and copy-drawings were exhibited at the University in Moscow and in the Synod in St Petersburg.

Sevastianov's studies of the Orthodox culture of Mount Athos coincided with the intentions of the official circles in Russia to maintain the Orthodox tradition. Russia, the successor of post-Byzantine heritage, in the middle of the nineteenth century attached great importance to its role as the Orthodox Empire. His Majesty Emperor Nicholas and the Most Holy Synod in the 1850s undertook the preservation of Russian ecclesiastical treasures (and Byzantine objects as its source), their scientific description and the making of drawings of them. Then the Synod proceeded to another task, namely, to the founding of a museum of Christian iconography and to the equipping for this purpose of an artistic–archaeological expedition to Mount Athos. At the same time in 1856, the President of the Academy of Arts, Grand Duchess Maria Nikolaevna, introduced at the Academy a new class of 'Orthodox icon-painting', the organization of which was entrusted to Prince G. Gagarin. In order to 'equip' the class, state funds were allocated for the purchase of books, icons and copies of Byzantine painting. Maria Nikolaevna also had the idea of sending an expedition to Mount Athos. It was decided to organize this expedition from the Academy of Arts, the cost to be shared jointly with the Synod.[4]

Thus Sevastianov's private activity became official. He first received money from Grand Duchess Maria Nikolaevna, and after the 1859 exhibitions in Moscow and St Petersburg from the Synod and the empress's personal fund. He was also given the task of reproducing the earliest monuments of Mount Athos as models of church art. These funds enabled Sevastianov to organize an expedition to Mount Athos in 1859–60, which lasted fourteen months. The Synod commissioned Sevastianov 'to engage primarily in making copies of icons of the eighth and ninth centuries and, if possible, to authenticate the dating of these icons with a certificate from the elder brethren of the monasteries where the icons were found'.[5] In the work of Mount Athos the recommendations of the Archaeographical Commission of the Academy of Sciences were also taken into account. It provided instructions as to which monuments of architecture, painting, sculpture and literature the collector should look for: 'The Archeographical Commission need primarily acquisitions which relate to Russia, from the earliest times up to the year 1700 inclusively … and documents relating to other Slavonic lands.'[6]

---

[4] A. Gavrilov, 'Postanovlenia i rasporiazenia sv. Synoda o sohranenii i izuchenii pamiatnikov drevnosti (1855–1880)', *Vestnik archaelogii i istorii Peterburgskogo archaeologicheskogo instituta* 6 (1886), 60–63; *Imperatorskaia Akademia hudozestv (1764–1914). Jubileiny spravochnik* 1 (St Petersburg, 1914), 44–5; G. Dovgallo, 'P. I. Sevastianov', 13–15.

[5] Gavrilov, 'Postanovlenia', 60–63.

[6] Dovgallo, 'P. I. Sevastianov', 13.

The expedition, which was an international one, included copyists, topographers and photographers. It was judged necessary to have an archaeologist with a knowledge of Greek and Latin and of the dogmatic significance of Byzantine antiquities. Archimandrite Porfiry Uspensky was to have joined the expedition in this capacity. In a letter to N. V. Isakov, the founder of the Moscow Public Museum, Sevastianov wrote: 'Father Porfiry ... did not take part in my expedition, and the whole burden of encyclopaedic labours fell upon me alone ...'.[7] However, Sevastianov's archives contain an unpublished paper by Archimandrite Porfiry regarding Athonite antiquities entitled 'Instructions to Russian artists when visiting the Holy Mountain Athos' with a list of items in the monasteries there. Sevastianov was guided by this document in choosing objects to be photographed and studied.[8] Archimandrite Antonin Kapustin, whose knowledge and advice were most useful, spent about three months with the expedition.[9] The expedition was based in the skete of St Andrew the First-Called, founded by Andrew Muraviev, where objects were brought temporarily to be copied as well as various acquisitions for the collection. When the expedition had completed its work, all the copies, photographs and medieval objects were sent by sea from Constantinople to Odessa and from there overland to St Petersburg.

In spring 1861 Sevastianov returned to St Petersburg, where an exhibition of the items in his collection was organized that April in the Museum of Early Russian Art of the Academy of Arts. This Museum founded by Prince G. Gagarin in 1859 was intended to educate Russian artists. The exhibits consisted of 135 original icons and fresco fragments, twenty-five items of church plate and applied art, over 5,000 leaves of original manuscripts, as well as copies, sketches and plans in the form of photographs, tracings and drawings. These included about 400 tracings of icons from twelve monasteries, more than 1,000 copies of miniatures, over 350 copies of applied art, and 200 architectural drawings, maps and views of monasteries.

In 1862, when the Moscow Public and Rumyantsev Museums were being set up, Sevastianov temporarily handed over almost all of his collection to them. The objects and copies took up four whole rooms in the Pashkov house. The exhibition was opened in June 1862. The collector dreamed of uniting his collections in Moscow by bringing back the part of it still in St Petersburg and organizing a public 'Byzantine Museum'. Towards the end of his life he handed over to the Moscow Public

---

[7] Dovgallo, 'P. I. Sevastianov', 14.

[8] A. Viktorov, *Sobranie rukopisei P. I. Sevastianova* (Moscow, 1881), 114–16.

[9] 'Archaeologicheskaia expedicia na Aphon', *Sovremennaia letopis russkogo vestnika* 1 (1861), 31; Pyatnitsky, 'Proishozdenie icon', 42.

and Rumyantsev Museums the items collected during his journeys of 1862–66 in Italy and Western Europe and other items. On 5 July 1865 he made over the full rights to the ownership of his collection to the Moscow Public and Rumyantsev Museums, but the will was not drawn up in time.[10] Pyotr Ivanovich Sevastianov died in 1867, in St Petersburg, and was buried in the Alexander Nevsky Lavra.

Sevastianov's collections included manuscripts of various kinds, including illuminated ones. There were one hundred Greek manuscripts, about ninety Slavonic-Russian, mainly Yugoslavian, and acts of the Athonite monasteries; more than three hundred icons, including not only Byzantine works, but a large number of post-Byzantine: Cretan, Italian, Athonite, Serbian, Bulgarian, Georgian and Russian.[11] Most of the icons and manuscripts in the collections bore special personal labels or *ex libris* of P. I. Sevastianov.[12] Apart from twenty-five items of applied art left in St Petersburg, the catalogues of the Moscow Public and Rumyantsev Museums contain descriptions of about two hundred architectural fragments, monumental sculpture, tombstones, mosaics, frescoes, plastic art, church plate and other metal articles, enamel work, including Limoges enamels, vessels, embroidered textiles, coins and gems.

In the words of J. Pyatnitsky,

> as the inventory of his collection compiled by Sevastianov shows, he began to collect objects on Mount Athos in 1851, but most articles were acquired in 1859–60 ... Antonin Kapustin ... left a detailed diary, which throws some light on the question of how Sevastianov built up his collection. One of his sources for adding to the collection was the Sunday market in Kariai ..., where the monks sold their ware ... Hearing that 'Russian general' ... collected ancient icons and other objects, they brought him anything they could find that was old and decrepit.[13]

Being a man of substance, Pyotr Sevastianov presented expensive gifts to the monasteries, monks and monastic libraries. His archives make it possible to establish the monasteries and sketes where he himself selected items, received them as gifts and blessings, purchased them, exchanged them for modern books needed by the monasteries, and sometimes simply rescued them from destruction.[14] These are, first and

---

[10] *Otchet Moskovskogo i Rumiantsevskogo museev za 1864 g.* (Moscow, 1865), 33, 37–9; Dovgallo, 'Sobranie P. I. Sevastianova', 144.

[11] Pyatnitsky, 'Proishozdenie icon', 42–4; Kyzlasova, 'Novoie o colleccii', 71–3; I. Kyzlasova, 'Iz istorii sobiratelstva grecheskih icon v Moscve', in L. Evseeva, ed., *Postvisantiiskaia zivopis. Icony XV–XVIII vekov iz sobrania Moscvy, Sergieva Posada i Riazani. Catalog vystavki* (Athens, 1995), 25–32.

[12] Dovgallo, 'Sobranie P. I. Sevastianova', 143; Kyzlasova, 'Novoie o colleccii', 72.

[13] Pyatnitsky, 'Proishozdenie icon', 42.

[14] Dovgallo, 'Sobranie P. I. Sevastianova', 143; Pyatnitsky, 'Proishozdenie icon', 42–4.

foremost, Chilandar, Xenophontou and Zographou, the sketes of Prophet
Elijah and St Andrew, the monasteries of Pantocrator, St Paul and
Philotheou, the Great Lavra of St Athanasius, a kellia which was once a
Moldavian monastery, and also other monasteries in which he was active:
Iviron, Koutloumousiou, Vatopedi, St Panteleimon and Esphigmenou.[15]
In addition to the Athos acquisitions, his collection is known to have
included antiquities from Constantinople, fragments from Daphni, near
Athens, and from Rome, Paris and Brussels.[16] Unfortunately, however,
the provenance of many items is not known.

Icons acquired on Mount Athos include the early twelfth-century 'Apostle Philip, St Theodore and St Demetrius', and the late twelfth-century
'Holy Warriors St George, St Theodore and St Demetrius' and 'The Virgin
with prophets' – all now in the Hermitage.[17] Two late twelfth-century
icons from the lavra of St Athanasius – 'The Descent into Hell' and 'The
Descent of the Holy Spirit', now in the Hermitage – come from the same
epistilia as the 'Baptism' and the 'Dormition' published by M. Chatzidakis.[18]
The late twelfth-century icon of the 'Transfiguration' now in the Hermitage is also from Mount Athos and from the same epistilia as 'The Raising
of Lazarus', from a private collection in Athens, which also came from
Mount Athos.[19] Two icons from the Pushkin Museum in Moscow, 'The
Virgin' (mid-fourteenth century) and 'The Dormition of the Virgin' (last
third of the fourteenth century) are also Athonite, as are 'The Dormition of
the Virgin' (second half of the fourteenth century) and the mid-fourteenth-
century Constantinopolitan icon of 'The Six Feasts' – both in the Hermitage.[20] The 1363 icon of 'Christ Pantocrator with the donor brothers Alexis
the great stratopedarch and John the great primicerius', now in the Hermitage, was acquired from the storeroom of the Pantocrator monastery.[21]
From the same monastery are fragments of frescoes of the 'Head of Christ',

---

[15] Dovgallo, 'Sobranie P. I. Sevastianova', 143; Pyatnitsky, 'Proishozdenie icon', 42–4.

[16] *Catalog otdelenia drevnostei. Moscowsky Publichny i Rumyantsevsky musei* 1 (Moscow, 1906),
4, 10, 13 ff.; Dovgallo, 'Sobranie P. I. Sevastianova', 142; O. Etinhof, 'I mosaici di Roma nella
racolta di Sevastianov', *Bolletino d'arte* 66 (Marzo-Aprile, Anno LXXVI, s. VI; 1991), 29–38.

[17] Pyatnitsky, 'O proishozdenii nekotoryh icon', 131; *Aphonskie drevnosti. Catalog vystavki
iz fondov Ermitaga* (St Petersburg, 1992), 48, cat. no. 1.

[18] Pyatnitsky, 'O proishozdenii nekotoryh icon', 128–31; *Aphonskie drevnosti*, 48, cat. no.
3; M. Chatzidakis, 'Icones d'architraves provenant du Mont Athos', *DChAE* 4 (3) (1966),
377–403; M. Chatzidakis, 'L'évolution de l'icone aux 11e–13e siècles et la transformation
de templon', *Actes de XVe Congres International d'études byzantines* 3 (Athens, 1976), 170.

[19] Pyatnitsky, 'O proishozdenii nekotoryh icon', 131; *Aphonskie drevnosti*, 48, cat. no. 2;
Chatzidakis, 'L'evolution de l'icone', 188.

[20] *Vizantia. Balkany. Rus. Icony konca XIII – pervoi poloviny XV veka. Catalog vystavki.
Gosudarstvennia Tretiakovskaia galereia. Avgust- sentiabr 1991 goda. K XVIII Mezdunarodnomu
Congressu vizantinistov* (Moscow, 1991), 214, 217–18, 221–2, cat. nos. 19, 26, 32, 34.

[21] *Vizantia. Balkany. Rus*, 222, cat. no. 35.

the 'Head of an angel' and an 'Apostle', thought by J. Pyatnitsky to be fourteenth century, which are also in the Hermitage.[22] The icon of 'The Dormition of the Virgin' (second half of the fourteenth century), in the Russian Museum in St Petersburg, was bought for a hundred gold pieces at the market in Kariai.[23] The 'Virgin of Tenderness with the marginal saints' (second half of the fourteenth century), now in the Hermitage, was also acquired on Mount Athos.[24] The early fifteenth-century icon of 'Sts Athanasius the Great and Cyril of Alexandria', also in the Hermitage, is thought to have been acquired in one of the sketes of the Xenophontou monastery.[25] The icon of 'St George the Diasorite' (second quarter of the fifteenth century), now in the Pushkin Museum in Moscow, belongs to Sevastianov's Athonite collection.[26]

Other icons from Sevastianov's collections are the early thirteenth-century 'Virgin Hagiosoritissa'; the mosaic icon 'Christ Emmanuel' produced in Constantinople (end of the thirteenth century); and two icons of 'St John the Baptist', one late fourteenth- to early fifteenth-century and the other mid-fifteenth.[27] All these icons are in the History Museum in Moscow. And 'The Virgin Hodegetria' (first quarter of the fifteenth century) is in the Tretyakov Gallery.[28]

Three fragments of ceramic icons of different periods from Nikomedia, of 'St Panteleimon' and 'St George' (tenth to eleventh century) and of the 'Archangel Michael (?) on horseback holding a spear' (thirteenth to fourteenth century), were a gift from the Athonite monk Panteleimon Sapoznikov.[29] All three are now in the History Museum of Moscow. Another item from Sevastianov's collections is the enamelled reliquary cross of the late twelfth–early thirteenth century, thought to have been made in Salonika and subsequently transferred first to the collection of M. P. Botkin, then to that of Mr and Mrs Bliss, and now in the Dumbarton Oaks collection.[30] The steatite icon with the 'Ascension' (fourteenth

[22] *Aphonskie drevnosti*, 55–6, cat. nos. 70–71, 74 b. In our opinion they could be post-Byzantine like most of the objects from his collection.

[23] Pyatnitsky, 'Proishozdenie icon', 42–4; *Vizantia. Balkany. Rus*, 231–2, cat. no. 54.

[24] *Vizantia. Balkany. Rus*, 221, cat. no. 33.

[25] Pyatnisley, 'Proishozdenie icon', 42–4; *Vizantia. Balkany. Rus*, 66, cat. no. 239.

[26] *Vizantia. Balkany. Rus*, 261–2, cat. no. 110.

[27] *Iskusstvo Vizantii v sobraniah SSSR. Catalog vystavki*, vol. 3 (Moscow, 1977), 100–101, cat. no. 966; E. Gromova, 'Vizantiskaia icona Bogomateri iz socrania Gosudarstvennnogo Istoricheskogo museia' in L. Sribnis, ed., *Musei. Hudozestvennye sobrania SSSR* 6 (Moscow, 1986), 76–83; *Vizantia. Balkany. Rus*, 112, 211, 231, cat. nos. 13, 53, 112.

[28] *Vizantia. Balkany. Rus*, 254–5, cat. no. 95.

[29] *Iskusstvo Vizantii*, vol. 2, 33, cat. nos. 476–7; vol. 3, 153, cat. no. 1003.

[30] *Catalogue of the Byzantine and early Mediaeval Antiquities in the Dumbarton Oaks Collection*, vol. 2: M. Ross, *Jewelry, Enamels and Art of the Migration Period* (Washington, DC, 1965), 109–10, cat. no. 159.

century), now in the History Museum in Moscow, was also acquired by Pyotr Sevastianov.[31]

Particularly noteworthy among the illuminated manuscripts is the Four Gospels of the first half of the twelfth century, No. 8 (gr.10), now in the Russian State Library in Moscow, with three surviving miniatures, representing Christ Enthroned and the evangelists Matthew and Mark.[32]

In 1863 five crates were dispatched from Rome through the agent Fabri to the Moscow Public and Rumyantsev Museums. They contained fragments of mosaics, reliefs, icons, lamps, glass vessels, carved and engraved gems and other items from the Roman catacombs. Among these antiquities were three fragments of monumental mosaics from the old basilica of St Peter's, namely, 'St Joseph' from the scene of the 'Nativity' from Pope John VII's early eighth-century oratory, the 'Head of the Virgin' from the early thirteenth-century deesis on the façade of the basilica, and the 'Christ Child' from the tomb of Pope Boniface VIII executed by Jacopo Torriti in 1299, which are now in the Pushkin Museum in Moscow.[33] All three mosaics were acquired from the antique dealer Bonieno's shop at 192, via di Ripetta. Sevastianov's diary contains a note to this effect, and also a diagram of the arrangement of icons and mosaics on the walls of the shop. The crates also contained a late thirteenth-century historiated Tuscan icon of the Virgin, now in the Pushkin Museum.[34] It is less certain, but possible, that the crates also contained three marble reliefs acquired by Sevastianov in Italy and now in the Moscow History Museum: 'Christ with Apostles', a fragment of a fourth-century sarcophagus and two eleventh- to twelfth-century relief panels depicting peacocks.[35]

Even during his lifetime Sevastianov's collection was split up between many institutions. Apart from the Museum of Early Russian Art of the Academy of Arts in St Petersburg and the Moscow Public and Rumyantsev Museums, items went to many libraries, private owners, societies and other depositories. Parts of the collections remained abroad, particularly in the St Andrew skete on Mount Athos. These collections were redistributed later as well. In the transfers after the Revolution the provenance of items from Sevastianov's collections was often not documented. The fate of a large part of the collection in the Moscow Public and Rumyantsev

---

[31] *Iskusstvo Vizantii*, vol. 3, 161, cat. no. 1013; I. Kalavrezou-Maxeiner, *Byzantine Icons in Steatite*, (Vienna, 1985), 219, cat. no. 151.

[32] *Iskusstvo Vizantii*, vol. 2, 60–62, cat. no. 516.

[33] Etinhof, 'I mosaici di Roma', 29–38. See there the reference to an unpublished article by J. Pyatnitsky.

[34] *Iskusstvo Vizantii*, vol. 3, 16–17, cat. no. 890.

[35] *Iskusstvo Vizantii*, vol. 1, 49, cat. no. 26 ; vol. 2, 76–7, cat. no. 534 a, b.

Museums is unknown to this day, and the provenance of many well-known antiquities in Russian museums has not been established. A special archive for Pyotr Sevastianov was set up in the Russian State Library in 1953 and classified by G. I. Dovgallo in 1980. Research on it by various specialists is of great help in reconstructing the collection.

In publications during his lifetime Sevastianov's activity was greatly admired, but reference was made primarily to his collection of copies and photographs.[36] F. I. Buslaev wrote: 'It is a great patriotic feat ... to have established in our country firm foundations for the science of Christian antiquities and Christian art in relation to the Orthodox tradition.'[37] Sevastianov's drawings and photographs were widely published in newspapers and magazines of the 1860s both in Russia and France. A few decades later, however, N. P. Kondakov was most critical of Pyotr Sevastianov's amateur activity, again meaning only the collections of copies:

> It seemed ... that this collection was to have a fruitful academic destiny, but in fact ... it has been of very little use ... The remarkable energy of the collector and his devotion to the idea made people ignore the lack of success... in the scientific selection of the monuments, and at that time there was not sufficient knowledge to make a critical analysis of them... people are accustomed to regard the collection as a useful manual for icon-painters and archaeological information on iconography.[38]

Yet many young scholars in Russia learnt from Sevastianov's photographs, including N. P. Kondakov himself and D. V. Ainalov when preparing for journeys to Mount Athos. And N. P. Kondakov, G. Millet and others made use of his isolated architectural plans and referred to the drawings and photographs of manuscript illuminations in their publications.[39] The fate of the collections has, however, to a large extent been a tragic one in Russia. The copies and photographs have never been published in general or even classified. The collection is broken up and partially lost, and only a small part of it has been professionally investigated.

---

[36] A. Didron, *Annales Archéologiques* 21 (Paris, 1861), 173–9; N. Langlois, *Géographie de Ptolemée. Réproduction photoligraphique du manuscript grec du monastère de Vatopedi au Mont Athos* (Paris, 1867), 98–103.

[37] F. Buslaev, 'K protokolu XVIII 10 (2 aprelia 1867 g.)', *Vestnik obschetva drevnerusskogo iskusstva pri Moscovscom Publichnom musee* 4–5 (1874), 41.

[38] N. Kondakov, *Pamiatniki christianskogo iskusstva na Aphone* (St Petersburg, 1902), 8–9. A Viktorov wrote about Kondakov's neglect of the materials gathered by P. I. Sevastianov. See Viktorov, *Sobranie rukopisei*, 87.

[39] N. Kondakov, *Pamiatniki ... na Aphone*, 22; N. Kondakov, *Istoria vizantiiskogo iskusstva i ikonographii po miniaturam gracheskih rukopisei* (Odessa, 1876), 116, 193, 249, 254–64; G. Millet, *L'école grecque dans l'architecture byzantine* (Paris, 1916; repr. London, 1974), 54–61.

It is interesting that the collections of original works of art were referred to extremely rarely by contemporaries in Russia. Even the published report of the expedition contains no information about them. On the one hand, the collection of objects was regarded as his private activity, unlike the official mission to make copies as models of Orthodox art. On the other, ownership disputes arose between the Academy of Arts, the Synod and Pyotr Sevastianov, so the publication of information about the composition and number of the collections of originals to which the Synod might make claim was not in the interests of the Academy.[40] The Academy of Arts considered that everything brought back by Sevastianov, including the collections of works of art purchased with his own money, should be regarded as the property of the expedition of 1859–60 and belong to the Academy of Arts. About 150 original items were left at the Academy after the exhibition of 1861. Sevastianov went back to Moscow in high dudgeon. Even in the Academy of Arts' *Catalogue of the Museum of Early Russian Art*, published by V. A. Prokhorov in 1879, Sevastianov's items are not marked.[41] Only in the publications of the Moscow Public and Rumyantsev Museums in the late nineteenth and early twentieth century is tribute paid to the distinguished Russian traveller's collections of genuine objects.[42]

Pyotr Ivanovich Sevastianov's unique contribution to the study of Christian archaeology and Byzantine art lies in the creation of first-class collections which included hundreds of items and were put together with a collector's intuition, artistic taste and understanding of the subject. The task of reconstructing these fine collections still lies ahead.

[40] Pyatnitsky, 'Proishozdenie icon', 44.

[41] V. Prokhorov, *Catalog museia drevne-russkogo iskusstva* (St Petersburg, 1879).

[42] *Otchet … museev*, 50–57, 97–106, 115, 123, 128, 130; Viktorov, *Sobranie rukopisei*; S. Dolgov, 'Otdelenie doistoricheskih, christianskih i russkih drevnostei', in *Piatisdesiatiletie Rumyamtsevskogo museia v Moscve. 1812–1912. Istorichesky ocherk* (Moscow, 1913), 187–8; *Catalog otdelenia drevnostei*, 1–13, 15–30, 32, 34–5, 47–9, 53, 55–6, 59–60, 64–7, 69–73, 75, 77–106.

Section V

Encounters with the imagined Byzantium

17. Simpering Byzantines, Grecian goldsmiths *et al*.: some appearances of Byzantium in English poetry

David Ricks

This chapter's subtitle is an evident disavowal of comprehensiveness: what follows consists of recollections from rather disorderly reading and has no claim to being a mature overview. Yet a more creditable, and indeed fundamental, reason for my choice of phrase, 'some appearances', is that Byzantium, though it has opened up some interesting avenues for poets, is far from being a constant point of reference in English poetry over the last two centuries: it does indeed make only passing appearances, and it is interesting, in the larger context of this volume, to see how such appearances come about.

The 'Grecian goldsmiths' will be familiar from Yeats. But Wallace Stevens's phrase, 'simpering Byzantines', reveals an initial problem for the Byzantines in English poetry – namely, how you pronounce them – which might at ground level seem to reveal them as rather unassimilated in the literary culture. I have little doubt that in any gathering of Byzantinists at least five pronunciations of 'Byzantine' are in use. The *Oxford English Dictionary* gives 'Byzant' ine' as Byron's pronunciation, hence with that poetic authority, while indicating that 'Byz' antine' is 'frequent with classical scholars'. But Stevens's pronunciation, 'Byz'antines' (rhyming with 'tambourines'), is important for what he has to say, as we shall shortly see; so I may be forgiven for beginning this discussion – as I shall end it – with an American.[1]

Stevens's first important poem was 'Peter Quince at the Clavier' (1915).[2] The poem has been seen as illustrating 'the complex interrelationships

---

[1] The only book-length poetic response to Byzantium this century that I have come across is by the American Gjertrud Schnackenburg, *A Gilded Lapse of Time* (New York, 1992).

[2] Wallace Stevens, *Collected Poetry and Prose*, eds Frank Kermode and Joan Richardson (New York, 1997), 72–4.

between sexual and aesthetic experience' – a theme that we shall find recurring in poetic uses of Byzantium.[3] Peter Quince, the speaker, compares in the first section the desire evoked in him by music to 'the strain waked in the elders by Susanna'. In the second section, Susanna's peaceful bath is (in every sense) rudely interrupted by the elders; the fourth and concluding section is a praise to her fleshly beauty. But it is the third section which comes to our point:

> Soon, with a noise like tambourines,
> Came her attendant Byzantines.

> They wondered why Susanna cried
> Against the elders by her side;

> And as they whispered, the refrain
> Was like a willow swept by rain.

> Anon, their lamps' uplifted flame
> Revealed Susanna and her shame.

> And then, the simpering Byzantines
> Fled, with a noise like tambourines.

What are the Byzantines doing in the ostensibly Biblical context? One function is of course Stevens's characteristically witty sound patterning, in a poem, moreover, with a musical theme. The tune made by the Byzantines, like their very appearance in the poem, is as spasmodic and inconsequential as a sounding cymbal, quite unlike the clavier at the poem's beginning and the viol at its end. Further, the Byzantines seem not only useless in the practical situation, in which Susanna needs to be calmed down, but fundamentally second-order to the aesthetic issue in the poem. If they symbolize something aesthetically, it will be the un- or even anti-poetic character of Byzantium as traditionally conceived of – not least by some Byzantinists.[4] Finally, the word 'Byzantine' has a dimension of word-play, and is not without a suggestion of 'epicene': in a poem about sexual attraction, the simpering Byzantines are sexless, fleeing the scene of sexual and aesthetic tension and creativity. In every respect, then, their appearance is a fleeting one – it is as if Byzantium has made one of its rare incursions into English-language poetry only to be consigned once more to the realm of the intrinsically unpoetic.

---

[3] Herbert J. Stern in Irvin Ehrenpreis, ed., *Wallace Stevens. A Critical Anthology* (Harmondsworth, 1972), 271–6.

[4] E.g., Cyril Mango, 'Byzantine literature as a distorting mirror', in *Byzantium and its Image: History and Culture in the Byzantine Empire and its Heritage* (London, 1984).

Stevens's ironic use of the word 'Byzantine', then, comes with certain culturally inherited resonances – inherited, no doubt, largely from that greatest of ironists, Gibbon. We have only to think of current English to see how far the disparagement of Byzantium goes. The *OED Supplement* adds the following definition of 'Byzantine': 'Reminiscent of the style, manner or spirit of Byzantine politics. Hence, intricate, complicated; inflexible, rigid, unyielding'. The first occurrence is given as 1937; a contemporary example may be taken from an issue of *The Economist*, which reported that Americans 'had long since lost faith in Byzantine, big-government plans to cure society's ills'.[5] Whether or not Byzantium was a victim of big government I leave to the experts; but the flavour of such remarks is at any rate revealing.

It is hardly surprising, then, that Byzantium seems in one way poetically unpromising, and is but rarely encountered as the subject of English verse – with some intriguing exceptions, as I hope to show. Indeed, the *Columbia Granger's Index of Poetry* has only two entries under 'Byzantium': Yeats's 'Sailing to Byzantium' (1927) and 'Byzantium' (1930).[6] This very much confirms the view that Byzantium in English poetry is in a significant sense a Yeatsian monopoly. But I shall show that Yeats does have precursors and successors in this area – with some necessarily briefer remarks on his own famous recourse to Byzantium in between.

As far as pre-nineteenth-century English literature is concerned, Gibbon more or less *is* Byzantium, so we are not surprised to find the most important poetic inaugurators of the mid-nineteenth century following in his wake. In his dramatic monologue, 'St Simeon Stylites' (written 1833, published 1842), Tennyson draws on *Hone's Every-Day Book*, but also on Gibbon.[7] The latter caustically remarks that

> A prince, who should capriciously inflict such tortures, would be deemed a tyrant; but it would surpass the powers of a tyrant to impose a long and miserable existence on the victim of his cruelty. This voluntary martyrdom must have gradually destroyed the sensibility both of the mind and body; nor can it be presumed that the fanatics who torment themselves are susceptible of any lively affection for the rest of mankind.[8]

Tennyson dramatizes this situation, giving us 220 lines spoken by Simeon himself, as he singles himself out for God's blessing and even, in the following passage (lines 143–54), boasts of his miracle-working powers:

---

[5] *The Economist*, 21 January 1995, 22.

[6] *The Columbia Granger's Index of Poetry* (10th edn, ed. Edith P. Hazen; New York, 1994), 1944.

[7] *The Poems of Tennyson*, ed. Christopher Ricks (2nd edn, London, 1987), 593–604.

[8] Edward Gibbon, *The Decline and Fall of the Roman Empire*, vol. 4 (London, 1954), 18–19.

> Yes, I can heal him. Power goes forth from me.
> They say that they are healed. Ah, hark! they shout
> 'St Simeon Stylites.' Why, if so,
> God reaps a harvest in me. O my soul,
> God reaps a harvest in thee. If this be,
> Can I work miracles and not be saved?
> This is not told of any. They were saints.
> It cannot be but that I shall be saved;
> Yea, crowned a saint. They shout, 'Behold a saint!'
> And lower voices saint me from above.
> Courage, St Simeon! This dull chrysalis
> Cracks into shining wings ...

This is an un-ironic version of Vespasian's dying statement: 'vae, puto deus fio'. But while Tennyson's poem is a brilliant one, it has (as he later conceded) no specifically Byzantine content. Interestingly, the poet at the end of his life wished to correct the balance by giving us a poem on a Byzantine saint in a very different spirit. Hence the poem of 1892 on St Telemachus, whose protest against the games and stoning by the mob was said to have led to the games' abolition by Honorius. The poem is a rather woodenly pious one, which deliberately expunges the attitude represented by Gibbon's acidulous footnote on the subject: 'I wish to believe the story of St Telemachus. Yet no church has been dedicated, no altar has been erected, to the only monk who died a martyr in the cause of humanity'.[9]

If Tennyson gives Simeon as a perversion of religious feeling, Browning in 'Protus' (1855) reveals a Byzantium that is the quintessence of political decline, mordantly captured in just fifty-seven lines, with a layering of invented sources.[10] Protus is a late emperor, 'Born in the porphyry chamber at Byzant', and his name is a highly ironical one: 'Hystatus' would be more fitting. His beauty is described in the first source, his supplanting by a John the Pannonian in the second, and his fate reported by a third fictional source, an annotation to the second (lines 43–54):

> Then a new reign. Stay – 'Take at its just worth'
> (Subjoins an annotator) 'what I give
> As hearsay. Some think, John let Protus live
> And slip away. 'Tis said, he reached man's age
> At some blind northern court; made, first a page,
> Then tutor to the children – last, of use

---

[9] Gibbon, *Decline and Fall*, vol. 3, 189.

[10] Robert Browning, *The Poems*, eds John Pettigrew and T. J. Collins (Harmondsworth, 1981), vol. 1, 704–5.

> About the hunting-stables. I deduce
> He wrote the little tract 'On worming dogs'
> Whereof the name in sundry catalogues
> Is extant yet. A Protus of the Race
> Is rumoured to have died a monk in Thrace, –
> And if the same, he reached senility.'

Significantly, both this poem and Tennyson's 'Simeon' were read and responded to, in Greek and from a Greek's very different historical perspective, by Cavafy, who, in one of his best unpublished poems, 'Simeon' (1917) views the same subject from ground level.[11] The speaker of this dramatic monologue is a young littérateur and pagan whose aesthete's attitude is shaken, for the greater part of the poem at least, by the sight of Simeon on his pillar. (Cavafy himself wrote admiringly of Simeon in a manuscript note of 1899: 'He was, perhaps, the only man who has dared to be alone'.[12]) It is worth noting that through Cavafy, whose collected poems first appeared in English translation in 1951, English poetic perspectives on Byzantium have been considerably adjusted and enriched, so thoroughly naturalized has Cavafy become in English.[13] Once we include Cavafy's Byzantine poems in translation, the diversity of responses to Byzantium in our verse is hugely enriched.[14]

A further variant on the Gibbonian approach, but, like Browning's 'Protus', fictionalized, is provided by a rather neat poem by Walter Thornbury (1828–78), written shortly before 1851, which is now little known and requires to be quoted entire. The poem has the title, 'The Court Historian' and is subtitled, 'Lower Empire. *circa* A.D. 700'.[15]

> The Monk Arnulphus uncork'd his ink
> That shone with a blood-red light

---

[11] For 'Protus' and Cavafy see most recently David Ricks, 'English influences on intellectuals of the Diaspora: C. P. Cavafy and Alexander Pallis', in *Proceedings of the First International Congress on the Hellenic Diaspora* (Amsterdam, 1991), vol. 2, 427–32. Cavafy's 'Simeon' in *Anekdota poiemata 1882–1923*, ed. G. P. Savidis (Athens, 1968), 175–7; translation by David Ricks, *Modern Poetry in Translation* (n.s.) 13 (1998), 11–12; discussion by Gregory Jusdanis, 'Cavafy, Tennyson and the overcoming of influence', *BMGS* 8 (1982–3), 123–36.

[12] Cavafy, *Anekdota peza*, ed. M. Peridis (Athens 1963), 70.

[13] See David Ricks, 'Cavafy translated', *Kampos: Cambridge Papers in Modern Greek* 1 (1993), 85–110.

[14] For constrasting overviews see Panagiotis A. Agapitos, 'Byzantium in the poetry of Kostis Palamas and C.P. Cavafy', *Kampos: Cambridge Papers in Modern Greek* 2 (1994), 1–20 and Anthony Hirst, 'Two cheers for Byzantium: equivocal attitudes in the poetry of Palamas and Cavafy' in David Ricks and Paul Magdalino, eds, *Byzantium and the Modern Greek Identity* (Aldershot, 1998), 105–18.

[15] *The Oxford Book of Victorian Verse*, ed. Arthur Quiller-Couch (Oxford, 1912), 439–40. For biography see *DNB*.

Just now as the sun began to sink;
   His vellum was pumiced a silvery white;
'The Basileus' – for so he began –
'Is a royal sagacious Mars of a man,
   Than the very lion bolder;
He has married the stately widow of Thrace –'
   'Hush!' cried a voice at his shoulder.

His palette gleam'd with a burnish'd green,
   Bright as a dragon-fly's skin:
His gold-leaf shone like the robe of a queen,
   His azure glow'd as a cloud worn thin,
Deep as the blue of the king-whale's lair:
'The Porphyrogenita Zoë the fair
   Is about to wed with a Prince much older,
Of an unpropitious mien and look –'
   'Hush!' cried a voice at his shoulder.

The red flowers trellis'd the parchment page,
   The birds leap'd up on the spray,
The yellow fruit sway'd and droop'd and swung,
   It was Autumn mixt up with May.
(O, but his cheek was shrivell'd and shrunk!)
'The child of the Basileus,' wrote the Monk,
   'Is golden-hair'd – tender the Queen's arms fold her.
Her step-mother Zoë doth love her so –'
   'Hush!' cried a voice at his shoulder.

The Kings and Martyrs and Saints and Priests
   All gather'd to guard the text:
There was Daniel snug in the lions' den
   Singing no whit perplex'd –
Brazen Samson with spear and helm –
'The Queen,' wrote the Monk, 'rules firm this realm,
   For the King gets older and older.
The Norseman Thorkill is brave and fair –'
   'Hush!' cried a voice at his shoulder.

The historical setting is fictitious, though with echoes of the much later Macedonian dynasty, simply summing up with comic compression every sort of dynastic complication. The picture of the writer plagued by interference prefigures similar motifs in Cavafy, including his poems set in Byzantium. There is also a certain pathos in the picture of the hack writer here when we reflect that after a short life producing books with titles like *The Monarchs of the Main, or, Adventures of the Buccaneers* Thornbury died of overwork.

It is not, of course, the case that the Victorians' stock response to Byzantium was an ironic one: the growth of interest in the arts and crafts from the mid-century is discussed elsewhere in this volume. Nor should I leave unremarked a parallel phenomenon in verse: John Mason Neale's extensive translations from Byzantine hymnography.[16] Here are the unmistakable Anglican accents of the last verse from his rendering of the hymn, Ζοφερᾶς τρικυμίας, still current in hymn books:

> Jesus, deliverer,
>   Near to us be,
> Soothe thou my voyaging
>   Over life's sea;
> Thou, when the storm of death
>   Roars, sweeping by,
> Whisper, O Truth of Truth,
>   'Peace, it is I'.[17]

Neale, it should be noted, was also the author of *Theodora Phranza* (1857), a novel on the fall of Constantinople, and of a history of the Orthodox Church.[18]

But the 1890s were undoubtedly the key decade for the poetic experience of Byzantium, with interest shown by Wilde, Arthur Symons and others. Eventually, after a visit to Monreale and Cefalù in 1925, the importance of Byzantium crystallized in Yeats's mind, as he indicated in the following famous passage (which I abridge) from his prose work, *A Vision*:

I think if I could be given a month of Antiquity and leave to spend it where I chose, I would spend it in Byzantium a little before Justinian opened St Sophia and closed the Academy of Plato …

I think that in early Byzantium, and maybe never before or since in recorded history, religious, aesthetic and practical life were one, that architects and artificers – though not, it may be, poets, for language had been the instrument of controversy and must have grown abstract – spoke to the multitude and the few alike. The painter and the mosaic worker, the worker in gold and silver, the illuminator of Sacred Books, were almost impersonal, almost perhaps without the consciousness of individual design, absorbed in their subject-matter and that the vision of a whole people. They could copy out of old Gospel books those pictures that seemed

---

[16] Bibliography in *DNB*.

[17] *Songs of Praise*, enlarged edn (London, 1974), 187.

[18] Samuel Johnson's tragedy *Irene* (1749) testifies to literary interest in the fall of Constantinople rather than in Byzantium *per se*. A fuller discussion of the presence of Byzantium in English poetry should embrace Richard Watson Dixon's long poem of 1888, *The Story of Eudocia and her Brothers*.

as sacred as the text, and yet weave all into a vast design, the work of
many that seemed the work of one.[19]

Now it is important to see that Yeats's Byzantium is not a historical
one; he tended to be extremely hazy about history in general. Yet the
passage above interestingly grasps the nettle that, paradoxically, a poetic
response to Byzantium is unlikely to be a response to the poetry produced in Byzantium – but that this fact may in some way set the later
poet free. What we have here is an *idea* of Byzantium, most famously
expressed in a poem whose successive drafts moved both further away
from history and toward the goal of impersonality Yeats had set for
himself, namely 'Sailing to Byzantium' (1927). Only the final stanza of it
need be quoted to jog the reader's memory:

> Once out of nature I shall never take
> My bodily form from any natural thing,
> But such a form as Grecian goldsmiths make
> Of hammered gold and gold enamelling
> To keep a drowsy Emperor awake;
> Or set upon a golden bough to sing
> To lords and ladies of Byzantium
> Of what is past, or passing, or to come.[20]

In this much-discussed poem Yeats appears to have synthesized the
artificial birds mentioned by Constantine Manasses and others with a
childhood recollection of Andersen's 'The Emperor's Nightingale'.[21] The
one thing I would like to stress here, by contrast with the plentiful
scholia on the timelessness of the theme, is its timeliness: Constantinople
had been continually in the news between 1919 and 1923.[22] Furthermore,
the campaign for the redemption of Hagia Sophia had brought into play
strong emotions: Constantinople was a Christian city which needed to be
saved – an eternal city, which was not Rome (and this latter fact was
rather important for Yeats).[23]

Yeats decided against giving his 1933 collection *The Winding Stair* the
title *Byzantium*, but the continuing importance of Byzantium for his personal mythology is demonstrated by the equally famous poem 'Byzan-

---

[19] In A. Norman Jeffares, *W.B. Yeats. A New Biography* (London, 1988), 282–3. Lady
Gregory visited Ravenna in 1898 and did a watercolour of it (pp. 112–13). Yeats's remarks
have an affinity with the views of Eric Gill.

[20] W. B. Yeats, *Collected Poems* (London, 1978), 217–18.

[21] Jeffares, *W. B. Yeats*, 282.

[22] David Roessel, 'The historical context of Yeats's Byzantium', *Perspectives on Contemporary Literature* 14 (1988), 55–63.

[23] Erik Goldstein, 'Holy Wisdom and British foreign policy 1918–1922: the St Sophia
redemption agitation', *BMGS* 15 (1991), 36–64.

tium'.[24] There is no space to discuss the poem here, and it may be seen in any case as having somehow cut loose from anything in Byzantium specifically and gone into a self-perpetuating symbolism. In his notes for the poem, Yeats does appear to be making it a darker counterpiece to the earlier poem, specifying the period of the setting as 'towards the end of the first Christian millennium' – but it is more natural to see this as a piece of number symbolism rather than any sort of historical reference.[25]

There is of course much more to be said about Yeats, and some of it would concern his use of the work of O. M. Dalton (discussed elsewhere in this volume – Chapter 13). The main importance for our purposes here is to acknowledge the force of Yeats's invention of Byzantium as a symbol for poetry.[26] After 1930, no reference to Byzantium in English poetry can be made without relation to Yeats. This seems to have inhibited a number of poets who by temperament or education might have been thought likely to respond to Byzantium. There are but glancing references in Auden and Roy Fuller, despite the fact that each had a long historical arm and indeed an interest in Cavafy; and we find almost nothing in the philhellenes Durrell, Plomer and Bernard Spencer.[27] MacNeice, as a Protestant Irishman, might be felt to have been to a high degree inhibited by Yeats, but he was also under the shadow of a classical education of which he had suspicions yet could not eradicate. His glum classicist's picture from *Autumn Journal* (1938) is worth quoting:

> And for a thousand years they went on talking,
>   Making such apt remarks,
> A race no longer of heroes but of professors
>   And crooked business men and secretaries and clerks
> Who turned out dapper little elegiac verses
>   On the ironies of fate, the transience of all

---

[24] Yeats, *Collected Poems*, 280–81. On the drafts of the two poems see Curtis Bradford, 'Yeats's Byzantium poems: a study of their development', in John Unterecker, ed., *Yeats: A Collection of Critical Essays* (Englewood Cliffs, N.J., 1963), 93–130; for further discussion, William Empson, *Using Biography* (London, 1984), 153–86.

[25] Bradford, 'Yeats's Byzantium poems', 94–6. Sir Steven Runciman confirms that Yeats was little interested in the historical Byzantium (personal communication).

[26] D. J. Gordon and Ian Fletcher, 'Byzantium', in Unterecker, *Yeats*, 131–8.

[27] Auden characteristically translates Cavafy's 'Alexandrian Kings' into the Western setting of the Merovingians in his 'Rois Fainéants', *Collected Poems* (London, 1976), 603. And while Julian in Cavafy's poems relates to a wider concern with Byzantium, this is not so in, e.g., Thom Gunn's 'Julian the Apostate', *Collected Poems* (London, 1993), 62–3. Some play is made with the Byzantine and the modern in Lawrence Durrell's 'A Portrait of Theodora', *Collected Poems* (London, 1960), 155–6; while C.A. Trypanis takes a surprisingly Western perspective in 'Meteora', *Pompeian Dog* (London, 1964), 22. (The same poet's collection title, *The Cocks of Hades*, is embarrassingly Yeatsian.)

> Affections, carefully shunning an over-statement
> But working the dying fall.[28]

Byzantium here is seen – perhaps not surprisingly, given the poem's date – in the traditional terms of decline from ancient Greece. More gloomily still, in a late poem, 'Ravenna' (1961), MacNeice concludes:

> What went wrong
> With Byzantium as with Rome went slowly, their fame
> Sunk in malarial marsh. The flat lands now
> Are ruled by a sugar refinery and a church,
> Sant' Apollinare in Classe. What do I remember of Ravenna?
> A bad smell mixed with glory, and the cold
> Eyes that belie the tesselated gold.[29]

The originality of Yeats had been in his refusal to see Byzantium essentially as decline, and the 1950s saw Pound endorsing and developing the Yeatsian view in a characteristically strange direction. (It would be artificial to exclude Pound, with his English connections and publisher, from this account.) Pound's interest in Byzantium went back right to the First World War, when the spectacle of 'a botched civilization' stirred in him dreams of unity and thoughts of the Council of Florence in particular. With Constantinople in the news, and Spenglerian theories of civilizations doing the rounds, this is not perhaps surprising. But it does not bear fruit – and then a rather poisonous one – until the late collection of Cantos, *Thrones* (1960). There, and in Canto 96 in particular, Pound, in what is surely the most bizarre poetic use to have been made of Byzantium, ransacks the Book of the Eparch for a conception of the ideal society.

The poetic roots are once again in Yeats, though here in the darker shades of 'Byzantium'. There is a private allusion to Yeats early on with the phrase, 'the wind in the holly bush'; and later on, in a rare moment of clarity clearly referring to some of the battier ideas of the interwar years, Pound says:

> 'Constantinople', said Wyndham 'our star'
> Mr Yeats called it Byzantium.[30]

But the way in which Byzantium appears here gives a whole new meaning to 'Grecian goldsmiths': they now figure in an economically

---

[28] Louis MacNeice, *Collected Poems* (London, 1979), 118.

[29] MacNeice, *Collected Poems*, 527–8. We may detect here a trace of Seferis: see the phrase 'sinking in marshes' from *Mythistorema* xxii as translated by Rex Warner (George Seferis, *Poems* [Boston, 1960], 30), in turn reviewed by MacNeice in 1960: see Alan Heuser, ed., *Selected Literary Criticism of Louis MacNeice* (Oxford, 1987), 220–23.

[30] Ezra Pound, *Thrones 96–109 de los cantares* (London, 1960), 5, 13.

regulated context such as Yeats, even with his fascistoid leanings, could not have conceived of.[31] The Canto is full of cracker-barrel economics: 'and of course there is no local freedom/without local control of local purchasing power'.[32] The symbolism of Byzantium for Yeats is here presented in a way close to Pound's key source – cited in Greek characters – but in a dottily annotative manner; let this reference to Hagia Sophia suffice:

θόλος a round building
καμάρα arched over
all ἀσφάλειαν to be unlikely to fall
ἐμπειρίαν & experience
θεμέλιος the foundation not wobbly σαθρός
After all Justinian's boy *had* built Santa Sophia
        'vurry,' says Pearson, N.H. 'in'erestin'.'[33]

The inclusion of Byzantium in English poetry from the nineteenth century represents an extension of the latter's range of reference, and Pound speaks up for such extensions in a prose passage in this Canto, saying that 'If we never write anything save what is already understood, the field of understanding will never be extended'.[34] William Cookson loyally praises 'the accumulation of realistic detail' in the poem, but even Pound's admirers – of whom I am one – might find it hard to see how such a poem represents any enduring appropriation of Byzantium.[35]

I turn, finally, to living poets, among whom references to Byzantium seem few and far between. John Heath-Stubbs has a poem called 'The Death of Digenes Akritas' (1954), loosely modelled on the Greek folk ballad of that name and reflecting an idea of Greek manhood, especially after the 1940s, rather than anything specifically Byzantine (though it does seem to refer to the Grottaferrata version as well as to the folk songs). The poem's Yeatsian ring is all too palpable in the following stanza:

I have seen the golden Emperor
Sitting under a golden tree,
Commanding Sappho and Anacreon
To praise me with their balladry.[36]

But the existence of such a poem is a reminder of just how little Byzantine verse has been translated, let alone translated well – in that sense too

---

[31] The goldsmith's long-awaited appearance: Pound, *Thrones*, 19.

[32] Pound, *Thrones*, 7.

[33] Pound, *Thrones*, 14.

[34] Pound, *Thrones*, 11.

[35] William Cookson, *A Guide to the Cantos of Ezra Pound* (London, 1985), 123.

[36] John Heath-Stubbs, *Collected Poems 1943–1987* (Manchester, 1988), 314–15.

Byzantium is marginal to English-language culture. In the early years of the century Pound translated a handful of epigrams of the Byzantine period, and Tony Harrison has given us a vigorous Palladas – who is, however, the anti-Byzantine author *par excellence*.[37] And there seems to be little else.

But Yeats's symbol is still there in our literary culture, inviting newer and inevitably oblique responses today. One such comes in a poem called 'Cruising Byzantium' (1993) by the Irish-American but London-based poet Michael Donaghy. The poet, speaking of his 'holiday snaps from Greece', blasphemously compares an icon of the Virgin which survived iconoclasm with a picture of his girlfriend 'in skintight scuba gear', linking the two categories in the lines,

> Each photo frames a door beyond which, deep
> Within the Patriarchate of my yearning,
> The marble pavements surge with evensong.[38]

The fact that Yeats never visited Constantinople is not without significance: here we have the Byzantine world (though not, as it happens, Constantinople itself) in the age of mass tourism. The combination of sexual and aesthetic preoccupations familiar from 'Sailing to Byzantium' is now in a very different idiom. Instead of the 'golden handiwork' of 'Byzantium', moreover, we have the democratic form of holiday snaps. 'The Emperor's pavement', the 'Marbles of the dancing floor', which for Yeats have ecumenical power, are here transmuted into the strictly personal: a patriarchate (with a sly pun on patriarchy) shrinks and recedes into an individual with no avowed claim to being more than that. This is an ingenious poem, based on the everyday life of the end of the second millennium, and once again cashing in on Byzantium's marginality to this literary culture: for it is the far-fetchedness of the comparison in which the wit resides.

Tourism is of course the parent of incongruity, and Donaghy has a precedent in relating this to Byzantium, a precedent which I shall do no more than mention, as it marks clearly the borders of the subject which might properly concern this chapter. In T. S. Eliot's *Poems* (1920) there is a poem in French, 'Lune de Miel', which contrasts some American honeymooners' European peregrinations with what the poem's closing words call 'la forme précise de Byzance'. The stones of the church of Sant' Apollinare in Classe crumble, yet the form persists, in a way the innocent

---

[37] Pound, *Selected Poems* (ed. T. S. Eliot, London, 1948), 154–5 (esp. IV from 'Agathas' [sic]); Tony Harrison, *Palladas: Poems* (London, 1975).

[38] Michael Donaghy, *Errata* (Oxford, 1993), 20.

and unhappy tourists were in no position to perceive.[39] Here Yeats's view of Byzantium as 'the artifice of eternity' has been anticipated by a decade, and with the lightest and driest of touches. Perhaps the most interesting thing, from the point of view of this volume, is why Eliot felt he needed to say this in French. Could it be that, when it comes to bringing Byzantium into relation with the modern, they order this matter better in France?[40] Can it be significant that there is no perfume called 'Byzantium' as there is one called 'Byzance'?

---

[39] T. S. Eliot, *Collected Poems 1909–1962* (London, 1974), 50; good remarks (yet without anything on Byzantium specifically) by Hugh Kenner, *The Invisible Poet: T.S. Eliot* (London, 1979), 69–70, and William Arrowsmith, 'Eros in Terre Haute: T.S. Eliot's 'Lune de Miel'', *The New Criterion* 1 (2) (October, 1982), 22–41. Eliot's poem is compared favourably with Yeats's 'Byzantium' by G. D. Klingopoulos, '*O W. B. Yeats kai to Buzantio*', *Anglo-ellenike Epitheorese* (2nd series) 6 (1) (summer 1953), 65–70.

[40] Pound, too, seems to find something evocative in the French (Eliot's French?), in his final reference to Byzantium (Canto CX in *The Cantos* [London, 1975], 780): 'Byzance, a tomb, an end'. On the general issue of 'The French construction of Byzantium', see Robin Cormack's article with that title in *Dialogos* 1 (1994), 28–41.

18. 'As the actress said to the bishop ...': the portrayal of Byzantine women in English-language fiction[1]

Liz James

'British Reflections of Byzantium' are not only available in travellers' tales and the writings of historians. Another very distinct perspective of Byzantine culture is offered by English-language novels about Byzantium. These byways of fiction provide a glimpse into the average reader's understanding of that state and its culture. They supply a snapshot of popular perceptions of the Byzantine world and offer us a means of exploring the ways in which that recognition of Byzantium both changed and remained constant over a period of some 150 years. Indeed, there are many more novels about Byzantium than is generally realized; most are rightly confined to the second-hand bookshop of literary history.[2] In this chapter, I have space to examine only a few of these fascinating romances. In order to make the material even more manageable, I have concentrated on the portrayal of women in these works. What attitudes do the novelists display towards the Byzantine women they describe, women who are almost invariably empresses, and how, if at all, do these attitudes change? What do these attitudes reveal about popular perceptions of Byzantium?

Gibbon's *Decline and Fall of the Roman Empire* was published between 1776 and 1788. The first English-language novel dealing with a Byzan-

---

[1] I should record my gratitude to the staff of the Interlibrary Loans Office at the University of Sussex who tracked down many of the works discussed here and to Jenny Marshman of the University Library for her help in obtaining novels.

[2] An appendix to this chapter contains details of the novels discussed here and of other fictional works on Byzantium. Any additions would be gratefully received. I discovered Paul Halsall's web-page of 'Byzantine' novels some time after this chapter was completed: http://www.fordham.edu/halsall/byzantium/byzbibs.html ('Modern fiction, plays and poetry about Byzantium').

From *Through the Looking Glass: Byzantium Through British Eyes*, eds Robin Cormack and Elizabeth Jeffreys. Copyright © 2000 by the Society for the Promotion of Byzantine Studies. Published by Ashgate Publishing Ltd, Gower House, Croft Road, Aldershot, Hampshire, GU11 3HR, Great Britain.

tine subject that I have come across so far is Sir Walter Scott's *Count Robert of Paris,* first published in 1832, the year before Scott's death.[3] Although literary critics claim that it is not one of his greater pieces, it was nevertheless an influential work, emerging as the first of the nineteenth century's so-called 'muscular' novels, a forerunner of works like Charles Kingsley's *Hereward the Wake.*[4] It also set the tone for much of what has followed in the field of Byzantine fiction.

Set at the time of the First Crusade, *Count Robert* is the story of the eponymous Norman knight who dared to sit down on the imperial throne of Alexios I Comnenos. It is also the tale of the count's Amazonian wife Brenhilda, of the courageous Anglo-Saxon Varangian guard, Hereward and of Hereward's long-lost love, Bertha. Opposed to these uncultured but heroic Westerners are the noble but duplicitous Alexios Comnenos, his scheming wife Eirene, their blue-stocking daughter Anna and Anna's lecherous, cowardly, base husband, Nicephoros Bryennios, the real villain of the piece. The novel deals with the clash of ideologies, with what happens when these two worlds, cultured but corrupt Byzantium and stalwart but rustic Western Christendom, meet. The classical world is in decay, capable of supporting itself only through guile and conspiracy; the Crusaders, rude and unlettered, are upheld by a new chivalrous energy. Significantly, Scott chose to bring this battle of ideologies to a head by portraying a struggle between the two female protagonists, Anna Comnena and Countess Brenhilda. In a battle of wits, the conceited refinement of Anna Comnena easily outmatches Countess Brenhilda; in the second stage of the contest, the two adversaries take on each other in hand-to-hand combat with swords. Hard pressed and virtually overcome, the indomitable Byzantine princess is on the verge of humiliating defeat when the Valkyrie-like Brenhilda swoons, leaving Anna again victorious. The unexpected collapse of Brenhilda remains to be explained: it is later revealed that she is, in fact, pregnant. However, this entire scene was omitted from the published text. Scott's editor called it highly offensive, considering the countess's interesting condition too indelicate for contemporary eyes.[5] For the first time, but by no means the last, a Byzantine novel dabbled with indecency.

---

[3] The edition I used was Volume 24 in the Waverley Novels series, published in 1843 by Robert Cadell of Edinburgh. A critical edition of the novel by D. Pohl and K. Gamerschlag is in preparation. I am most grateful to Tony Inglis for his advice about Scott and *Count Robert.*

[4] See, e.g., C. A. Simmons, 'A man of few words: the romantic orang-utang and Scott's *Count Robert of Paris', Scottish Literary Journal* 17 (1990), 21–34, especially 21–6. Simmons's view is that in *Count Robert,* 'the search for a subject had taken him [Scott] to an obscure area of medieval history, eleventh century Byzantium', suggesting some of the problems with *Count Robert* may be the critic's rather than the author's.

[5] On the fight, the pregnancy and reactions to both, see K. Gamerschlag, 'The making

Scott's sources for *Count Robert* were essentially Gibbon, Charles Mills's *History of the Crusades* and a Latin text of Anna's own *Alexiad*.[6] From these, he built a picture of a complex degenerate society which set the tone for much of what was to follow. Many of his themes remain a continuous presence in novels about Byzantium: devious, cultured, superstitious Byzantines, essentially cowardly and afraid to fight, are opposed by straightforward, heroic Westerners, who appear regularly as Varangian guards, get the girl, save the empire and then return in triumph to their misty homelands. This, in turn, establishes a 'them' and 'us' scenario, offering the Western novel-reader some point of identity in the alien, oriental, corrupt, Gibbonian world of Byzantium.

Count Robert of Paris was followed by two works from each end of the Byzantine Empire: Charles Kingsley's *Hypatia*, published in volume form in 1853, and J. M. Neale's *Theodora Phranza*, published as a single volume in 1857. *Hypatia* is the story of the pagan philosopher–teacher who came to an unfortunate end in Christian riots in Alexandria in 415. It focuses on her encounters with Christianity in its various forms: the noble but naïve monk Philammon; the fanatical and power-crazed Bishop Cyril and his evil minions; the cynical aristocrat Raphael, redeemed by the love of a good Christian woman; and the semi-heroic bunch of Arian Goths who consort with the theatre dancer Pelagia (who is, inevitably, the long-lost sister of Philammon). *Theodora Phranza*, on the other hand, is an account of the fall of Constantinople in 1453 and the love affair between the beautiful Theodora Phranza, daughter of the emperor's chief adviser, and Sir Edward de Rushton, the exiled English knight and captain of the Varangian guard.

Both authors work to their own, specifically Christian, agenda. Kingsley's sub-title for *Hypatia*, *New Foes with an Old Face*, underlined his comparison between religion in fifth-century Alexandria, with its loss of true Christian values, and nineteenth-century England and Protestant apologetics. Convinced, like the Byzantines themselves, that the study of history was the study of God's developing plan for mankind, he aimed to establish Christianity as the only really democratic creed.[7] To achieve this, in *Hypatia* he created a world in which unity fragments into cults and parties and where the poor and the fallen are ignored by all but true

---

and un-making of Sir Walter Scott's *Count Robert of Paris*', *Studies in Scottish Literature* 15 (1980), 105–6, 108–10 and J. A. Sutherland, *The Life of Walter Scott: a critical biography* (Oxford, 1995), 342–3.

[6] See the Advertisement by J. G. Lockhart, Scott's son-in-law, to the 1832 and subsequent editions and J. Mitchell, *Scott, Chaucer and Medieval Romance* (Kentucky, 1987), 201–5.

[7] On Kingsley's agenda in *Hypatia*, see L. K. Uffelman, *Charles Kingsley* (London, 1979), 84–6 and S. Chitty, *The Beast and the Monk* (London, 1974), 151–6.

Christians. In this world, the three female protagonists, all young and beautiful, carry a different meaning. Hypatia herself is a coldly intellectual woman whose spiritual difficulties are only resolved through encountering true Christianity: the ultimate irony in Kingsley's novel lies in Hypatia's acceptance of Christianity just before her lynching by the fanatical Christian mob. Pelagia, the circus dancer, is the Alexandrian sister of the nineteenth-century fallen woman. Despite a life of wanton pleasure and indulgent sensuality – though only in a Victorian novel could Pelagia be seen as totally disgraced because she danced in the amphitheatre fully clothed in a garment sister to the crinoline – Pelagia is seen by Kingsley as a true woman at heart, capable of a profound abiding love, seen in her repentant conversion and afterlife as a hermit. Victoria, the good Christian woman, is as beautiful as Hypatia and as passionate as Pelagia but a devout Christian who achieves fulfilment through an idealized family life. It is perhaps little wonder that Queen Victoria and her Albert wholeheartedly approved of this novel.

Neale's line in *Theodora Phranza* is less insular. The novel stands partly as a testament to English interest in the Orthodox Church and to sympathy for Russia at a time when she was Britain's bitterest enemy. Partly it stands also as a polemical piece focusing on the state of Orthodox Christians under Ottoman rule, a theme again pertinent to the Crimean War.[8] *Theodora Phranza* herself symbolizes Constantinople; her marriage to the Englishman, de Rushton, effects a symbolic union between East and West, and offers Eastern Christianity a harbour after the sack of Constantinople. Theodora and de Rushton escape from the sacked city to England, where Theodora has a son, named Constantine. In this way, Neale established a link between England and Constantinople which, it seems, the reader is supposed to assume lasted firm in the intervening 400 years. In *Theodora Phranza*, although the Byzantines are portrayed as effete and idle, it is the Ottomans who are the cruel, deceitful, brutal oppressors, in the same way that nineteenth-century propaganda represented them as the torturers of Orthodox Christians.

As in Scott's tale, both novels take the outsider as hero: the barbarian Goths and the world-weary Jewish convert Raphael for Kingsley; the English Varangian, Edward de Rushton, for Neale. These characters act as a focus for the reader in this alien, decadent world of Byzantium. Both authors also stress Christianity and the importance of God, the contrast between 'true' Christianity, with its emphasis on Victorian philanthropy, and monkish fanaticism and superstition. In following this line, both consequently offer much criticism of the attitude of their major source,

---

[8] See L. B. Litvak, '*Theodora Phranza*; or, Neale's fears revisited', *Victorian Review. Journal of the Victorian Studies Association of West Canada* 15 (1989), 1–14.

Edward Gibbon. Many of these themes are conveyed through the representation of female characters in the books. All three novels portray Byzantine women through different strategies, which are cleverly organized to make a point. In *Count Robert of Paris*, the female protagonists are all unnatural women: Eirene, the woman ruling her husband; Anna, the scholar and writer; Brenhilda, the woman warrior. In *Hypatia*, three contrasting women are portrayed; it is the Christian home-maker who survives best. In *Theodora Phranza*, Theodora herself is little more than a cipher, what Virginia Woolf might have called 'the angel in the house'. The tricky issue of female sexuality rears its head in the 'fallen woman' Pelagia, the pregnant Brenhilda, the virginal Theodora Phranza.[9]

It is this issue of female sexuality that dominates the most common type of 'Byzantine' novel, those that retell the story of the sixth-century empress Theodora. In their portrayal of Theodora, these novels struggle with one fundamental issue: the 'fascination and the dilemma' presented by the character of the woman drawn in Procopius's *Secret History*. The issue which has obsessed writers has not been that of a plausible recreation of Byzantium but the discovery that, in Byzantium, a whore, a 'bad woman', could become an empress, a 'good' or perhaps 'powerful woman'. This theme of women and power is, in fact, the basic plot of most television soap operas: for Theodora, read Joan Collins's portrayal of 'Alexis Carrington'.

There are two approaches to this theme. Procopius's portrait is always accepted as close to the truth; in responding to it, either Theodora is drawn as evil and depraved, or, at least, as doing everything Procopius said she did and enjoying it,[10] or writers prefer to believe that she did it because she had to. It is this last category that I shall focus on here. Several basic strategies are employed.

---

[9] I regret that space does not allow me to discuss this theme in relation to the group of novels which deal with women saints and especially, unsurprisingly, with repentant prostitutes. Paul and Thekla form a popular subject – one can hint at love whilst talking about conversion – and several of the Paul and Thekla novels are published by bodies such as the SPCK and the American Baptist Publication Society. Clearly, such works are of an improving nature. Repentant prostitutes slide around uneasily on the ground between sex and God, thus uniting the two basic themes. Most are essentially derivative; Anatole France's *Thais* was translated into English in 1909 and novels such as T. Everett Honoré's *Behold the Woman* (1916) are clearly reworkings of this work, with different whores. The heroine of *Behold the Woman* is Mary of Egypt, but the plot is fundamentally the same as that of *Thais*: the whore repents and is saved; the fanatical monk falls into temptation and is damned. Similarities with *Hypatia* are also apparent.

[10] This is the line of F. Dahn's *Struggle for Rome* (New York, 1878) and even of Robert Graves's *Count Belisarius* (London, 1938). Averil Cameron also reminded me of the existence of *Theodora, She-Bitch of Byzantium*, by the author of *Vampire Lesbians of Sodom* and I regret having been unable to trace this classic.

First, 'she didn't really do it'. John Masefield's sickly pair of novels fit into this category admirably.[11] In *Basilissa* (1940), Theodora, linked with the prima ballerina of the Byzantine stage, Macedonia, restores the sacredness of the stage and the ballet, a noble art form approved of by the patriarch.[12] Clearly the Mary Whitehouse of her age, she meets the young Justinian, nicknamed Prinny, and the two spend many a pleasant hour discussing theology, clearly what the actress really did say to the bishop. She also saves Justinian from a wicked plot hatched by the evil Greens and the two plight their troth. In its turgid sequel, *Conquer* (1941), Theodora saves the empire at the time of the Nika Riots. As for her Procopian past, all the reader is told is that Theodora had wanted to be a ballerina but, lacking talent, had ended up as a mime artist.

The second approach claims that 'She didn't really mean to'. Sir Henry Pottinger's three-volume tome, *Blue and Green, or The Gift of God. A romance of Old Constantinople*, first published in 1879, is the earliest example of this tactic, and reveals how far popular fiction has travelled in the forty years from the 'offensive' pregnancy of Scott's Brenhilda. *Blue and Green* opens cheerfully enough: 'One Sunday morning in the Year of Our Lord 514 ...', but from this sunny beginning, it is all downhill. The year of Our Lord 514 is a time when, according to Pottinger, 'the eastern empire was approaching the lowest stage of that degradation from which, under the rule of Justinian, it recovered for a brief period', a time when 'the licentiousness of the age was incredible. Effeminacy and ultra-refinement walked hand in hand with brutality and ostentation. The corruption of morals extended through all ranks of society'.[13] This is a familiar world: Pottinger explains that his chief sources were Edward Gibbon, Niebuhr, Lord Mahon on Belisarius, and the *Secret History*.[14] He is keen to stress, however, that his Theodora is 'in many respects opposed to the traditional one as rendered by Gibbon on the evidence of Procopius'.[15] She is 'the victim of circumstances', a woman with a 'nobler side to her nature', no Messalina. As Pottinger says, 'Poor Theodora! I confess to great sympathy for her, and were I not cheered by the knowledge that she will at last emerge triumphantly out of all her troubles and wipe away the degradation of her early

---

[11] Masefield's interest in Byzantium perhaps derived from his friendship with David and Tamara Talbot Rice; see C. Babington Smith, *John Masefield. A Life* (Oxford, 1978), 212.

[12] As the Empress Euphemia memorably remarks of the pair, 'I like both these girls; they do their hair so nicely' (Masefield, *Basilissa*, 141). Muriel Spark remarked of this novel that it 'is the story of a young woman dancer of Byzantium and her historical progress'; M. Spark, *John Masefield* (London, 1953), 174, which evokes something of Masefield's success in depicting Theodora.

[13] Pottinger, *Blue and Green*, vol. 1, 15.

[14] Pottinger, *Blue and Green*, Preface, xi.

[15] Pottinger, *Blue and Green*, Preface, vii.

days by her subsequent career, I should be doleful of the end of the book, which contains the outlines of that degradation'.[16] Of course, this does not stop him from devoting two and three-quarter volumes to getting Theodora into a suitable state of repentance, though he does not soil his pen with details of her licentiousness, and a mere fifty pages to marrying her to Justinian and getting her through the Nika Riots.

Some eighty years later, Kathleen Lindsay's effusion, simply called *Theodora*, shares the same conclusion: 'Procopius the historian did his utmost to blacken her character and present her to the world as a wanton empress, but her good deeds shine like a brilliant light in a dark age. Yet she was very much a woman and yielded to the impulse to avenge herself on those who sought her ruin. Who can blame her?'[17]

Version number three suggests that 'she's a tart with a heart of gold'. James Wellard's offering of 1966, *You with the roses, what are you selling?*, fits this category admirably. According to the publisher's blurb, the book purports to be a free rendering of the *Secret History*, with some 'surprising adventures'. For those acquainted with the *Secret History*, these adventures are indeed surprising. As Wellard begins, 'As soon as she entered the house, Theodora saw that it was to be one of those nights ...' So it was. Kidnapped that very night from Constantinople, Theodora is immured in a cave with fanatical monks. Seducing her way out of this, she is taken to Africa and abandoned in a deserted fort in the Sahara with a handsome British prisoner, Julian, an envoy of King Arthur, huge and fair with splendid arms and legs, as Wellard puts it, as companion. Escaping to Alexandria, she meets one Peter Sabbatius who is learning how to paint icons; returning at last to Constantinople, she re-encounters her old friend Sabbatius, now nephew to the emperor Justin, and the rest is history. Just one of those nights, really ...

Finally, there is the 'she can't help it/she can't help herself' school of prostitution. Perhaps the outstanding example of this group is Paul Wellman's *The female city. A novel of another time* (1954), dedicated 'to the women in my life'. The opening sentence again sets the tone: 'Some cities are by nature male, being full of smoke and bustle and making a virtue of the prosaic. Others are equally female, given to frivolity, vanity and the gay pursuit of trifles. If this be true, never in history was a city more like a woman in her opulence, waywardness and beauty than Constantinople ...' Wellman tells the usual Theodora story with the usual emphasis on the brothel in a mildly titillating no-mention-of-breasts-but-lots-of-naked-alabaster-bodies sort of way, a rather breathless Mills and Boon of the fifties. He ends with the Nika riots, concluding that

---

[16] Pottinger, *Blue and Green*, vol. 2, 46.

[17] Lindsay, *Theodora*, 183.

> Theodora had a woman's mind, desires, necessities and viewpoints ... Her errors and weaknesses as well as her strengths and achievements are attributable to the essential femaleness in her. Woman is first and primarily the guardian of the race, the giver of life. Since, in renewing the race, she approaches each time the raw primitive frontiers of death, she is, underneath all her frivolities, froths and frills, more unswerving, more remorseless in the pursuit of the end of her being than any man.[18]

In this instance, nature wins out over nurture.

In all of these 'Theodora novels', sex is ever present but prurient. Nothing is ever spelt out; the Procopian geese never appear. They provide an interesting angle on what makes up the titillating, daring and pornographic in the nineteenth and twentieth centuries, and how it changes. Fascinatingly, the same problem seems common both to the sixth century and the nineteenth and twentieth centuries. Procopius wrote his *Secret History* to demean Theodora and Antonina, to denigrate their characters, to show them as dangerous women in sixth-century terms. His piece attempts to control them through the strategies he employs to portray them.[19] They are subject to none of the controls imposed by nature or society on their sex, they have no feminine concern for their children, they indulge in their whims and emotions in an unrestrained fashion, they are sexually aggressive and voracious, they control and dominate their husbands. These are the indications of a 'bad woman' in Byzantine terms.

Yet in turn, Procopius's approach is too dangerous and threatening for our age. In the 'Theodora novels', the trick is to downplay Theodora's sexuality, to disempower the Procopian disempowering of the empress. It is a question of strategies, of how to deal with powerful and/or sexual women. For all of the novelists writing about Theodora, the concept of Theodora as successful prostitute is an issue that has to be covered or controlled in some way, through excuses, repentance or avoidance, through a rewriting of the *Secret History* which both succeeds in denigrating Theodora and in denying her sexual power.[20]

---

[18] Wellman, *The Female City*, 488.

[19] See the arguments of E. A. Fisher, 'Theodora and Antonina in the *Historia Arcana*: history and/or fiction?', *Arethusa* 11 (1978), 253–79.

[20] Significantly, in no Theodora novel is Justinian ever the hero. The real lead is the Western outsider. Belisarius is the champion in several novels: 'strong, brave and staunch as a thorough-bred' according to Pottinger (*Blue and Green*, vol. 1, 206), 'a tall fair man of Germanic origin' in Lindsay (*Theodora*, 10); in both cases, Theodora has an affair with him. Elsewhere, Masefield has one Count Atorios, from Britain, 'a most unusual man, in whom courage and beauty balanced and made something divine' (*Basilissa*, 130), and there is the unfortunate leggy Julian of *You with the roses*. Even in Robert Graves's *Count Belisarius*, a notable exception to the general standard of Byzantine fiction, Belisarius is a Thracian outsider in Byzantine society and the narrator, the eunuch Eugenius, is, despite his name, the kidnapped son of a British chieftain.

Pottinger in 1879 defended his Theodora with the phrase 'The tale of Theodora's excessive depravity in her earlier years, unrelieved by any redeeming qualities or circumstances, rests entirely on Procopius' libel ... She elevated herself to be the fit consort of a disciplinarian ... like Justinian'.[21] In 1988, John Julius Norwich said of his empress, referring to Procopius, '[H]is authority can only be the gossip of the market place, and that, we may be sure, lost nothing in the telling. All the same, such billowing black smoke must presumably issue from some sort of fire; and there can be no doubt that Theodora was, as our grandparents might have put it, no better than she should have been.'[22] Different centuries but the same strategy: Procopius was wrong and a pervert, but there must be something in it. By citing Procopius at length, while claiming to disbelieve him, both authors succeed in titillating the reader while claiming a moral authority of disgust. The stereotypes of abuse have, however, changed little.

Although she dominates 'Byzantine' novels, Theodora is not the only empress fortunate enough to gain a place in popular fiction. The eighth-century Empress Eirene appears in two novels with distressingly similar plots, in so far as the fiction goes; the actual history employed by the novelists is rather more variable. In Rider Haggard's masterpiece, *The Wanderer's Necklace* of 1912, the Empress Eirene falls in love with a Scandinavian adventurer who joins the Varangian guard and loves another and is persecuted for it by her and helps to depose her. Some seventy years later, in Caecilia Holland's *The Belt of Gold* (1984), she falls in love with a Frankish adventurer who joins the Varangian guard and loves another and is persecuted for it by her and helps to depose her. There is no mention in either case of icons or of Constantine VI. This same fate of love for a Scandinavian freebooter awaits a different empress in Michael Ennis's 1989 bonkbuster, *Byzantium*, the non-stop sex 'n' shopping novel of life in eleventh-century Constantinople. It might be more accurately entitled 'Zoe's Breasts', since these dominate the action, which revolves around the torridly tedious, but ultimately unconsummated affair between the ageing and desperate Empress Zoe and the heroic Varangian guard, Harald Hardrada, who, inevitably, loves another and dies bravely in battle at Stamford Bridge.

Some small variety is offered to other empresses. Leo III's otherwise anonymous wife is the nominal heroine of W. S. Davis's 1924 masterpiece, *The Beauty of the Purple*. Virtuous but kidnapped, she spends much of the plot being rescued from evil scheming eunuchs by that Bulldog Drummond of the eighth century, Leo the Isaurian, with his trusty sidekick, the red-

---

[21] Pottinger, *Blue and Green*, Preface, vii–viii.
[22] J. J. Norwich, *Byzantium, the Early Centuries* (London, 1988), 192–3.

haired Breton, Fergal (another Western hero), when the pair can tear themselves away from the Avar siege of Constantinople and their heroic defence of the city. Theophano in Frederic Harrison's novel of the same title,
published in 1904 and dedicated to J. B. Bury, has much more fun. Evil,
duplicitous and scheming throughout, she is the Messalina of her age, the
new Theodora, a veritable Clytemnestra, going through husbands, plots
and, inevitably, an athletic blond Varangian guard from Norway called
Eric, in a desperate unwomanly bid to keep power. Rightly, she suffers for
it. In the last sentence of the book, John Tzimisces banishes her: 'I acknowledge my sin in that I was seduced by the woman … The evil one is put
away from Rome'.[23] In turn, Theophano departs invoking a familiar litany:
'Mongrel priest, bastard child, false lover, slaves, eunuchs, I defy ye all, I
curse ye all'.[24] Even the virgin empress Pulcheria is not exempt from
fantasy. Helen Mahler's novel, *Empress of Byzantium*, with its soft-focus
pornography and daring hints of homosexual love between Pulcheria and
Athenais, between Theodosius and Paulinus and heterosexual hanky-panky
between every conceivable couple, was doubtless very risqué in the 1950s.[25]

Such portrayals of empresses share a similar theme. She may be an
empress, but underneath it all, she is a woman like any other, one placed
in a more exotic setting. The whole thing is a wonderful fantasy: the hero
arrives in Constantinople, sleeps with the empress, saves the empire,
usually by replacing the empress with an emperor, and goes home again.
In all cases, female power is sexualized. Sex is used to control the portrayal of these women and their power. There is, after all, something
slightly ludicrous from a historic perspective about this continual line of
Scandinavians entering the Varangian guard and having their wicked
ways with the various empresses. It does mean that these empresses
need not be taken seriously as rulers.

As for what these works tell us about popular perceptions of Byzantium, we are essentially offered a Gibbon's-eye view. As Davis put it in
The Beauty of the Purple, 'He [Leo III] had saved them … despite luxury,
avarice and corruption in the palace, despite treason among the mighty,
despite twenty years of demoralisation and anarchy'.[26] Luxury, avarice,

---

[23] Harrison, *Theophano*, 337. For Harrison's views on Byzantium and his admiration of
Bury, see chs 10 and 11 in his *Among my Books. Centenaries, reviews, memories* (London,
1912), 180–248.

[24] Harrison, *Theophano*, 337.

[25] In contrast, Ada Teetgen's supposedly serious work of history, *The Life and Times of the
Empress Pulcheria* (London, 1907), refers to the empress throughout as Saint Pulcheria: 'She
had something of the English Elizabeth's delight for character and might indeed be
described as a masculine-minded woman did not that term rob her of the nun-like grace
and humility with which her actions were stamped' (3).

[26] Davis, *Beauty of the Purple*, 526.

corruption, treason, anarchy, demoralization: that is Byzantium, the by-word for servility and intrigue. The only noun Gibbon might have added is 'superstition'.

Even today, this is a perception of Byzantium not only found in fiction. I offer two quotations, one drawn from a history and one from a novel; they bear remarkable similarities of tone.

> The present work may be justified in that it tries to depict the events as they may have appeared to the emperor himself and to his astonishing consort ... Like many women, [Theodora] never revealed her age and she had a chequered and rather disreputable past.[27]

> Surely in all history, no woman ... certainly no man ... ever accomplished so mighty an upward step as did [Theodora] ... This grave injustice has been done by history: though Justinian, far her inferior in mind and spirit, has come down to us as 'the Great', the only title given to Theodora is 'the Notorious'.[28]

The perception of Byzantium offered by popular fiction is very different from that which we as Byzantinists would like to believe in; it is perhaps a sad reflection on post-structuralism that the history of the Byzantine state still depends on Ostrogorsky.

In all the works of fiction I have discussed here, Byzantium is always the other. It is an unnatural world and one of the manifestations of its unnaturalness is the role of women within it. From Scott's *Count Robert of Paris* with its three unnatural women, the dominatrix, the academic and the sports star, through Kingsley's repentant prostitute, Neale's 'angel in the house', the different actress–whores and the pitifully limited personifications of sex-starved empresses, female figures serve to mark out very strongly the perceived difference between Byzantium and ourselves. In fictional terms, it is still Gibbon's Byzantium. As Lecky put it in 1869, 'The history of the empire is a monotonous story of the intrigues of priests, eunuchs and women'.[29] Base, despicable, ridiculous and above all effeminate, was it any wonder that it was portrayed as an empire of decline and fall?

---

[27] Robert Browning, *Justinian and Theodora* (London, 1971; revised 1987), 7 and 38.
[28] Wellman, *The Female City*, 497.
[29] W. E. H. Lecky, *History of European Morals* (London, 1869).

English-language novels about Byzantium

G. Bradshaw, *The Bearkeeper's Daughter* (London, 1988) [Theodora]

M. Brion, *Crowned Courtesan* (translated W. Bradley Wells, London, 1936) [Theodora]

W. W. Collins, *Antonina or The Fall of Rome* (London, 1896)

F. M. Crawford, *Arethusa* (London, 1907)

F. Dahn, *The Scarlet Banner* (New York, 1903) [Belisarius and the Vandal war]

F. Dahn, *The Struggle for Rome* (New York, 1878) [Theodora]

H. F. Daringer, *Yesterday's Daughter* (New York, 1964) [fifth-century Greece]

W. S. Davis, *The Beauty of the Purple* (London, 1925) [Anthusa and Leo III]

W. S. Davis, *God Wills It: A Story of the First Crusade* (London, 1901)

P. Dixon, *Glittering Horn* (n.d. found)

A. Conan Doyle, *The Last Galley* (London, 1911) [collection of short stories including Byzantium]

G. Ebers, *Serapis* (1885) [Theodosius I]

M. Ennis, *Byzantium* (London, 1989) [Zoe]

F. W. Farrar, *Gathering Clouds* (London, 1896) [Chrysostom]

A. France, *Thais* (first published 1890, translated R. B. Douglas, Oxford, 1909) [Thais]

N. Gallizier, *The Lotus Woman* (New York, 1922) [Theophano and Nicephoros Phocas]

N. B. Gerson, pseud. S. Edwards, *Theodora* (New York, 1969) [Theodora]

G. Gissing, *Veranilda* (London, 1905) [Byzantine war in Italy]

R. Graves, *Count Belisarius* (London, 1938) [Theodora]

H. Rider Haggard, *The Wanderer's Necklace* (London, 1913) [Eirene]

F. Harrison, *Theophano. The Crusade of the Tenth Century* (London, 1904) [Theophano]

C. Holland, *The Belt of Gold* (London, 1984) [Eirene]

W. G. Holmes, *Theodora and the emperor. The drama of Justinian* (Garden City, 1952) [Theodora]

T. Everett Honoré, *Behold the Woman* (London, 1916) [Mary of Egypt]

E. Hubbard, *Justinian and Theodora* (London, 1906) [Theodora]

Mrs Hypatia Karidia, *The Very Pious Theodora, an historical play* (London, 1956) [Kassia and Theodora]

C. Kingsley, *Hypatia* (London, 1853) [Hypatia]

H. Lamb, *Theodora and the Emperor. The Drama of Justinian* (New York, 1952) [Theodora]

K. Lindsay, *Theodora* (London, 1964) [Theodora]

J. M. Ludlow, *Sir Raoul: a tale of the theft of an empire* (London, 1905) [Fourth Crusade]

H. Mahler, *Empress of Byzantium* (New York, 1952) [Pulcheria]

J. Masefield, *Basilissa* (London, 1940) [Theodora]

J. Masefield, *Conquer* (London, 1941) [Theodora]

C. A. Mason, *The White Shield* (Philadelphia, 1904) [Thekla]

G. Musgrave, *Paul and Thekla. A love story of the first century* (Heathfield, 1988) [Thekla]

J. M. Neale, *Theodora Phranza* (London, 1857) [Fall of Constantinople]

J. H. Newman, *Callista: a sketch of the third century* (London, 1856)

R. O'Connor, *The Vandal* (New York, 1960) [Theodora]

J. Olek, *Theodora* (London, 1971) [Theodora]

J. Paton Walsh, *The Emperor's Winding Sheet* (London, 1976) [Fall of Constantinople]

W. C. Perry, *Sancta Paula* (n.d. found) [Valens and Valentinian]

E. Philpotts, *Eudocia* (London, 1921) [Eudocia and Romanos Diogenes]

H. Pottinger, *Blue and Green, or, the Gift of God. A Romance of Old Constantinople* (London, 1879) [Theodora]

D. L. Sayers, *The Emperor Constantine* (play) (London, 1951) [Helena]

W. Scott, *Count Robert of Paris* (Edinburgh, 1832) [Alexios and Anna Comnena]

C. Underhill, *Theodora, the Courtesan of Constantinople* (New York, 1932) [Theodora]

J. W. Vandercook, *Empress of the Dusk. A life of Theodora of Byzantium* (New York, 1940) [Theodora]

A. C. Vaughan, *Bury me in Ravenna* (New York, 1962) [Galla Placidia]

A. Vlachos, *Their Most Serene Majesties* (n.d. found) [twelfth century]

E. Waugh, *Helena* (London, 1950)

J. Wellard, *You with the roses, what are you selling?* (New York, 1966) [Theodora]

P. I. Wellman, *The Female City. A novel of another time* (New York, 1954) [Theodora]

Index

251